Single to Sirkeci

by
Linda Rushby

Damson Tree 2016

ISBN: 978-0-9929048-2-1
Designed, typeset and published by Damson Tree Publishing, Southsea, England.
Typeset in Palatino Linotype
www.damson-tree.co.uk

Contents

Contents - continued

Acknowledgements

So many people helped me on this journey, the thought of trying to thank them all individually terrifies me. What order should I list them in? What if I miss somebody out? Would they ever forgive me?

Well, here's a simple list in chronological order. You know I love you all, and if you happen to read this book, I hope you enjoy it.

First, my wonderful children, without whose support I would never have set off: Simon Hadfield, Laura Hadfield and my granddaughter Felicity. Then my friend Sue Walker, the first person outside the family who I confided my plan to, and who helped with packing up the flat; and my ex-husband Brian Hadfield, who patiently stored all the junk which I wasn't quite brave enough to abandon completely.

My brother and sister-in-law Ian and Penny Rushby, who gave me a staging post at each end of the journey, and sister and brother-in-law, Gill and Neil Spooner, who hosted me in Brittany. Nicolas and Yves Mathieu, who welcomed me to Brussels, and then a long list of friends who offered me hospitality across the continent: Eduardo Malagon and family; Irina Rachieru and extended family; Gabriella Taborossy and István Paréj; Petra and Eva Zallmannova; my daughter-in-law Dina Ottesen; her mother Kari-Anne Moen and Kari-Anne's partner Håkon Andresen who welcomed me into their home; and Daniel Egonsonn, who shared a coffee with me at Lund station.

The journey of bringing this book to publication was a much longer one, and involved even more people. Many thanks to blogfriends from the now sadly defunct blog.co.uk (especially Marian Barker, who invited me to stay but had to cancel); the University of Exeter online Life-Writing course, Spring 2014; the life-writing forum (special mentions to Gill Kimber and Dani Hilliard); the Writers of Lovedean, and numerous friends who responded to my posts and sketches on Facebook.

And I can't not mention a little person who only came into my life (and the world) while this book was in the final editing stage, my grandson Stephen.

Prologue

Mostar station, Bosnia-Herzegovina, Sunday morning. A small grey and white cat picks its way delicately along the rail. Red poppies glow by the tracks. White houses cling to the hillside and a deep green cypress pokes above the skyline in front of the freshly risen sun.

The 8.02 for Sarajevo pulls in, and passengers (surprisingly many) cluster round the doors. I hang back a little, in my English way, not wanting to hold anyone up too much when I load the Wardrobe.

An older lady moves out of the queue for the next door down and shamelessly pushes in front of me. She grabs onto the vertical bars either side of the door and starts to heave herself up the metre or so of steps into the train. Despite being probably little heavier, and certainly no more than ten years older than I, it takes three male relatives to load her on board.

I am getting twitchy now. The neighbouring doors are closed already, and the Wardrobe and I are still platform-bound. I've turned it on its long end, and grabbing the handle I lift it, slide it into the train next to my fellow-passenger, then clamber up the steps and squeeze in myself. The door clangs behind me. If I've deprived her of a tearful farewell with assorted family, well, that's tough Grandma. Don't mess with me and my luggage.

Rewind almost three months, to Valentine's Day, 2012; the station is Ebbsfleet, Kent, the train is Eurostar, the male relative is my brother, and the grandmother is me, in my long black boots, black leather jacket, purple scarf and red beret.

I'm still wearing the boots, re-soled and heeled by a darkly sexy cobbler in Split. The leather jacket got left behind in the rack when I had to change buses at the border between Croatia and Bosnia-Herzegovina. I was ready to ditch it anyway, it was getting too sweaty to wear and too heavy to carry around, and I can buy something more lightweight before I get to Scandinavia. It had a narrow escape a couple of weeks previously when it got moved on the train between Florence and Turin and I almost didn't find it, which would have been a disaster given the miserable weather I had for some of the time in Turin. The red hat and purple scarf are safely stowed in the inner recesses of the Wardrobe (of which more later).

But I'm rambling. I guess the real question is – what am I doing here, and why? What took me from a rented flat in Bedford, to catch the Eurostar to Brussels and then keep going, through Paris, Brittany, south through France to the Basque country and Catalonia; from Barcelona through the Languedoc and Provence to Italy (where I spent April); out of the EU and into the patchwork of the Balkans; to arrive, blinking and befuddled on the bus from Kapikule to Sirkeci Station in Istanbul at six in the morning, thirteen weeks to the day after leaving England?

In some places, I have stayed with friends; in others, I have found lodgings online, rarely knowing exactly where I'm going to be staying more than a day or two in advance. I've slept on a stationary yacht moored off the Camargue (with resident cat); within the (reconstructed) walls of the mediaeval city of Carcassonne; in a comfortable apartment with a terrace overlooking the shell of a bombed-out house in Mostar, Bosnia; and in a couchette on the Balkan Express from Sofia to Istanbul. I've lain in bed and listened to the bells of San Marco in Venice; those of the Duomo in Florence; the muezzin of the Blue Mosque in Istanbul; and the mewing of gulls on coasts from the Bay of Biscay to the Sea of Marmara.

And this is how it all happened…

I

Running Away

Bedford - Kent - Brussels

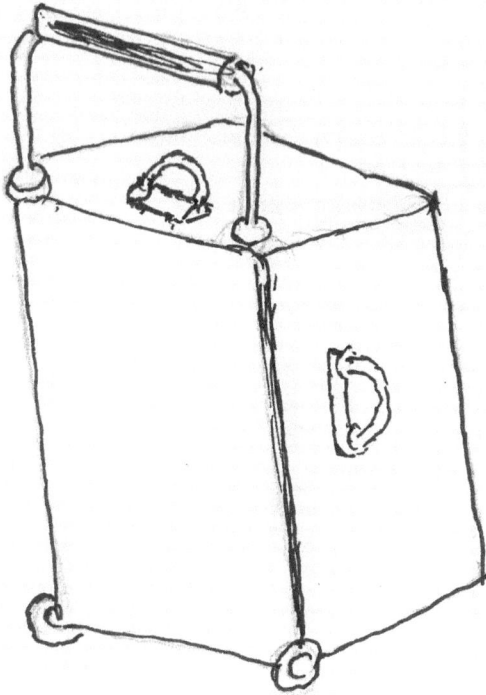

Chapter 1 – How I came to run away

Brussels - Tuesday 14 February 2012

Push open the wrought iron gate and enter the mews. Tall buildings, staggered around an irregular courtyard, red bricks within a grid of white mortar, window panes within a grid of white frames, grey tiled roofs slicked with rain, black lampposts and railings, bare winter trees and shrubs in raised beds. Steps, cobbles, hidden corners. Can I remember which house it is? Then I see the sign in the window above the door, white lettering on blue: '2012 re-elect Obama'. This has to be the place.

I first fell in love with this house, and this city, in October 2005. I loved the location, so close to the city's heart, with everything you need from a city – cafés, galleries, parks, shops, bars – lying just outside the wall and gate that set apart this little cluster of flats and terraced houses and made it feel like a secret haven of homeliness. I loved the quirkiness, the sense of chaotic comfort, welcome and friendliness, which was not at all what I expected from a city stereotyped in my imagination as grey, dour and bureaucratic.

On the walls of the living room were two posters whose messages have stayed with me. The first says:

'je suis chez moi. je suis arrivée'

I am home. I have arrived.

The other conveys in English the following advice:

'Be here now. This is the only place you need to be, and from this place, all things are possible.'

That autumn day over six years ago, my life was in crisis, though I didn't recognise then what a turning point it would turn out to be - I guess that's the nature of turning points. But in these words I caught a glimpse of other possibilities. I gave the label 'surreality' to that imagined life, and invented an alternative persona for myself: Melinda, the free-spirited, creative, loving, wild and slightly crazy girl who had buried herself long ago inside the soul of a sensible wife and mother.

And although Melinda longed to believe that '...*from here, all things are possible*', sensible Linda knew that life isn't like that. Marriages are there to be worked on. They may go through sticky patches, but sensible people stick with them. Husbands, even ones who raise your hopes by threatening to leave and then back down and stay, are for life, not just for Christmas.

So, I stuck with it. We stuck with it. We did all those things couples are supposed to do: counselling, reviving common interests, communicating... well, that last one was a bit too much to hope for. And after a few more years had passed by, we agreed to separate. I found a flat and moved out, and after a decent interval we started divorce proceedings.

That was the first stage of my running away, and for a while it seemed that life was full of possibilities. I discovered at the age of 55 that not only could I live alone, but I loved it, that sense of closing my own door on the world, and being responsible to and for no one but myself. I would get a new job, start a new business, make new friends, meet a new man. Melinda had come into her own at last, and everything would be great from now on.

Wouldn't it?

Bedford - December 2011

Except that – somehow the dream didn't quite go according to plan. Here I was, three years later, still living alone with my ginger cat in that rented flat in Bedford. The divorce settlement dragged on interminably, the business had never really taken off and I was smarting over the messy ending of my first relationship with a man after two years of being alone. My employers had cut my hours in response to the funding crisis, and I was applying for jobs but with no success. Somehow I'd managed to get through the summer with what little savings I had left, but then came the final blow.

Ten days before Christmas I walked into my boss's office for my annual appraisal in the small charity where I worked part-time as an administrator. The tiny room was usually freezing, but that December day the heating was on full and it was stuffy. The boss was sitting behind her desk and I took my usual seat on the side of the meeting table, spreading the self-assessment form and my notebook in front of me. She was smiling and affable, but there was no preamble:

'There's no easy way to say this, so I'll get it out of the way. We're going to have to cut your hours - again. I can offer you ten hours a week.'

There was a throbbing behind my right temple, as though a small woodpecker trapped inside my skull was hammering to get out. My mind, shocked and dazed, did what it often does when nothing else in the world makes sense, and took refuge in the comforting predictability of mental arithmetic.

Ten hours. Eighty five pounds a week. Three hundred and forty a month. When I started this job, it paid enough to cover my rent and council tax. Now it was barely going to be half that.

I didn't hear another word she said. I have no idea how I responded. She gave me the papers to read and sign, I left the office and wondered what the hell would happen now.

Two days later, the Sunday before Christmas, I woke after a broken night, dragged myself out of bed and into my dressing gown and then into the living room. I huddled on the sofa, with the cat nestled against one hand and a cup of coffee in the other, my shoulders hunched not so much against the cold as against the future, and stared at the laptop, at the spreadsheet where I kept track of my spending and my budget. At the back of my mind I knew about the lump sum which would come to me when the divorce was sorted out, but it felt unreal, intangible. I tried to think how many months' rent it would pay for. Would it keep me going till I reached pension age, if I couldn't get another job?

The internet was full of the imminence of 2012, and all the myths and theories about the Mayan prophecies. 'The world might end next year' I thought wryly, 'So why worry?' The gremlin of failure perched on my shoulder, ticking off the list with its bony fingers. I had failed in my marriage. I had failed to get a job which matched my qualifications and brought in a liveable income. I had failed in my business. I had failed in my new relationship. Everything was falling apart, and how could it be anything but my own fault? Brooding, I took a sip of coffee, and grimaced as the cold, bitter liquid coated my tongue. Outside, a relentless drizzle fell from the winter sky onto the stationary traffic, stuck on the one-way system, waiting for the green light.

This was no good. I was going to meet my son, daughter and grand-daughter for lunch, and I needed to make an effort. I dragged myself off to the shower.

Bombshell – Sunday 18 December 2011

A few hours later I was sitting in the local Wetherspoon's with my son Simon, dark and stocky (me with testosterone), Laura his sister with her blonde bob and her Dad's blue-eyed grin, and little Felicity, her daughter, perpetual motion and non-stop chatter.

There was the usual buzz of Sunday-lunching families, swelled to crushing point by glassy-eyed Christmas shoppers. Felicity, refusing the high chair, perched on the edge of the bench seat next to her Mum, crayoning on the back of her paper menu and giggling as Uncle Simon made silly faces.

My heart racing, I didn't even bother to look at the menu, I didn't care what I ate. I'd made a decision, and I had to share it, get it out into the open before reality hit me and it faded back into hopelessness. And everything would hinge on how they reacted.

'Right, what's everyone having?' I asked breezily. Ribs and a pint of Guiness. Scampi and a diet Coke with ice and slice. Kids' fish-fingers with beans and blackcurrant squash. Before I went up to the bar with the order, I dropped my bombshell:

'I've decided that when the money from the divorce settlement comes through, I'm going to quit my job, quit the flat, and go travelling by train across Europe.'

I expected a stunned silence, but Laura, bless her heart, came back straight away: 'Go for it Mum. You should have done it years ago!'

I felt light-headed as I went up to the bar with the order. Give them a chance to think it over, talk between themselves. But I had a feeling it was going to be all right. I bought myself a large Merlot and went back to the table with the drinks.

'When do you think you'll go?' asked Simon.

'Haven't decided. It'll depend on when the divorce gets settled and the money comes through.' That wasn't strictly true. I had got a date in mind – 14th February, Valentine's Day, and the third anniversary of the day I picked up the keys for the flat – a gesture, a token of independence and autonomy, of putting up two fingers at the idea that what I needed was a man in my life. Sheer bravado, of course, and given all that needed doing, it hardly seemed feasible. I took another large swig of Merlot and put that out of my mind.

'I've worked it out' I explained as I crunched my fish and chips. 'The money from the job is less than the rent I'm paying on the flat, so I may as well give in my notice, get rid of a lot of my stuff and put the rest in storage, and then I can just take off. The only other worry is Murka. Would you be able to look after her for me?'

'No probs, you know we'd love to have her' Laura answered. 'Won't we, Flick? Grandma's puss cat can come and live with us.'

'Pusscat!' yelled Flick, splatting baked beans into orange mush with her fork.

'I've set myself a budget of ten grand' I went on. 'I'll put the rest of the lump sum in a savings account for when I get back and see how far I can get.' And anyway, the little voice at the back of my mind was saying, who knows what will have happened by then? New places, new opportunities, new man maybe? The end of the world? The end of my world might happen tomorrow for all I know. Why wait?

'Will you go to Norway?' Simon asked. He was flying to Kristiansund the next day, to stay with his girlfriend Dina and her family for Christmas.

'I don't think so. Most of the friends I was thinking of going to see are down in the central and southern parts.' Melinda had planned out the itinerary many times – Brussels, Paris, Brittany, Bordeaux, San Sebastián, Barcelona… after that it grew a little hazy, but Italy was in there, Prague and Budapest, and finally Istanbul.

It was a week later, on Christmas Day, that the final bit of the itinerary fell into place. Simon emailed from Kristiansund:

'I told Dina's family about what you're doing' he said. 'Her Mum says you sound like her kind of person, you can come and stay with them.'

Then it became obvious. From Istanbul I would come back diagonally North West across the continent, via Budapest, Prague and Germany, then up through Scandinavia for midsummer. After that it would be back south again to Brussels and home for the beginning of August and Felicity's third birthday.

All I had to do now was do it.

Time to go – Kent, Monday 13 February 2012

Red flames crawl and crackle round the fireplace, nipping at the logs and making them spit and hiss like angry cats. None of this disturbs Dottie, the old black Labrador, sprawled blissfully across the rug, dreaming, no doubt, of the real things.

Outside the window, a Kentish landscape, the snow like white blankets thrown over the hills, or swept and heaped into brown and white piles around the edges of the farmyard and the path through the garden to the house.

Ian, my brother, appears in the doorway from the kitchen – still every inch the Captain of Industry, even in his Barbour and wellies and with a dog lead in his hand. Dottie lifts her head and stares at him mournfully.

'Come on you' he says sternly. 'Time to go.'

As the old dog drags herself to her feet, I glance up from my laptop.

'Can we do this printing some time?' I ask.

'Of course. Sort out what you need onto a stick and let me know when you're ready.'

My itinerary is planned for the next couple of weeks. Eurostar to Brussels tomorrow, where I'll stay at my friend Yves' house. I met Yves, as I did most of the people I'll be visiting, on a project I got involved with in 2005. He was working as a facilitator for a Citizens Review Panel, recruited online with volunteer representatives from all the EU member states to take part in workshops and review environmental policy – that might sound dry, but it certainly wasn't, and the friendships that were formed on that panel transformed my life and opened up my mind to the adventure I'm about to embark on.

Yves is working in Paris now and won't be in Brussels till the weekend, but his son will be there to greet and look after me. On Saturday I'll catch a train from Brussels to Paris and stay for three nights in a hotel, then another train to Carhaix-Plouguer in Brittany, to spend a week with my sister Gill and her husband Neil. From there I'll head south to stay with my friend Marian, a Yorkshirewoman who lives near Bordeaux. The station is Angoulême, a place I've never heard of before.

All those trains are booked, except the one from Brussels to Paris. Because it's an international journey, the SNCF (French national railway) website won't let me book and print out the ticket, and it's too late to get it by post. That's okay, surely I can buy it at the station in Brussels? That gremlin appears on my shoulder, asking what I'm going to do if this happens everywhere, but I brush it off.

Should I even try to describe the last week? Highlights? Well, there was waking at 3.30 on Friday morning realising I had no idea where my passport was. All the main furniture had been moved the day before, in a van driven by my ex, from my flat to his house, with help from Simon, Laura and my friend Sue. Which meant that all drawers, boxes, and my usual putting-stuff-down-in places had gone too, leaving me with a fold-out bed, a fold-up table and stools, some sofa cushions on the floor and no bloody passport. In panic, I started to question where other things were too. My international roaming phone sim card? My international ATM card, pre-loaded with €1,000? My printed-off Eurostar ticket for Tuesday – that wasn't a problem, at least, it was folded up in my backpack. I ran round the flat screaming and berating myself for my stupidity for a while, then checked in my wallet and found my cash card. The sim was on the folding table under some other bits of paper, so I took that and carefully put it into my wallet too.

I calmed down enough to start thinking in a semi-rational fashion. I took my passport to the sorting office on Monday to use as id for a recorded delivery letter. I had my laptop bag and not my handbag – and that probably got packed and taken to the house. Plan: go over in the morning and go through the boxes till I find my laptop bag, and if it's not there I have Friday and Monday to get to the passport office in Peterborough. Luckily, it was in the third box I looked in.

I'm a terrible packer. I always take things that I'll never use, but knowing in advance which those are is impossible, and if you only take the essentials you can end up cursing yourself just as much over what was left behind as what was taken unnecessarily. It's an inevitable outcome of the uncertainty of life.

Ian came to collect me from the flat yesterday (Sunday). When he arrived, Laura and I were still finishing off emptying everything out and cleaning up. He took one look at my over-sized, ultra-light case standing in the corner, and pronounced:

'That's not a suitcase, it's a wardrobe!'

'It's a wardrobe on wheels' I pointed out, but it was too late. The Wardrobe it became.

He carried it down the stairs and got it into his car, as well as the backpack, the fold-out table, the fold-out bed and two bags of clothes and things to be stored in his barn. In the car park behind the flats, I hugged Laura as tightly as though she were still my baby, and we were being parted for the first time.

'The only way I can cope with this is by not actually believing it's real' I told her.

I remember nothing of that first, preliminary journey – in Ian's car, down the A1, round the M25 and over the Thames bridge to Kent. I haven't slept well for weeks and am desperately overtired. But what's done is done, *que sera, sera*, the die is cast, and all that crap.

By the time Ian and Dottie return from their walk, I have assembled all my tickets, bookings, directions and itineraries for the next fortnight onto a memory stick, and we print them out. I file them neatly into plastic wallets, the ones for tomorrow slotted in the front of my back pack and the rest in the Wardrobe.

Departure – Tuesday 14 February
I'm awake just before 6.00 feeling ridiculously calm, get up and have my shower, check and double-check that everything is in its place, dry my hair and put the hairdryer back in the Wardrobe.

Down in the cosy farmhouse kitchen, sister-in-law Penny - blonde, petite, and nobody's stereotype of a farmer – pours me a coffee before she goes out to see to the animals.

'All ready?'

'*Comme ci, comme ça!*' I answer with a grin and a wriggle of the hand.

'You look more rested than you did yesterday.'

'I don't know about rested, exactly, but I feel more ready.'

'Well, have a lovely time' she reaches her arms out for a hug.

'Won't I see you again?'

'No, I'll just say goodbye now.'

So many goodbyes.

'The journey of a thousand miles... has to start somewhere' I say to Ian as we pull up at Ebbsfleet station and I get out of the car into the damp grey chill of a February morning.

At the Eurostar check-in desk, the left hand strap of my backpack pops undone. Ian fiddles with it to get it back in again. There's really no queue to speak of. A rail employee wanders over to ask if he can help.

I smile and thank him, then stand and breathe.

When the bag strap is fixed, Ian hugs me and says:

'When you feel blue, which you will sometimes, just think what the alternative would be like!'

'I know! I will!'

At security, I take off my coat but not my waistcoat, and set off the alarm. A nice lady does the body search. I empty my waistcoat pockets and put the contents in a tray to go through the scanner. I collect my suitcase, coat and other things. But where's my backpack?

'It's got to be searched' says another friendly lady.

Everything comes out, laptop first. But at least it's reasonably well organised. The corkscrew is put into a red tray, and I think it's being confiscated, but it goes through the scanner and then gets put back into my bag.

There's a story behind that corkscrew. When we were sorting everything out last week Laura found it in the cutlery drawer. She asked what to do with it, and I said pack it away, but somehow it got left on the kitchen counter, and was still there when we were finishing off on Sunday, so at the last minute I threw it into the backpack and tweeted: 'You never know when you might have need of a corkscrew.'

Back in Ebbsfleet, I feel such a girly with my huge suitcase. It is heavier than I thought.

I get through to the departure lounge and into the queue for Caffé Nero. The queue, though not long, moves very slowly. By the time my mocha comes, there's only 10 minutes to departure. I get as close to the gate as I can. This is the first time I've joined the train at anything other than a terminus. We're allowed through and down the escalator. Coach 14, seat 54. The coach entry points are marked on the platform. I find the space for coach 14. To the left there's an arrow for 15, to the right, 12. There's no coach 13.

Over the tannoy comes a voice: 'due to icy conditions, be aware that the platform is slippery'. But the conditions aren't icy. The temperature was 4°C on the display in the car on the way here.

'The train will stop for 2 minutes only. Please board immediately.'

I've finished my mocha, but I can't see a bin. That friendly guy from the check-in is there again.

'Do you mind taking my rubbish?' I thrust the empty paper cup into his hand as the train pulls to a halt, then grab the Wardrobe. The doors open, but no one is getting off here. This is it. I heave the Wardrobe in and stand it on end in the narrow corridor, scanning for a space in the luggage shelves between the carriages, and manage to shove it in at the bottom.

I find my seat and pull the laptop out of the backpack.

Down in the tunnel, there's no wifi, of course, no signal at all. I send a frantic last few texts of farewell to assorted people before we go under, and then, too late, think that I should have tweeted as well. Never mind. I will when I get there As long as I can find some wifi, I'll be fine.

And now we emerge into daylight again. A beautiful morning here in… where are we now? Normandy?

'It looks just like Essex!' says the guy in the seat behind.

I try to tweet from my phone, but no connection.

I hear the ring tone on my old phone. It has updated the time. There is a text:

'Hi from Orange. Make a call for 36p/min & receive a call for 11p/min in France & the rest of the EU. Send a text for just 10p and MMS for £1. Browse the mo* some text missing *'

We haven't reached Lille yet. It's 11.25. We're due to arrive in Brussels at 12.05.

Time to stop typing and just travel.

II

Near Neighbours: Belgium, France, Northern Spain

Brussels - Paris - Brittany - Angoulême
- San Sebastián - Barcelona

Chapter 2 - Brussels

Bienvenue à Bruxelles – **Tuesday 14 February**

Riding up the escalator from the Bourse Metro station into the bustling heart of the city, my pulse starts to race. Which exit do I need? I can never remember - not even sure which side of the road I'll come out. I pull the Wardrobe into a stream of busy humanity, all shapes, sizes and colours, parting and flowing around me. Intoxicating music pours from the Cuban bar, and traffic roars, honks and fumes along the street. I look from side to side, trying to recognise landmarks (the comic book shop? the Irish bar?) and get my bearings. I've been coming to Brussels for six years, so I know roughly how to get to Yves' house. I'm sure I'll recognise it when I see it.

Nicolas meets me at the door and carries the Wardrobe up to the attic room, rather shocked by the size of it.

'I'm going to be travelling for six months' I tell him. 'Didn't Yves say?'

'No, I thought you were only coming for a few days!'

It's very comfortable to be sitting here, in the living room. I feel a little disoriented, but safe. I've got a few plans for the next few days, familiar things and familiar places. 'Be here now'.

Yves has left me some notes: the wifi password, his mobile number, stuff like that. I set up the laptop. Need to do something with this phone. Ask Nicolas to swap the sim card for me (I'm hopeless with phones). It asks for a PIN, I try twice and get rejected. Shoot, only one chance left, and then what? Better try calling the UK number on the back. I read it out to Nicolas, who dials, does something on his mobile then passes the house phone to me. The customer service lady tells me how to reset and we go through the rigamarole again. Still no luck.

'I'll have to ask tech support' she says. 'Can we call you back on the number you called from?'

'I guess so.' I hang up, and tell Nicolas: 'They're going to call back'.

'Oh, that won't work' he says, looking concerned.

'Do you think it might be okay if I just switch my phone off and on again?'

'I doubt it. It sounds like a problem at their end.'

After he's gone, I turn my phone off and on again. It asks for the PIN code, I enter it, and this time it works perfectly.

I never did get that call back.

I text Yves to let him know I've arrived, and he replies:

'Hi Linda! Happy you are happy. I will arrive around 6pm Friday. May I invite you for *diner*?'

'*Merci beaucoup!* I'm delighted to accept.'

Morning in Brussels – Wednesday 15 February
Walking through familiar streets, damp but shining under sunlight, the cobbled and crowded tourist streets behind the Grand Place, where I buy post cards and stamps. Then into the Place itself, on either side the gothic fripperies of the Hôtel de Ville and Maison du Roi, solid but incongruously intricate, like Bruges lace rendered in stone. In front of me the neat row of flat-fronted guild houses, their windows and balconies consistent and restrained, giving way to wild individuality when it comes to the competitively ornate gables. They are all shops or restaurants now, with an even row of red awnings over the ground floor windows. Over the years I've been coming here, the buildings of the Grand Place have been cleaned and renovated one by one, so some are gilded and shining while others are covered with scaffolding and *trompe l'oeil* curtains.

The morning is well worn as I walk through the cobbled streets up the hill to Le Pain Quotidien in the Place du Grand Sablon. Even though it's gone 11.00 they're still serving breakfast, and I make the most of it – a basket of croissants and bread, juice, a boiled egg (the only time I ever eat them is at breakfast in cafés), butter and preserves and coffee. The fresh fruitiness of strawberry jam is the only accompaniment for a warm croissant, while the dark bitterness of the chocolate spread goes on the crusty warm baguette. Breakfast at Le Pain Quotidien is a small ritual for me, a sense of being here, in one of my favourite places.

After the second cup of coffee, I leave behind sticky red croissant crumbs and the cosiness of the café for the chilly damp of a February morning. I walk across the square and past the grey gothic church of Notre Dame du Sablon, then over the road to the little park at Le Petit Sablon. The statues of the sixteenth century Counts of Egmont and Hoorn, executed for opposition to the Spanish rulers, stand resplendently chilly in their doublets and hose on top of the partly frozen fountain. At the top of the steps I turn to look back downhill across the park towards the church. At the Royal Art Museum I wander from room to room, and find two 16th century paintings of landscapes which are also the faces of a man and a woman. It pleases me to think that they might have inspired Magritte - even Surrealism had roots.

I stop at Les Halles Saint-Géry, the old market hall which is now a community centre, gallery and café, for a hot chocolate and to write postcards. I have promised cards to so many people, they will have to be satisfied with a nice picture and 'Greetings from Brussels!' And there are others I haven't even told about my travels - it seems a good way of spreading the news.

When I get back to the house, I flop onto the sofa. I am so tired. But it's okay. I'm here now, all the preparation and stress are behind me, and everything is going to be fine.

Le Jardin Botanique – Thursday 16 February

Today I'm heading for the Botanical Gardens. I vaguely know the way, but really I'm just following my nose, past the elegant shops and cafés of the Galeries St Hubert and through the less than elegant streets on the other side. It seems everywhere is being dug up, or knocked down, or rebuilt, the sound of drills and smell of concrete dust are everywhere. In a dishevelled back street I find Sterling's English bookshop, and can't resist going in for a browse around. The travel books are upstairs. They've got just what I need - a guide to Barcelona.

The Botanic Garden is on the other side of a nasty dual carriageway. The last time I was here was June 2008. Today the ducks are walking and skidding on the ice of the frozen pond. The parterres are neatly geometric, but empty. Still, the sun's shining, and everywhere seems full of promise. I must come back again in the summer, on my way home.

Heading back to the house, I wander into the main shopping streets, full of chain stores named after foodstuffs: Mango, Paprika, Cerise (or was it Framboise?). There's gridlock on a narrow one-way street with cars parked along the right hand side. One of the parked cars has its hazard warning indicators going, and a young woman has stopped a couple of car lengths behind it, presumably because she thinks the driver is indicating to pull out, and she's waiting to take the space. Someone keeps hooting – I'm not sure if it's the young woman trying to get the parked car to move, or one of the other drivers piled up behind her. But there's no one in the parked car, so it's not going anywhere. There's nowhere for the waiting cars to turn around or get past her, but she doesn't seem inclined to move. Maybe I should come back later and see if they're still there.

Last day in Brussels – Friday 17 February
I've spent this morning sorting out (or trying to) online banking and phone top-up. This is the kind of crap I'm running away from. 'If you have forgotten your security details, call this 0845 number and we will send a new code to your registered address'. I swear, I entered it correctly, I've used it a million times, don't do this to me now.

'In order to top up online, enter the 4 digit pin we texted to you when you first bought the phone'. But this is the third phone I've used this sim in, the original one is back in the drawer at home… no it's not, it's in a box somewhere, the box that has the stuff that came out of that drawer. Whatever, it's not here.

Digits swim through my head, forming themselves into random clusters of four. I need coffee and carbohydrates. Walk the damp streets. By the church of St Nicolas, a busker strums the chords for 'Knocking on Heaven's Door'. I dawdle, window shopping in the ethnic jewellery shop, I like that black and white bracelet, €5, but I don't need more stuff. And when his voice joins in, disappointingly, it's not strong enough to stand up to the guitar.

The guy at the waffle stall is selling *churros*, hot sweet fried batter, I buy a cone of 4 for €3 and walk through the maze of streets behind the Grand Place, going nowhere, doing nothing.

'When you feel blue think of the alternative' my brother said, but I'm not blue, just aimless, reminding myself that this is what I'm here for, observing, absorbing. A window box of white creamy flowers, what's the name? I used to have them in the garden, when I had a garden. It begins with h, helio something? But these are winter flowers, why would they be named after the sun?

Sweet cannabis smoke drifts in the damp air. That young man, thin as a splinter, tight leather jacket, close cropped hair, I wonder if he's a rent boy? I pass the café I had in mind, then pass on. Why do I plan a destination, then think better of it and change my mind? Often my plans are arbitrary anyway, so why not? Contingency is what this trip is all about.

It comes to me – the flowers are hellebores.

I end up at the Arcadi Cafe, and because it's the lunchtime rush and they are packed, I feel obliged to order a meal, not just a coffee. I have their bacon and mushroom omelette, the omelette comes flat, not folded, plate size, like a pizza. The bread is good and comes with real butter mmm, the simplest things are always the most delicious. And now I've finished, the lunchtime rush has died down, there's hardly anyone else in here, might as well order another coffee. The cups bear the logo: 'Caffé Vergnano, 1882' like my favourite coffee shop in Charing Cross Road.

Young couple on the table in front of me, knees touching, he casually puts his hand on the underside of her thigh, near the knee joint, as though he were touching her shoulder.

Back at the house, I check my horoscope online:

'Have you got a big unanswered question? Good! Does tension and uncertainty hang in the air? Even better! Racked with doubt? Great!... It would somehow be wrong now if you felt that everything was sorted, settled and straight. But from now until August, you are on a journey. It began late last year and already has taken you through many twists and turns. Now it can only take you towards one eventual outcome. Happiness.'

Moving on

I feel a little flat. It's gone so quickly, and I'm moving on already. I've written hardly anything, and I haven't got my ticket to Paris. I meant to ask at the station when I arrived, but I still haven't got round to it.

There's the sound of the front door opening. I stand up, and it's Yves, tall, balding, in black framed glasses, oozing Gallic (or Walloon) charm as always. After we've caught up, he asks:

'What time is your train to Paris tomorrow?'

'I haven't got my ticket yet.'

'I could drive you over the border to Valenciennes and you can catch the train from there to Paris. I'm running a seminar tomorrow and Valenciennes station is on my way. But it will be an early start.'

'How early?'

'Seven.'

'No problem. I can be ready for then.'

'Where are you staying in Paris?'

'Near the Place de le République'.

'That's only three stops on the Metro from the Gare du Nord. But I suggest you pack now, because you might be drunk when we get back from dinner.' Huh, as if – anyway, most of it's already done.

We walk to the restaurant, in a part of town I don't recognise - not on my mental map, though no doubt one day in the future I'll find myself there and slot it in.

'You must have whatever you want' he says. 'I'm trying this restaurant out, I have a special pass for 30% off 40 different restaurants in the city, and I want to know what you think about it. It's typically Belgian food, but he gives it his own twist.'

The chef comes out and speaks to Yves in rapid French. I pick up the words *'boudin noir'* and *'un explosion de goût'*, which sounds good to me. The latter phrase is even accompanied by the classic chef's fingers-to-lips-and-hand-opened gesture, though somehow it seems unforced and not a cliché. He's youngish, probably in his thirties or early forties, and nice looking but a little chubby, as befits a chef.

When the food comes, Yves tells me to photograph it '…for your blog. I told him you write a blog. He gets mentioned on lots of food blogs and restaurant reviews.'

'Mine isn't really like that...' But I do it anyway.

Then it's time for dessert - the chef is called out again and quizzed. I think I pick up the words: '…*crêpes Suzette*', but when I ask Yves, it's blinys with Clementine sauce '…in the fashion of…'

I hesitate.

'Or I could have the crème brûlée …'

'You can have that in Paris!' says Yves dismissively. So I go for the blinys *'au façon de crêpes Suzette'*, and the flavour of the sauce is so intense, I'm glad I did.

Chapter 3 - Paris

Brussels to Paris - Saturday 18 February

Uurgh, awake at 4.30 – not that that's unusual, but I wonder how tired I'm going to be by the time I get to Paris? Pass the time by reading – I've just started 'Pure' by Andrew Miller, set in Paris in 1785. Many of the characters are miners from Valenciennes – quite exciting to think I'll be catching the train from there later today.

I'm still awake at 6, so get up and dressed and head down to the kitchen. Yves does a double-take when he comes down the stairs and finds me ready and waiting for him, just as I was for Ian on Tuesday.

'Is your case still upstairs? Shall I get it for you?'

'Oh, yes please.'

By the time he's manoeuvred the Wardrobe down two flights of stairs from the attic, he's out of breath and probably wishes he hadn't offered.

'Better take a taxi in Paris' he grumbles.

We leave about 7.15, driving from Brussels in a rented car.

'I don't have a car of my own, it's not worth it living here. I just hire one when I need to' he says as we negotiate the city traffic. It's good to have a little extra time to chat.

'You know, I took a round the world trip with my family in 2007, though we weren't away for so long as you. The good thing is, normally when you leave somewhere you are sad, but when you're leaving to go somewhere else, it's exciting.'

'I know just what you mean.' He's summed up my feelings perfectly. I've got some regrets over leaving Brussels so soon, but nothing like the heart-sinking I normally feel when I have to go home, and anyway I'll be passing through again in the summer. It's something I've always felt, that regret at leaving places and reluctance to go home. It's only through talking to other people that I've realised not everyone feels that way. Maybe I really am a traveller at heart, always wanting to be somewhere else.

'We had to have a stopover in Europe half way through' Yves continues 'so we chose to come back to Brussels, but even that was exciting, because we came as though we were tourists.'

'I know that feeling too. We lived in the States in the 1980s, and when we came home as visitors, I saw the place very differently. It made me much more appreciative of England.' Maybe by the end of this trip my attitude will change again.

At Valenciennes station Yves speaks to the lady in the ticket office.

'You need to change at Lille. You can't buy your tickets for the Metro here, but when you get to Lille, go to the relay and you can get them there'.

I have no idea what the relay is, but no doubt I'll find out.

When the train pulls in, I turn and hug him, English fashion, rather than the continental peck on each cheek. He seems a bit taken aback. Between us we haul the Wardrobe onto the train. I stand hesitantly in the corridor. There are steps up to the carriage.

'Leave it there' he says. 'It will be fine. No one will steal it - it's too heavy!'

This feels like the first real leg of the journey. Eurostar doesn't count, it's too familiar. To my eyes, my fellow passengers have a Flemish look: large, blond, florid with round cheeks and chubby faces, like extras from a Breughel painting.

At Lille station I have forty five minutes to kill before my connection to Paris. There's a shop, the French equivalent of WH Smith - called Relay. Suddenly Yves' comment makes sense – so I buy my ticket for the Paris Metro. When we reach the Gare du Nord in Paris, I trudge for miles trying to find the right Metro platform. Twice I stand at the bottom of a flight of stairs and kind passers-by offer help. Don't let anyone tell you the Parisians are rude and unkind.

At last I emerge into daylight, drizzle, and the roar of cars and construction in the centre of the Place de la République, a huge roundabout with endless traffic orbiting anti-clockwise. So which exit do I need to get to my hotel? Better get the printout of my reservation out of the backpack

– okay, it's on Boulevard Voltaire, but where the hell is that?

I have to get to the other side of this whirlpool of cars, and here's a crossing – and when I get over, there's a map too – Voltaire is about three junctions clockwise. The rain is smearing my glasses and my arms are starting to ache - even pulling a case on wheels is exhausting after a while if it's heavy, especially if you're tired already and in an unfamiliar city, surrounded by strangers and wondering what you're doing here and what the hell possessed you to come.

At the hotel, the guy at reception looks at the Wardrobe and shows me the lift. The floor area is probably smaller than the cross-section of the Wardrobe. He pulls the metal grille back for me and I step inside, trying to pull the Wardrobe in after me. No chance.

'Ah no' he says 'You get out.'

I stand in the lobby while he pushes the Wardrobe in. Now there's a place for me to squeeze in beside it. Don't ask why it worked that way and not the other, it just did.

I press the button for the third floor. The lift creaks and groans – is it going to take the weight? At last it stops and the doors open. Somehow I manoeuvre the Wardrobe across the corridor and into my room. There's a bed, a bathroom with a shower and a toilet, a bedside cabinet, a desk, and just about enough space between the bed and the wall to leave the Wardrobe standing on its long end, but not to lay it flat. But I'm safe, dry, I've got a bed for the night, and best of all - I'm in Paris.

Chasing dreams - Sunday 19 February

Can you ever escape from yourself? In part, I guess, this journey is about trying to answer that question. Will this experience change me? Will I come back as someone different? Or even at the end of all this, will I still be the same person, no escape, no running away?

The last time I was in Paris, I walked down to the river on Sunday morning, heading for Shakespeare & Company, the famous bookshop on the Left Bank, and heard the bells of Notre Dame ring in all their glory. The shop's claim to fame is that its American owner, George Whitman, allowed struggling writers - names like Hemingway and Ginsberg spring to mind - to live in the attic free in exchange for working in the shop. On my previous visit, that May morning in 2008, I made a pilgrimage there, and listened to the bells, and it all became part of the fantasy, of the other life that I would live if I wasn't so caught up in the one that was starting to crumble around me. So when I was planning this trip, I made sure that I'd be in Paris on a Sunday morning to do it again, although I heard on the radio just before Christmas that Whitman had died at the age of 98.

So here I am, standing on a bridge over the river to the Île de la Cité, watching the sun making light-and-shadow patterns on the Gothic stone of the cathedral, but why can't I hear any bells? Am I too late, or don't they ring every Sunday? It's beautiful, everywhere is beautiful and I'm in Paris, and I damn well ought to be happy, so why do I feel so cross with myself?

Well, for a start I slept in late, I missed breakfast, and to cap it all, there are no bloody bells. So much for my fantasy now, being here on Sunday morning to listen to them. Well, that's what happens to fantasies, isn't it? Suddenly the whole thing, everything, seems ridiculous.

This is the city of romance, and what relevance does romance have to me? I'm still the woman no one wants. I'm still running away. I hoped I'd feel better, but here I am in Paris, for God's sake, and I'm still managing to feel sorry for myself.

I guess I've still got to eat. There's a cafe in the shadow of Notre Dame, where I order scrambled eggs with crusty bread and coffee that makes my heart pound and my head buzz, even without the romance. Through the window I watch the queue to get into the cathedral – I assume it's moving, every time I look it seems exactly the same, but I suppose it's different people.

I finish my breakfast and walk over the bridge to the Left Bank, and Shakespeare & Company, but somehow that's not quite the same as last time either, and I can't buy any books because I don't want to overload myself - or the Wardrobe.

I forgot when I booked my weekend in Paris that the museums don't open on Mondays, so as I've only got two full days here, I'd better do my museum-visiting this afternoon, tick that box. I'm going for the Musée d'Orsay, because in my memory I enjoyed it more than the Louvre. I can't help feeling that once in a lifetime is enough for the Louvre, but the Musée d'Orsay holds the essence of Paris.

I queue for half an hour to get in but that's okay, as we shuffle towards the entrance I'm reading 'Pure' by Andrew Miller, a novel based on the destruction of the cemetery and church of Les Innocents in 1796. Once inside, I go looking for the Toulouse-Lautrecs, suitably Parisian, the Van Goghs and the Gaugins.

The Impressionists are on the fifth floor, and the lift isn't working. Still, at least that makes me walk through four floors on the history of Art Nouveau, which is quite enjoyable, and I might have skipped it otherwise. But by the time I get to the top, I don't really feel that interested in looking at the paintings. I'd rather sit in a cafe and read some more – but if that's all I'm going to do, what's the point of coming all this way? I could have done that back in Bedford.

On the way back to the hotel, I stroll through the Tuileries, very pretty in the late afternoon sunshine, children sailing boats on the lake, and men in berets playing *boules*. I've got half an idea of looking for the locations from 'Pure', I know it's somewhere near the underground shopping centre at Les Halles, but I'm not sure exactly where.

Near the church of St Eustache (mentioned in the book) I find a restaurant for dinner, then take the Metro back to the hotel. I have to walk so far to find the right line and the right platform, it feels as though I might as well have walked the whole way.

Boules **players in the Tuileries**

Parisian notebook - Monday 20 February
Monday morning sunshine, pollarded plane trees, and the self-important growling of scooters, like tom cats who think they're tigers.

Respectable people are starting the week's work – and here's me, window shopping, wandering, sitting with a coffee and watching the world go by – this is what it's all about.

I've pieced together the information in the back of 'Pure' with my guidebook and the free map from the hotel, and found my way to the site of the cemetery and church of Les Innocents, now the Place Joachim-du-Bellay. The square is draped with orange plastic fencing, and resounds with the noise of pneumatic drills and cement mixers. Doesn't look much like I imagined - but there in the centre is the Fontaine des Innocents - arches, domes, nymphs and steps down which no water is cascading on this February day.

As I eat lunch, a lady passes the *crêperie* window wearing turban hat, coat, leggings and ridiculous 6 inch patent heels, all in matching pure, primary blue. Impossible to see her face clearly from this angle, but from occasional glimpses I'd say she's at least my age.

On the Pont Neuf, I stop to watch the river flow, and eat the clementine I bought earlier. The flesh is blood-orange red, the flavour sharp and intense, like the sauce I had with the blinys on my last night in Brussels.

I notice the bases of the lamps look very like those by the Thames in London, dolphins at the four corners and the face of the river god on the flat sides.

What now? A trip on the Batobus which glides up the Right Bank as far as the Eiffel Tower, down the Left Bank to the botanic gardens, and back again. The Left Bank drifts slowly by. From the top walkway a Japanese man feeds the birds, gulls and pigeons, then photographs them as they fly over our heads.

Sitting on the wall, a young couple, facing one another, the girl looking in the same direction as us. She has a sketch book, props it against her legs. Is she going to draw her partner?

Another couple, the man is walking along the wall, the girl holds his hand, stretching up. When they reach steps, he walks up the ramp. At the top, the wall has disappeared, and now they walk side by side, he pushes her hand into his coat pocket.

A mother on the boat with a baby about ten months old on her lap.

He sucks his mother's finger, and twirls his mother's hair around his hand. They leave at Notre Dame. I move to the seat behind so that now I am looking forward, no longer squinting into the sun, which is low and dazzling.

I leave the boat at its furthest point, the Jardin des Plantes, and walk for half an hour or so among winter trees until the next boat stops. The light is starting to fade as we chug back along the Right Bank to the Place de l'Hôtel de Ville, where an ice-skating rink has been created in the square. This is the closest stop to my hotel, so I leave the boat - I'm nervous about being out alone after dark.

The low winter sunset floodlights the skating rink, which is filling up as off-duty office workers and students join the tourists. I'm not brave enough to follow them, but to one side there's an old fashioned carousel, so I buy a ticket and mount a russet painted charger, grasping the gilt pole as we start to move.

I feel comfortable at last, I feel as though I've got my bearings, I know my way around, this small part of the city at least. And now that I've settled, ironically, I'm leaving in the morning.

Back near the hotel I find a restaurant and see *'piece de boucher'* on the menu. 'Butcher's piece' I think, in my school French.

'Excuse me, is this steak?'

'Yes madame.'

'I'll have that, *s'il vous plait.*'

The waiter brings me a salad, and as I'm eating it I start to panic – what if it's code for horse? Or maybe it just means a cheap and slightly ropy bit of steak which doesn't deserve any special name? The steak comes – it looks like beef - and tastes as though my second guess was correct, thank goodness.

Au revoir Paris – Tuesday 21 February

I've decided to follow Yves' advice and get a taxi to the station, after my experiences of the Metro, with and without the Wardrobe. It's a different receptionist, but I ask him:

'Can you arrange a taxi for me to Gare Montparnasse at 10.30?'

'Taxi?' he says helpfully. 'You can get a taxi from Place de la République. There is a taxi station there.'

'Oh. Can I leave my bag here for now?'

I set off with my backpack for McDonald's, to use the free wifi, as it costs a fortune in the hotel. I need to check an email from my sister, to try to find her phone number. She hasn't responded to the one I sent last week giving the train details. And what with swapping around sim cards, I seem to have lost the contacts from my phone, or some of them. So I don't have confirmation that she'll be there to meet me at the station and I have no way of contacting her.

I look out for a taxi rank on the Place, but in among the roadworks I can't see anywhere that could be one. I must ask for better directions when I pick up the Wardrobe from the hotel.

In McDonald's, there are no free tables, so I take my breakfast to the bar with the stools, and set up the laptop. Across the bar, and to my left, there's a man, also with a laptop. I don't take much notice until I realise he's speaking to me. Then I shake my head. 'Don't understand…'

'Aah, English! How are you finding the wifi?'

I glance back at the screen. 'It's not started yet.' I open Chrome; the tabs that were open last time all re-open, all with the green McDonald's screen. I hit *'j'accepte'*.

'It's okay. It's working now.'

'I find it's very slow' he says. I pull a face.

'It's slow everywhere in Paris' I say, with the benefit of three days' experience. I focus on the screen. I need to get onto Yahoo to find the email with my sister's phone number. I know they don't have wifi at the farmhouse so I'll be dependent on McDonald's for a week, and not in walking distance. I have to check my emails. Check my horoscope. Check the map. There must be other things I need to do.

I concentrate on the laptop. But I feel bad now. He's a good looking guy, he seems harmless. Quite Latin, brown eyes and thick dark hair starting to turn grey, younger than me, but not too young. I should have made a bit more effort to get into conversation, not bring down the shutters. Why do I always do that? I have to start being a bit more open.

He says something else, so I respond, smile, we get into conversation. He's staying in Paris with his sister, but he's travelling, trying to find a good place to be. 'I think maybe Amsterdam, what do you think?'

'I don't really know it.' Not at all.

'Everyone wants to go to London, but I think it's a bit hard.'

'Hard? Well, it's expensive.' I wonder if he means 'unfriendly'.

'Expensive, difficult to find work, difficult to find a place to live.'
'That's true. I've just come from Brussels. I like it there.'
'I haven't been there. How is it?'
'Very friendly, very open. Very comfortable, for me, but I've been lots of times. More comfortable than Paris, but that might be because I don't know Paris very well.'
'Paris is beautiful. I lived here for twenty years.' But not now, now he's just passing through, staying with his sister. He's Italian originally, 'from Milano', but he has a French passport too. He pulls them both out and shows them to me, along with an id card. I see his name is Marc, or Marco. On the French one, his hair is cropped, on the Italian, up in front in a quiff, on the id card, he points out: '*une barbe*', stoking his chin: 'what do you say?'
'Beard.'
'Ah yes, beard.'
I tell him I'm going to Brittany.
'You must go to the Mont Saint-Michel. Very beautiful. My girlfriend told me to go there when I went to Brittany.' I hope my expression hasn't changed when he says 'girlfriend'.
I fish around in my backpack for my passport to show him, then, a little panicked, to convince myself I haven't lost it. In the end I find it in my small handbag,where I'd already looked once.
'Ah, it looks the same as mine! Not special for England?'
'No, it's a European passport, just like yours, except it says "Great Britain" on the front.'
'England seems a strange place, not really part of the continent, but not really anywhere else. How is it there? And Ca-me-ron' - he separates the syllables – 'do people hate him? There is big change there I think?'
'Well I don't like him.'
'Nor me. I preferred the other one, Tony Blair.'
'I didn't like him either' I say. Not towards the end, anyway.
'But not Thatcher?'
'No definitely not Thatcher!' I agree.
He is looking at my passport.
'Ah your name is Linda, that's a lovely name.'
'Thank you!'
'And you were born in the same year as my mother.'

'Well thank you again!' I say laughing.

'Ah, I am sorry! French men are not very polite!' So now he's French. Just how old is he? I wonder. His mother? It's depressing. He doesn't look that young, especially with that irresistible touch of grey in his sideburns. Hey ho.

He gives me back my passport, we shake hands, say goodbye and good luck.

'I will go to Amsterdam.'

'I'll probably be there on the way back, maybe July' I say.

'It's a good place, a friendly place, and you can get the drugs. Not bad drugs, the sweet drug, the one that helps you sleep. Enjoy Bretagne.'

'You too. Enjoy Amsterdam.'

Back at the hotel, the usual receptionist is on duty, and as soon as I mention 'taxi' he offers to call one for me. From the hotel I ride through the Place de la Bastille, then over the bridge and up through Montparnasse to the station.

On the wall there's a notice with 'Waiting room' in several languages. In Spanish it says: *'Sala de espera'*. *Espera* – doesn't that mean 'hope'? 'The room of hope'. I like that idea. 'It's better to travel hopefully than arrive', so the saying goes, and there's a lot of truth in that. While I'm moving, I feel as though I'm in a bubble, my own little space, I am the still point at the centre of the universe, while everything passes by my window. The inverse, perhaps, of sitting in cafés and watching the world go by, but from my point of view, the feeling is the same.

So, with hope in my heart, I say goodbye to Paris, under glorious sunshine which lends a golden glow to its handsome white art nouveau apartment blocks, snaking river and pretty bridges. The train passes through woodlands, rows upon rows of tall skinny winter trees, in such neat lines that they must be some kind of plantation, with green balls of mistletoe on every bare trunk. Ah, that's the French for you.

Chapter 4 - Brittany

Bienvenue en Bretagne – **Tuesday 21 February**

Travelling hopefully is one thing, but arriving, by contrast, can sometimes be a bit of a challenge, bursting the bubble and disturbing the status quo, requiring action and movement.

And dragging the Wardrobe from a train in a strange town in a foreign country and wondering whether the people you're relying on meeting you are actually going to be there is probably the most unsettling feeling I've experienced so far in my journey.

All around me, people are being greeted, hugged, welcomed in French. I walk slowly across the platform and to the exit, then out into the station concourse, looking around me. I still haven't got Gill's phone number, and just for a moment…

'Linda! Over here!'

'I lost your number… didn't know if you'd got my email… You didn't reply…'

'That's because we talked on the phone, remember? On Monday evening, when you were at Ian's?'

Of course.

'Did you come over the viaduct?'

'I don't think so.'

'How could you miss it?'

Brother-in-law Neil isn't impressed with the Wardrobe.

'This isn't going to last five minutes… The handle's only attached to the fabric, that's never going to survive… There's nothing to it… What you want is something more robust… Why couldn't you have a backpack like everyone else?'

Chapter 4 - Brittany

Half of the back seat is folded down, and the Wardrobe gets wedged in, with me on the other half of the seat beside it. But somehow the trimming gets torn, either getting it in or getting it out.

'See? What did I say?'

Lovely to see you too, mate!

Gill grins.

'Don't take any notice of him.'

'Don't worry, I won't!' I never do.

Families, eh?

Ten minutes outside the town, we pass the viaduct. From this angle, it looks amazing, great arches stretched across the sky. Now I remember coming through the hills, looking down on the town. But bizarrely, when Gill asked if I'd seen it, I didn't realise that was what it was.

The drive from the station is longer than I thought. Three things surprise me about Brittany. In my head, I was expecting a French version of Cornwall, but the first two surprises come when I look at the map. Now, I did 'O' level geography, and it's not as though I'm unfamiliar with the map of Europe, but sometimes you take things for granted. So, the first surprise is how big Brittany actually is, stretching across half the south coast of England, from Portsmouth westward. And the second is, how far west it is. This is weird, because the time zone for France, and Spain come to that, is an hour ahead of the UK. Whenever I've been to mainland Europe before, I've always been further east, so I've never questioned this before, but it's really quite bizarre.

'I hope you like trees' Neil says. 'You're going to get a lot of them in the next few days.' So the third thing is – how different the countryside is from Cornwall – where are those bare, wild moorlands of my imagination?

'No problem' I say, as we wind through dense forest roads. I love trees, late-winter, early-spring trees, conserving their strength, psyching themselves up, biding their time. Trees full of mistletoe and birdsong. Familiar birds with French accents – I swear, they look the same but they sound different. And yellow blossom.

'What are those yellow trees?'

'I think they're mimosa. They smell lovely. I remember Mum used to love it, you get it in flower arrangements.'

As we pull in between the farm buildings, an elderly man in a beret comes over to the car.

'That's Alexi' says Gill. I've heard about him, the neighbour, and past owner of the farm where they live. 'He's got to come and check you out.'

Alexi has a modern comfortable house, Gill and Neil have the old farm house and outbuildings, partly renovated by a previous English owner, and continued since by them, their daughter and son-in-law.

We pull up in front of the farmhouse and unload. Grey stone blocks, small windows, a deep arched doorway, like the back door of a church, but behind it, not a vestry but a living room with a wide stone fireplace, sofas, television, table, stairs up to the next floor. Neil is busy lighting the fire as I dump the Wardrobe in the space by the side of the staircase and decide not to try taking it upstairs. I follow Gill through the door to the right, which leads into a big modern kitchen, an extension on the side of the old house.

'Sorry the house is a bit cold' says Gill as she puts the kettle on. 'We only came over from England last week, it's not had a chance to warm up yet.'

We go out for dinner to the pizzeria in Carhaix-Plouguer, the nearest town. Everybody knows Gill and Neil, the proprietor's not there, but I'm introduced to his wife and daughter. It feels nice and homely, after being on my own in Paris, hand-made pizzas cooked in the stone oven at the back of the room, red wine in a carafe, family chat.

'Let's come back here next Monday, on my last night' I say. 'My treat!'

'What do you want to do while you're here?'

I shrug.

'Haven't really thought about it.' I've never been to Brittany before, so everything's new. Actually, just about everything about this trip is new, from now on. I haven't got much in the way of plans about what to do, just a general outline of where I'm going, and a few specific places where I'll be visiting people.

'Well do you want to come with me to the *boulangerie* tomorrow morning to get breakfast? How does that sound?'

'Sounds good to me!'

When we get back to the farmhouse I'm a bit light headed, slightly woozy. Not drunk, I've only had two glasses of wine. Just a bit strange, almost as though I was still swaying on the train. We sit around the fire for a while watching (surreally) English local TV on satellite, until I make my apologies and go up to my room. I'm in the attic bedroom again, as I was at Yves' house in Brussels, with a pointed ceiling and dormer windows. I snuggle down under the duvet and listen to the owls calling, feeling snug and safe.

Change of plan – Wednesday 22 February

I'm awake about 7.30, but Gill and Neil take their retirement seriously, and rarely get up before 10.00, unless there's a specific reason for it. So it's quite late, from my point of view, before we get to the *boulangerie* on my first morning, but the bread is still warm and wonderful, with the butter melting into it and strawberry jam.

'Have you had any more ideas about what you'd like to see while you're here?'

'Well, there's one place, but I think it's probably a long way away.' I've been giving it some thought, but I don't really know much about Brittany, and as I said earlier, it's much bigger than I was expecting. 'How about Mont Saint-Michel?'

'Ah, that is quite a long way away. What do you think, Neil?'

'Why don't we make a weekend of it, book a couple of rooms in Saint-Malo and stay there overnight?'

'Sounds great!'

I'm planning to be in Brittany for a week and then next Tuesday go to stay with my friend Marian, a Yorkshirewoman who lives further south, near Bordeaux. She's in the UK at the moment, but she'll be flying back while I'm in Brittany. I've got my train ticket to Angoulême, and after a week with her, I'll be heading for San Sebastián, on the north coast of Spain, to stay with another friend, Eduardo.

We go out for a drive and to visit a nearby market. Sadly, I seem to have left the sunshine behind in Paris, and the scenery and drizzly mist both remind me of Wales, rather than Cornwall. Grey stone buildings, grey roof tiles, grey skies, streams bubbling over grey rocks, but with bright blue paint on the shutters and sudden splashes of yellow mimosa. I don't really mind the weather, I'm enjoying being here, seeing new places, quiet little towns and harbours full of furled sails waiting for summer.

In Locronan, we visit a church, where the inner contentment I'm feeling is reflected in the following inscription in English:

'Friend, believer or not, freely entering this church, extraordinary beauty of Man's work, witness of his faith in God, let us respect Silence, disposing to meditation and prayer. May this visit stay with you as a moment of peace.'

But my peace is rather disturbed when I check my phone and find the following text:

'Hi Linda, just had a phone call to say my mum has been taken ill so I am not flying back to France tomorrow. Don't know when I will be back home. Sorry, please text back. Marian.'

Oh shoot, what happens now? I feel bad for my friend, of course, but also - what do I do now? Doesn't sound as though she expects to be back by next Tuesday, when I've got a ticket to Angoulême. And Eduardo isn't expecting me until the week after.

I send a reply to Marian, giving her my sympathy and telling her not to worry about me: '… will check my ticket and have a think about my plan B.'

I'm scarcely a week into my journey, and already my itinerary is starting to come apart at the seams. I guess I could cancel the ticket and stay in Brittany for another week, but that seems like grinding to a halt. Am I going to have to change plans already?

Home thoughts – Thursday 23 February
In a *crêperie* on a misty Breton hillside, over a cup of mulled cider, I am enthusing about my Kindle, when Neil asks: '…is there anything you haven't got?'

I take a deep breath.

'I haven't got a home and I haven't got a husband.'

'Well you don't seem very bothered about not having either of them.' And it's true. There are lots of things that bother me at the moment, but neither of those two is a big issue.

'That's what I couldn't do' says Gill. 'I admire you but I don't envy you. Not to have a home, a base to go back to. I couldn't do that.' They have two bases now, one in England and this one in Brittany, two homes, two places to hunker down.

I've only been away for ten days. I'm still sleeping badly, which is a pain, but I don't suppose I'll ever resolve that. I'm used to it - a chronic insomniac - but I am tired all the time and it drags me down.

We're taking a drive around lovely tourist sites, grey in the mist but still beautiful. 'You should see this place in the summer, it's heaving, you can't see anything' Gill remarks, not for the first time. Even in February, there are a fair few people around.

Pont Aven for lunchtime, quaint with harbour and water mills, and sounding (and looking) to me as though it should be in Wales. A stop off at the beach at Cabellou: sand, waves, rocks and pools. 'We bring the grand kids here when they come. Once we saw a French family bring their pet rabbits in cages and let them out for a run around.'

'My favourite kind of beach. I always liked beaches with rock pools where you could climb and poke around in the pools and see what was there.'

'Yes, I remember that' says Gill.

Maybe it was a reaction to growing up near the Lincolnshire coast, with its flat, tedious beaches where the sea disappears into the distance at low tide, leaving acres of slippery mud behind.

'If I found a pool with sea anemones, that made my holiday.'

Not much of a day for sitting on the beach though, so we move on to the harbour and walled town of Concarneau, and watch the ferry boat pottering around the harbour.

I've decided that rather than try and change my ticket for Angoulême, I'll go there anyway, find a cheap hotel for the night, and travel on to Spain the next day. I text Eduardo to check the best station, and he suggests Hendaye - another place I've never heard of.

Mont Saint-Michel and Saint-Malo – Saturday 25 February

I went to Saint Michael's Mount in Cornwall over thirty years ago, with my then fiancé, and I'm expecting Mont Saint-Michel to be similar, a causeway, a rocky island and a castle. But when we approach, it seems much larger than my recollections of its name-sake; a mediaeval town looming out of the fog as we pull into the car park, its highest turret covered by the low lying clouds. It's atmospheric on this wet February day, but still busy with tourists.

Gill and I climb up some of the way into the town, leaving Neil in a café. The tide is low over the estuary, and we gaze out through fog and drizzle across mudflats with channels running through them. It's an impressive but not exactly glamorous sight, a reminder, as with the

Jardin Botanique in Brussels, of the northern winter I'm hoping to leave behind.

At the hotel in Saint-Malo, while Gill and Neil go to their room to freshen up, I sit in mine with my laptop hooked up to the wifi, searching for a hotel room in Angoulême for Tuesday night; booking my train ticket from there to Hendaye; and logging on to my online banking to transfer some money. It's doing the same thing it did in Brussels: I know I'm putting in the right details but it keeps rejecting them. I've got to transfer money to another account to pay my credit card, and top up my euro cash card, but I can't do either of these things. What the hell do I do now? Think Linda, try to calm down. The credit card bill doesn't need to be paid until the beginning of April, and I've still got a few hundred euros available. It's a Spanish bank, maybe I can find a branch in San Sebastian and ask them for help with the logon? And worst case, I can buy an air ticket home, or at least to the UK, as I don't have a home to go to. But it probably won't come to that.

There's a knock on my door, and I'm still crouched over the laptop, hair dishevelled, distinctly unfreshened, as my spruced-up relatives wait to walk over to the restaurant. *Que séra, séra*, I think, and join them.

In the hotel reception, there's a pile of travel magazines. One has a cover feature about Istanbul, in French, of course, but I flick through it anyway. Am I really on my way there? Maybe, I think. Maybe.

Brittany to Angoulême – Tuesday 28 February

Tuesday morning, 6.30. It's pitch black outside. I'm on the move again.

'Is the caravan ready?' Neil asks.

'Just about'. I shove my toiletries bag, nightie, last minute bits and bobs into the Wardrobe, where it lies on the floor at the foot of the stairs – has been lying for the last week, as no one could face trying to get it up to the attic.

'This is better' he acknowledges as he picks it up.

'That's because it's all upstairs' said Gill. 'We're taking it back to England with us when we go'.

'We've only got a little car, remember?'

'It's only one bag' I say. I took everything out yesterday afternoon and had a purge, in an attempt to make life easier. The leave-behind bag is pretty heavy, but the Wardrobe still feels hefty, too.

Chapter 4 - Brittany

At the station, there's no lift. Between the three of us, we get the Wardrobe down the steps, through the tunnel and up the other side. There's an electronic display showing the carriage numbers with a letter beside each. Mine is C, and there are letters on the lamp posts lined up beside the track.

'When it comes in' Neil says, 'you get on and I'll hand the case up to you.'

The train pulls in and I jump on, turn to pull up the Wardrobe, and stow it in the luggage compartment. I turn back to the door, but now a crowd of teenagers is boarding the train.

'Gill!' I call, at first I can't see her. I didn't give her a hug, but I can't get out again now.

I spot her as she waves and blows me a kiss, and I reply. The youngsters are still boarding. I spot Neil at the back of the crowd, wave, and blow him a kiss too. Then the doors close.

Grey morning hangs over the little towns, the trees with their nests of mistletoe, the grain silos. And here and there, the sudden yellow splashes of mimosa blossom.

I've only got 10 minutes to make my connection at Paris. Ah well, expect the best. There have been several times already in the last fortnight when events have had the potential for disaster. Expect the best, the worst doesn't always have to happen. Maybe I am changing my famously (among friends and family) gloomy attitude.

There is colour outside now, not just from the neon signs, green on the fields. At Saint-Brieuc, it's almost full daylight, of another rather grey and grizzly day. We are travelling towards the sunrise, but I have my back to it. Sad that my abiding memories of Brittany will be of grey skies and mist. 'You're not seeing it at its best.' No, I guess not.

Chapter 5 – Angoulême

*Bienvenue en Angoulême –***Tuesday 28 February**
For the first time, I feel like a real traveller. This is the first place I've been to which isn't either a tourist city I've visited before, or staying with friends/family.

It's about arriving in a place where the sun is warm against your face. Leaving the station and finding your hotel across the road, where you push down on an old fashioned (and tuneless) bell to get the attention of a receptionist whose English is as faltering as your French, and yet you communicate and smile and laugh with one another. About wanting sunglasses, longing to change jeans and boots for sandals and a flowing summer skirt. Finding a table in the sun outside a café on a square where bells mark the quarter hours and the small son of the family on the table to your left blows bubbles through a straw into his glass of lurid green pop. Where you stop to look at the shape of a chimney pot, and take more photos of graffiti and backstreets than you do of churches and civic buildings.

La vie est belle.

I know nothing about Angoulême, hadn't even heard of it till Marian suggested it as the station to aim for. Wikitravel describes it thus: *'Angoulême is the capital of the Charente department. It lies about 135km north of Bordeaux in south west France. See: The cathedral; The ramparts (old medieval city walls); The* hôtel de ville; *The* murs peints *(walls painted with cartoons); comic strip museum; paper-making museum.'*

It's mid-afternoon, and the sun is warm to my skin and my soul, though the townspeople obviously think it's nothing special and are resolutely wrapped up with scarves and gloves over their winter coats.

The hotel restaurant isn't open till dinner time, and the size and price of the set menu makes my eyes (rather than my mouth) water. I walk uphill, away from the hotel and the railway lines, feeling self-conscious but rather excited to be alone in a French provincial town for the first time. Behind a bog-standard shopping mall, there's a sunlit square where I sip *café crème* at a pavement café, then stroll to the ramparts and admire the views over the town and the distant mountains.

The '*Murs peints*' really are quite impressive. I've seen and enjoyed them in Brussels, but here they're everywhere, covering buildings of all shapes and ages. Some are jokey, some amazingly skilful *trompe l'œil* images reflecting the surrounding scene, or drawing phantom windows, inhabitants and street furniture on the outsides of buildings. I walk around in a happy daze taking a ridiculous number of photos. Fate has brought me to this place, and surely Fate wants me here for a reason? Maybe so that my path will cross the person or opportunity, the moment of destiny that will change my life forever?

'Errr... have you got any idea where you are?'

It's that gremlin again, breaking into my happy reverie. I've been wandering vaguely, and... well, down there in the valley, a couple of hundred metres below me, are the railway tracks. I guess if I keep heading towards them I can navigate my way back towards the station – yes, look there's a sign for '*La gare centrale*' – that's got to lead me back to the Hotel Terminus.

Angoulême to San Sebastián – Wednesday 29 February

A giant Mickey Mouse balloon is grinning manically at me over the seat back on the other side of the aisle.

More people pile into the carriage. A young couple get on carrying a suitcase and backpack between them. I move my backpack from the seat beside me and wedge it between my legs under the table, so the girl can sit down. Still more people are pushing down the aisle, and there is much checking of seat numbers. My ticket doesn't have a seat reservation, not even for the train I should have caught.

Heading south, with my back to the engine and the setting sun shining in through the window. I wonder about the Wardrobe: Did it get disturbed by the crowds who got on after me? Is it still there, or has it been flung out in disgust by some SNCF employee?

Single to Sirkeci

Outside the window, we're passing a plantation of Christmas trees. Not expected. Now they seem to be Christmas trees on stilts. Long, long bare trunks with Christmas trees at the top, and then another field of normal sized Christmas trees in front of them.

The day started well. I thought I could spend the whole morning taking advantage of the hotel's free wifi, before my train left at 13.55. But that seemed a bit sad. The sun was shining, and I knew how pretty the town was.

I had a shower, looked in the Wardrobe for my hairdryer, unpacked and repacked and tried to redistribute the weight a bit so everything doesn't fall to the bottom now it's not completely jammed any more.

I was combing out my wet hair in front of the bathroom mirror, when the light went out. Power cut.

I took this as a sign that I should get dressed, finish repacking, close the laptop down, and get out for some breakfast.

In the spaces between the pine plantations, the orange sun bounces along the perfectly flat horizon. It doesn't look real. I've been staring at it for too long and now the page I'm writing on jumps in front of my eyes.

A field of horses. And another – I'm sure that's what they are. I peer with red-dazzled eyes. This isn't the Camargue, is it? I'm sure that's further east. If I've thought at all about this area of the border between France and Spain, I thought of the Pyrennees, of mountains, but this is monumentally flat, and yet not in the dreary, East Anglian fashion that I'm used to from home. And is that the sea over there, where the sun is setting? It must be there somewhere, of course, but how far away? I have no idea. Don't they breed horses in the Camargue, or just white cattle? I haven't seen any of those.

When I'd packed my bags and left the hotel room, the power had come back on, and I thought perhaps I could sit in the reception area and use the wifi. I had to press the creaky old bell to get Madame's attention. I asked if I could leave my bag. Her English was if anything even worse than my French, but we got by, probably because it forced me to be more careful with my French, to make more effort to concentrate.

Little flat towns now, with flat white houses, and the sky full of pink light behind them, then back among the trees.

Madame commented on the size of the Wardrobe, and I explained, in slow, careful French, that I am travelling for 6 months all across Europe, visiting friends, by train. Then she says that it's fine to leave it because she'll be there all day, and I say my train is at *deux heures* from *la gare*, and suddenly she gets all animated and starts trying to tell me something. I think it's just to do with getting my ticket validated, but she calls up the stairs for someone to explain to me. A middle-aged lady appears on the landing.

'There's a strike' she says, in English-accented English. 'Not all the trains are going, but if you go into the station and turn left and go to the desk at the end and talk to the young lady there, she'll sort you out. Where are you going?'

'Hendaye' I say, then I think. 'Bordeaux', because that's where I need to change.

'I think the trains to Bordeaux are okay, but I'd go and check. Anyway, they'll make sure you can get where you need to.'

'Thanks, I will.'

I checked at the station, and confirmed that my train to Bordeaux would leave as expected, then walked up the hill towards the café I sat in yesterday, and had breakfast. On the way back down, I met a crowd marching the other way, with banners and loud chants. The strikers, of course.

Suddenly, there is movement on the train, the young couple stand and assemble their luggage. The Mickey Mouse balloon and attendant family leave the carriage. I am about to move my backpack into the space vacated by the young woman, when another young man sits down in it. He must have been standing – or sitting on his luggage – for over an hour, since we left Bordeaux.

The lady at the hotel was quite correct – there was no problem with the trains to Bordeaux. It was the connection from there to Hendaye that was the issue – a four hour wait.

In the ticket office at Bordeaux station, there is a map - actually, it's a mural that covers the wall, over an archway – a map showing *'Chemins de fer du Midi'* – the railways of the south. Routes served from the station. To the left of the archway, the Bay of Biscay, where the Atlantic coast of France turns a corner into the northern coast of Spain, from Bayonne, Biarritz and Hendaye to San Sebastián and Bilbao. To the right, across the isthmus of the Pyrenees, like a mirror image, is the northwest corner of the Mediterranean coastline, from the Costa Brava to the Côte d'Azur:

Perpignan, Narbonne, Sète, Montpellier, just names to me at the moment. The station was full of disgruntled people, squabbling families, long queues at the information desk and buffets. In the ladies' toilet I was harangued by the woman at the entrance when I innocently tried to walk past her and into a cubicle without paying for the privilege. I suppose I could have found a left luggage locker for the Wardrobe and stepped out into the city, seen some of the sights of Bordeaux and maybe even sampled the local produce, but I felt safer staying put, so I found a seat, texted Eduardo to warn him about the delay, and pulled a book from my backpack.

When the train arrived, I had no reservation of course, so I stowed the Wardrobe and settled myself where I could.

The train terminates at Irun, another place I've never heard of. At least seeing 'Hendaye' on the map at the station confirmed to me that it really existed. I'm not sure how many more stops there are, and hence when I can expect to get there.

By Biarritz, it's dark, and all I can see is a confused blur of lights on water which convinces me that it's probably a very pretty town if only I could see it clearly. A couple more stops, and I'm virtually alone in the carriage, just a mother and two children, and I wonder if they're going as far as me.

I hope Eduardo's going to be there. To 'arriving at a station in a strange town in a foreign country', add the further qualification – 'in the dark.'

I step off the train and into a gloomy, and empty, station. At the exit, a dark man under the influence of alcohol, or worse, is accosting other passengers.

A young boy speaks to me in very precise English.

'Hello, I am Mikel, the son of Eduardo.'

I turn to see where he's pointing. Behind the open boot of a car Edu appears, smiles and waves as relief rushes through me.

After what feels like only about ten minutes down the road, we cross a bridge.

'Are we in Spain now?' I ask.

'We have been since just after we left Hendaye.'

I've reached the third country of my itinerary.

Chapter 6 – San Sebastián

Bienvenidos a San Sebastián - **Thursday, 1 March 2012**
The sun wakes me, shining onto my face on the spare bed in Eduardo's study and filling me with a surge of excitement. A new country, a new city, an old friend. I've got this far. And it's a new month.

Before Eduardo goes to work, he gives me the low-down.

'If you go out the front door and turn left, you'll see the river at the end of the road. Turn right there and you'll come to the bus station. Turn left, keep walking past the bridge and you'll come to the sea. You can climb the hill or keep walking along the sea front till you get to the harbour. Here are the keys, this one is for the apartment and this one for the front door. I'll be home about six. Have a good day.'

Coffee and freshly squeezed oranges. 'Life is good' I think, and head for the sea. The wind is brisk and chilly, throwing up waves over the rocks. Old codgers in berets sit with fishing rods out over the foam, gulls shout to one another. A bright wintery morning at the seaside and the day opens out ahead of me. Deep green pine woods to my left on the hillside, paths leading up through them, but I stay close to the water. I can't see anything round the headland, so I just keep following the sea wall, listening to the gulls, watching the fishermen, feeling the spray from the waves.

A path leads up the hill, and there's a café – the first one I've passed. Just what I need: sit in the sunshine, write in my notebook, soak up the atmosphere.

'Err.. *café? Por favor?*'
'*Si.*'
'*Merci - er – gracias.*'

The pocket guide to Barcelona I bought in Brussels, has 'handy phrases' in the back, but I left it at Eduardo's. All I have in my head is my school French, and my Spanish is even more primitive than that.

I want to sit and listen to the gulls and the waves and the impenetrable babble of Basque from the people around me and soak up the sunshine, like a bud preparing to open, like a lizard on a rock, blinking in the first intimations of spring.

In Angoulême yesterday I had this feeling – to let go of the story and find the still place. But my life is the story, and that is why it's so hard for me to be still. I can't let it go.

There are layers, like an onion. There is the life that stops me from writing. There is the life that compels me to write, which becomes stressful in its own way, the need to capture, observe, record. The compulsion to hold on.

Perhaps, if I don't try so hard…

I finish my coffee and walk over to the other side of the terrace. Suddenly, there below me is the harbour, which has been hidden by the headland until now. I walk down the steps and along a path, looking down across white buildings with terracotta roof tiles, the grey stone harbour walls enclosing rows of boats and beyond it the almost perfect circle of the bay, the chilly, pale sand lapped by grey-green water, the tall, elegant buildings along the promenade and across to the opposite headland. The sun shines through the bare branches of a plane tree, black bobbles of last year's seed pods silhouetted against the dazzle.

I'm looking for a restaurant on the seafront for lunch, but what I find is more than I bargained for: a three course set menu of soup, seafood platter and *crema catalana*. A bit much for lunch, but hey, why not? I sit in a quiet upstairs room and savour every morsel. Most of the tables are empty, just a few businessmen in suits discussing deals, a smartly dressed couple who arrive separately (sneaking from work for a clandestine lunch together perhaps?) and me. This is not a tourist café, and it's not tourist season.

There are people and dogs walking on the beach, but I just lean on the railings and watch the patterns of the waves crashing into the curve of the sea wall, which sets up another wave that comes from the side and intersects with the one coming directly to shore. I could watch them forever, bumping and blending into one another.

I think I'm falling in love with this place. Why bother trying to find anywhere more perfect?

Tapas
'You like to eat tapas?' Eduardo asks.
'Ooh yes, sure, that sounds lovely.'
'We can't go out till the grocery delivery man has been, he should be here by eight o'clock'.
'I'll just carry on with my blog if that's okay? You don't think I'm being rude?' I've been crouching over my laptop since he got home from work.
'No problem at all. I'm glad you feel so comfortable.'
How could I not feel comfortable, ensconced with my laptop and internet access in this lovely flat in this beautiful town in this friendly country?
I finish off a post and notice it's about half past eight. Eduardo is working on his laptop in the kitchen, as I've temporarily displaced him from his study.
'Is this the famous Spanish "by 8 o'clock"?' I ask. He winces.
'They've texted to say it will be later, sometime between 8 and 10. Do you want to do something else for dinner? Are you hungry?'
'I'm okay, thanks.' I remember that great lunch, in the restaurant overlooking the harbour.
'Well, I'm starving' he grumbles.
'If you don't want to wait…'
'No, it's fine, we can go later'.
Eventually Señor Ocado (or whatever his name is) turns up. We stack the boxes on the kitchen table and step out into the night.
'I think it's a bit late to go to the Old Town now, but there are a couple of bars near here who do a special deal on Thursday nights.'
We find somewhere and order two glasses of red wine. The food is laid out on the counter.
'I recommend these' says Eduardo. 'These' are soft warm fritters made from potato with ham and cheese in the middle and a crispy coating. They go down a treat. As we talk, Eduardo's eyes keep sliding past me to the end of the bar, and the television, where a basketball match is in progress.

We move on. The next bar seems a bit more classy. The barman hands us a menu in Basque with Spanish translations.

'What do you want to try? Do you like anchovies?'

'Oooh, now you're talking!'

The barman overhears us and passes me a menu with English translations. We go for anchovies marinated in oil which has had lots of garlic and chillies fried in it.

The TV here is behind the bar where we're standing, so it's hard to avoid watching the basketball game, but as it's in front of us both, it feels more sociable.

When the anchovies are gone, so is the wine.

'Same again?' Two more glasses.

'What do you want to eat this time?' I've spotted some rather nice looking pastries topped with prawns further along the bar. 'Just take one' Edu says, 'you don't have to ask.'

The local team is winning, but it's very close. The guy standing at the bar to my left starts talking to Eduardo. They speak rapidly, I assume in Basque. Suddenly he turns and looks at me, and I hear him say '... *Español?*'

I shake my head 'English.'

He says something, but I don't catch it.

'No, no' Eduardo is saying. 'Just friends.'

'He's your boyfriend?' asks the stranger.

'No, just a friend' I say laughing.

They are still talking past me. I take a step back with my glass of wine, and reflect that when two men are talking about sport, it doesn't really matter what language it is, it's equally unintelligible as far as I'm concerned. The stranger is youngish, with dark eyes and curly black hair.

Eduardo looks at me again.

'He wants to buy us a drink. Are you okay with that?'

'I am if you are' I say with a grin.

Curly has a half pint tumbler. The barman throws some ice cubes into it, then three quarter fills it with J&B whisky, then hands it to the guy with a bottle of water. I get the feeling he's a regular. He takes a slug of the scotch then tops up the glass from the water. Eduardo and I look at one another.

'This is getting surreal' he says to me under his breath as the barman produces two more glasses of rioja. I just laugh.

Curly pulls out a packet of fags.

'You wanna smoke?' he says to me.

'No *gracias*.'

'Take one' he pushes one up and holds it out to me.

'No, really. It would make me sick.'

We pull coats on and all go out into the street with our glasses. I hear the word 'discotheque' pass between them, and wonder if he's trying to get us to go on somewhere.

'He says he works in a disco, on the gate.'

'A bouncer?' I ask.

'Is that what you call it? Someone who stops people who shouldn't be allowed in?' This guy doesn't look as though he could bounce anybody. He's about the same height as me, but a lot slimmer. Rather sweet.

Eduardo has his phone out. Curly is telling him to check something online.

'He says he was a boxer. He says he played football for...' he mentions the name of a team. 'He says he's from Marbella, but his accent is from Galicia.' Not Basque after all then.

'I'm a crazy guy' Curly says. 'This is my grandfather' pointing to Eduardo.

Somehow we finish our wine, take the empty glasses back into the bar and escape.

'Oh my god' says Eduardo as we walk home. 'I couldn't understand half of what he said. He talks so fast, and it's a difficult accent, they slur over all the consonants and it's hard to follow.'

I still think he's cute.

Bilbao - Friday 2 March 2012

Coffee in the sunshine outside the Guggenheim Bilbao.

Café con leche. Now I know what to order. I was afraid it might be latte, which I hate, it's so insipid, just frothy milk with a very faint coffee flavour. Yuk. But espresso is too short, I like the intensity but I need something that lasts a bit longer. It's like drinking shots. I'd rather have something to sit over, to make it last. But I still like to be able to taste it. Anyway, the *café con leche* is good.

Eclectic music comes out of the café, and rolls across the plaza.

When I arrived, a jazzy violin, maybe Stephane Grappelli. Then Lennon ('Woman'), Springsteen ('Streets of Philadelphia'), Santana ('Black Magic Woman'), now the Sinatras ('Something Stupid').

I came here on the bus, leaving San Sebastián in the morning mist. Flashes of sun, but just as the first patch of clear blue appears, we plunge into a tunnel. Feels as though we are going down and down but suddenly we emerge, the blue sky still there behind a misty veil.

Mountains, sheep, lambs, chalet-style buildings. Palm trees, pine trees, a patch of cabbages. Dusty beige apartment buildings with rainbow lines of washing hanging to catch the sun, grey factories, football pitches, multi-storey car parks, all crammed into deep valleys. A small blue train, a derelict viaduct, mimosa blossom.

Another bus, on the other side of the road, the passengers passing my window as I pass theirs, but no one is watching me as I watch them.

Cows among the sheep, a field of white goats, horses. And then the city, flyovers and high-rises. The bus station.

When you get to a new town, how do you work out which way to go? Remember the breadcrumbs. This is from a thought I had in Angoulême, or maybe it was even earlier than that, in Paris. Don't forget to leave the breadcrumbs behind you, so you can find your way back. Metaphorical breadcrumbs, that is. Make a mental note. I always forget.

Out of the bus station, right, then left, over the tram tracks. Walk downhill, away from the mountains, and I must be going into the town. A golden statue in the centre of the road. A park with a fountain. Teenage boys shouting as I stop to take photos, maybe at me, but why should I care?

Geese and peacocks. The geese parading across the water with their tails in the air, the peacocks nonchalantly trailing theirs across the grass. With tails like that, you can afford to be careless. The geese make such a show of theirs, it's comical. On the other hand, they can swim, they can glide across the lake. The peacocks are stuck on the grass. That's their problem.

I'm beginning to wonder if I'm going the right way. Before the park the streets seemed rough and down at heel, an old industrial town. But now, much more upmarket, a contrast, fancy shops, I still feel out of place, but for the opposite reason. Window shopping, antiques, a beautiful turquoise glazed jug, curving sinuously up to the spout. I take a picture, then look at it and see my face holding the camera, reflected in the glass of the shop window.

I turn left at the next junction - in the distance at the end of the road, light bounces from a shining, silvery building. This is what I'm heading for, of course. Huge before it, the flower dog, spring green now, not really blooming yet. There's the museum entrance, but I can see the café is down the steps. I pass it and walk on a little further, to lean on the rail and watch the river. To my right, unexpectedly, I see Louise Borgeois' giant metal spider. I wasn't expecting it here. I saw it when it was shown in the Tate Modern during the first six months of it opening in 2000. I didn't know this was where it had come to rest.

Then I head for the café, to drink *café con leche* and scribble in my note-book. And now I've finished writing, it's Sinatra *père* on his own, singing 'My Way'.

Inside the museum, I walk through the sinuous windings of Richard Serra's rusted steel plates, and start to feel sickly, vertiginous even. Maybe it was the journey on the hot bus, sitting in the sunshine at the café, or maybe just being inside this metallic box, however beautifully shaped and shimmery it might be. In the lift up to the higher levels, I grow even more disoriented and dizzy. I daren't look down in case I can't stop myself from jumping.

When I get back to the flat, Eduardo introduces me to an elderly gentleman in the hallway.

'I am Eduardo the second' the gentleman explains. 'This is Eduardo the third, and you've met Eduardo the fourth.'

'Ah no', Edu says. 'Linda hasn't met Eduardo yet. He's in there' he points to the living room 'watching television.'

Edu's older son has been at his mother's ever since I arrived two days ago, so I haven't met him yet, just the younger one, Mikel.

'I've been to Bilbao today' I say, making conversation. 'It's an interesting town. Big contrasts.'

'It used to be a steel town, an industrial town, but the industry has gone and the city suffered.' Eduardo Senior knows about Sheffield. I explain that I grew up in Scunthorpe, also a steel town which has seen better days.

'And what did you think to the Museum?'

'It's very beautiful, but it made me feel ill. It was very strange.'

'We say it is like a beautiful present, but what is inside is not so lovely as the packaging!' he says with a smile. I laugh.

A very charming old man, a real gentleman.

Edu's parents live in the same apartment block. He moved away for a while and lived in Bilbao, the boys were born there, but he came back to San Sebastián and the same place. It seems strange to me to think of being in the same place all your life, and so close to your parents. But to him it seems strange that I moved away, and my brother and sister, that we've all lived our lives in different places.

Endlessly fascinating - Saturday 3 March 2012

Walking out into San Sebastián again, I remember the analogy of falling in love, and it occurs to me how good a metaphor that is. The thrill of finding a new place is like the thrill of meeting a new lover – blind to the risks of disillusionment and over-familiarity.

Aha, my cappuccino has arrived. The waiter comes back for my money. '*Merci madame.*' Maybe, unlike the French, the people here don't recognise how bad my accent is, so just assume when I accidentally speak French that that's where I'm from. It's quite funny.

I walk up the headland, reach a fork, and glance to my left, to catch sight of a ginger cat stretched out on the bench in full sun.

I approach slowly. He (or she) turns his head and sees me. I stop dead. '*Hola*' I say softly. He doesn't move so I take a picture and walk a little closer. Now he sits up, still looking at me. No closer then. I sit on the bench, eyes closed to the sun, thinking I will email a picture to my daughter with the caption 'guess who I saw today?' When I open my eyes again, he's gone.

Everything, everything is endlessly fascinating. The sound of the waves, the seagulls, a dog barking in the distance, a clanking chain on a boat in the harbour.

I am hit by a small shower of twigs and clods of earth. This bench is set into the hillside, and something behind me is disturbing things. The cat, perhaps? Surely cats are more sure-footed than that - well, by reputation they are, though it doesn't apply to some I've known.

Endlessly fascinating? What else was I thinking of earlier? The pattern of the waves as they hit the curve of the harbour wall then bounce back again and intersect. The winter trees, pollarded hard into shapes like multi-armed cacti. I first noticed them in Brussels, then Paris, and Angoulême, and now here. I thought they were plane trees, but maybe this is a method of management, not limited to any particular species. An old carousel, bright in reds and golds. Elderly people in wheelchairs being pushed by young people who don't look like relatives. Could this be one of those seaside towns where people come to retire, a place with lots of nursing homes?

Something behind me sneezes. And again, no mistaking it. I sit up and look round. The ginger cat trots down the path, giving me as wide a berth as possible, but never taking his eyes from my face. At the end of the wall, he pauses.

'Hola' I say. 'Puss-puss. *Hola!*'

He turns and is gone. Maybe I should do the same.

Surf and peacocks – Wednesday 7 March
Chez Eduardo, the internet is down. I hope it's not my fault, but he assures me it isn't.

'It's not just here. It's bigger than that'.

The sun is shining again, after yesterday's rain.

'I think I'll go over the river, to the surfers' beach.' I haven't been that way yet, but Eduardo has pointed it out to me, and I've seen it from the headland.

'If you turn right when you get over the bridge, you'll see the gate to the park. It's like a British park.'

That sounds a bit boring.

'Well, maybe not like a British park. Your parks are so beautiful and so big, I think. It has those turkeys with the big tails.'

After a moment's startled confusion, I nod.

'Peacocks' I say. It's a pretty good description. 'I saw some in the park in Bilbao.'

When I cross the bridge, I don't see any park gates. I cross the road, and realise I'm at the railway station, maybe the one where I'll catch the train to Barcelona on Sunday.

I walk downriver towards the next bridge, the last one before the sea. Still no sign of park gates. I wander through back streets vaguely parallel with the beach, past shops full of cheap tat and, bizarrely, a vegan restaurant.

Here's the beach. Out on the sea I can see what look like large birds, dark triangular shapes. Then I realise they're surfers in wetsuits, waiting for a wave.

Walking back through slightly shabby streets, I find a path leading uphill past a playground. Path leads to path among the trees, I keep going upwards and then I find the peacocks. At the top is a building that seems to be a research/education centre, and rows of tree ferns that make me think perhaps it's a botanic garden. It's pleasant, but not what I'd think of as a 'British' park, I was visualising formal flower beds.

I head back to the harbour and the main beach, looking for a bench to sit in the evening sun and read my book. An old man in a wheelchair has been left by the side of a bench, facing the opposite way, while his carer sits facing forward on the bench next to him. When I get closer I realise he is asleep, or at least he has his eyes closed, while she is texting on a red phone.

Most of the benches are occupied, mostly by couples. I make for one facing the beach, which I can see is empty. A man sits with his back to the sea wall, replacing a guitar string. After I sit down, he starts to play. He is singing but it's drowned out by the strumming, like the guy in Brussels. People walk past and ignore him, while the seagulls call behind him.

All sorts of people are alone, in all sorts of ways, for lots of reasons, I think.

Excursions on the Basque Coast – Friday 9 March 2012
When I let myself into the apartment, there's no reply to my cry of *'Hola'*. I drop my bag in my room, and check to confirm that there's no one in the living room or kitchen. In the gloom of the hall, I notice a folded sheet of paper propped on the sideboard. I switch on the light and read:

'Dear Linda,
Unfortunately, we cannot share the evening with you. Maite's mother has already come and we will spend the weekend with her. Feel free to take anything you want for dinner from the fridge... I'll see you tomorrow morning.
Best regards,
Edu'.

So Maite's mother has arrived from Madrid. I knew she was expected today from a conversation I had with Maite, Edu's girlfriend, yesterday evening, so it's not that much of a surprise. And the boys, presumably, are at their mother's place. An evening to myself.

So, what have I been getting up to for the last week? I've been lazy, sleeping late. I ride buses and trains, walk, sit in cafés, watch the waves, get lost, find my way back, read, come home tired and mess around with photos or answer emails. Somehow, I never quite get round to writing. And yet there's lots to be said, and if I don't write it down, I'll lose it, and then I'll regret it.

Yesterday, for example, at Edu's suggestion, I took the local train to Irún and then the bus to Hondarribia. I walked down to the harbour and saw a boat with a sign for trips to Hendaye leaving in 10 minutes, so I took it across the bay and found myself back in France. We landed at a marina, quiet in the low season, I found a café where I ate pizza and drank wine, while a television on the wall showed coverage of the French presidential election campaign. I wrote the following in my notebook:

'The world is so full of joy – of red-roofed, white-washed houses, and blue sea, and green hills, and yellow… yellow mimosa. And lizards on stone walls. And birdsong. And boat rigging that sounds like cowbells.'

The harbour at San Sebastián

Chapter 7 - Barcelona

San Sebastián to Barcelona – Sunday 11 March

Tiredness crashes over me in waves. I swear the floor is still moving under my feet. Probably the sensation I had while walking along La Rambla earlier this evening, that the pavement was ridged like a ploughed field, was an illusion brought on by the wave patterns in the paving stones and exhaustion from the journey. I kept getting the distinct feeling that I was going to fall. But I'm here, I'm okay, I've got a bed for the night and it's been paid for, I've eaten dinner, I've even got wifi, and I might have a bath. And tomorrow, a new city, new things to explore.

I came to Barcelona with high expectations – it's been one of my 'must see' places for years. My friend Douglas came here when he was at a difficult point in his life, and it turned things around for him. Which I guess is really what I'm looking for – something to start me off again, on a new track. But high expectations, by definition, are difficult to match and prone to be disappointing. So I guess it's not surprising that I didn't instantly fall in love with the place, as I did with San Sebastián.

Twelve hours ago, 7.30 Sunday morning, walking by the river to the station, Eduardo pulling the Wardrobe. He seems subdued – I'm not sure if he's emotional at my departure or still half asleep. I'm awake and raring to go. I think I should feel sadder than I do, I tell myself it's because I have to focus. I have a train to catch. But the sadness was yesterday. I can't help thinking it's all about the next place now, the next stage.

A beautiful morning, a big moon still in the sky. On the bridge, a group of youngsters pass us as we wait to cross the road. Eduardo says quietly:

'Haven't been home yet. They were talking about cocaine.'

'Ah' I say. 'I thought I could hear people in the street when I woke up.'

When we get to the station, he sees someone he knows.

'Excuse me a moment.'

While they're talking I go to the desk and show my home-printed ticket. I'm chivvied through, and when Eduardo comes over we are standing awkwardly on opposite sides of the gate.

'Have a good trip – well, a good journey!'

'Thanks! And next time you're in England, if I've got anywhere you can stay, you're welcome to come and visit.'

'Well let me know if you're even in England!'

'Yes, who knows?'

We're blocking the gate, other people wanting to go through. I turn.

'Give my love to the Balkans!' he calls with a grin. 'Oh, and the people!'

On the platform, I look at the houses opposite, the shabby part of town, where I was walking on… what day was that? Wednesday? The day I went to the surfers' beach and the park with the peacocks. On the back of the ground floor of a grubby tower block, the stencilled words: 'Akademia Hair' make me smile. A pigeon waddles towards me across the opposite platform, hesitates as it reaches the edge, fluffs it, jumps, and flutters awkwardly up into the rafters of the station.

The train pulls in. I grab the Wardrobe and hoist it in, then find my seat – the window glass is shattered on the outside. No chance of taking photos from the train then. I settle down, get out the laptop and start to write.

The announcer mentions Zaragoza and Barcelona, I wonder if those are the only two stations, in which case perhaps I can change to one of the empty seats. I pick up my stuff and get myself settled again, across the aisle and a couple of seats further back. I start to get into the rhythm again, when a railway employee comes along the aisle and asks to see my ticket. Should have known it was too good to be true. He says something in Spanish, points to 14D, my old seat. I'm closing the laptop down to move again. I point to the shattered window. He's still talking rapidly in Spanish. 'All right, all right, I'm going as fast as I can' I grumble. I pick up my laptop, and return to my old seat. He goes down into the next carriage, then he turns and comes back, still talking to me. Now what? I'm getting really irritated. Suddenly he breaks into English:

'You want to move seat? Because of the window?'

'Yes please!' I feel bad about snapping at him.

'Come this way' he leads me to the first seat of the other carriage, same side as my original ticket. Evidently the one I'd moved to was reserved, but this one isn't.

'Thank you!' I flash him my best smile to make up for my grouchiness. *'Muchos gracias!'*

We have left the grotty suburb behind, passed through the tunnel and out into the mountains. The morning is misty around us. I settle myself into my seat, but leave the laptop in its bag. I don't feel much like writing.

I pull out my Kindle. I'm reading 'Homage to Catalonia'. Orwell is crouching in a filthy trench, bemoaning the cold and tedium of war, the inhospitality of the mountains. Outside my train window, there is snow in hidden valleys, and later, when the sun comes out, battalions of swirling white giants marching over the hilltops, and I wonder if I should have downloaded Don Quixote, but there are so many books I want to read, and somehow I don't have as much time as I thought I would.

I become so engrossed in the machinations between the Communists, Anarchists and Fascists, the POUM, the Popular Army, the Assault Guards, the CNT and the UGT and who is fighting with whom, and who against, that I don't notice when the landscape changes. There are fields outside the window and rows of what look like vines but surely they're not because they're not pruned bare like the ones in Bordeaux, and orchards of trees – olives? – no, I don't think so – and some that are long and spindly and I don't have a clue what they are, some on cordons (might they be oranges?) then one orchard of small trees covered in pink blossom – maybe they're cherries, because Orwell describes a scene in a cherry orchard.

I see a pair of storks nesting on a red rooftop, and then the land is yellow and drier and before I realise it we are stopping at Tarragona and now I try to catch glimpses of the sea through the hills and we've hit the suburbs and people are getting up and standing in the aisles. I pull on my coat and back pack, although the thermometer on the carriage display that started at 6°C when we left San Sebastián is now showing 19°C.

CRBO

Bienvenidos a Barcelona

On the station concourse, I pull the directions and my phone from the pocket of my backpack, dial the number and ask for Rebecca, as instructed in the booking agency email.

'This is Linda Hadfield. I've just got into the station.'

'Where are you?'

'At the station. Sants Station. I'm about to take the Metro'.

'You're taking the subway?' She doesn't sound American. Do I sound American? Why call it the 'subway'?

'Yes. Well, I haven't got my ticket yet.'

'Okay, you've got the directions? It will take you 45 minutes to get your ticket and get to the apartment. I'll arrange for Erik to meet you there at 2.30. But if you're going to be late, call me again.'

'Okay.'

I make my way down into the Metro station, buy a ticket from the machine, get on the train and stand, hanging on to the Wardrobe. Four stations, get off at Verdaguer, exit Diagonal. Go two blocks up Girona, turn left and go 50 metres. That's the directions.

I'm standing on Girona. But which way is 'up' and which 'down'? I walk over one block, check the name of the cross-street, and have a look on the map. Can't see it there – must have gone the wrong way. Okay, walk back again, past the entrance to the metro, wait to cross four lanes of traffic, walk to the next block - oh bugger, according to the map this road is on the other side, so I must have been right the first time - walk back again - should I call Rebecca? If I stop to pull out the phone and find the number, I'm wasting even more time.

At last, this is the building. It's 14.29. So I wait. At 14.35, I start to call again. As Rebecca answers, a red scooter with a blonde pillion rider passes on the street, the driver waves and pulls in.

Erik (for it is he), unlocks the front door. There is just enough room in the lift for the Wardrobe, with my backpack balanced on top of it, and the three of us (including the pillion rider).

I paid a deposit online with my credit card when I booked, but the balance is to be paid in cash on arrival. So, when Erik has shown me to my room, we talk money.

'It's €77 to pay, but for another €3 I can give you a ticket for the tourist bus, it goes all round the city, hop-on-hop-off as many times as you like, and you get a book of discounts for all sorts of other things, restaurants, attractions, shops. Sounds good, yeah?'

'Sounds great!' Too good. To be true. And you know what that means.

I have a €50 note and two €20s, but I don't have €10. So I give him the €90. He makes a fuss over getting change, and gives it to me as a fiver and assorted small coins. I wonder if he's giving me the opportunity to leave him a tip, but if so, I ignore it.

When he's gone, I read the small print on the 'bus ticket' which I've just paid €3 for, and discover that it's actually a voucher for €4 off the full price – which is €24.

I have the distinct feeling of being had – serves me right for thinking I could get a trip like that for €3. Still, I've only lost €3. I don't have to fork out the additional 20. I could skip the whole thing. And I skim through the book of discounts just in case there's anything that I might use, to get my €3 back. There isn't.

La Rambla

I set off walking vaguely in the direction of La Rambla, the street known as the heart of the city, the place to be. I know it's south and west from where I'm staying, so I go down the road, then right, then left, deciding at each junction whether to turn or keep going as the fancy takes me, trying to keep in the sun as much as possible, or just crossing where the light is green and carrying on if it isn't. And everything is great, so many lovely houses just sitting casually in nondescript streets, little details like the balconies or gates being shaped just-so, sometimes a mosaic or painting on a wall, no two alike. The pastel-painted stucco frontages sparkle in the sunshine, pink, green, cream and white like peppermint candies, and unlike San Sebastian it's warm enough to walk without a coat. Shady little back streets, pavement cafés everywhere, funny little shops.

The first thing to hit me as I approach La Rambla proper is a sign for McDonald's. Then KFC. Then a young woman walks past wearing a Burger King crown. Crowds. More living statues than you could shake a stick at. Sex shop. Wax museum. Peep show. More conversations in English (other than ones aimed at me) than I've heard for a month. Tourists! Nothing could be further from the utopian atmosphere described by Orwell in the first chapter of 'Homage to Catalonia' than this tacky commercialism.

Chapter 7 - Barcelona

Well, my brother once pointed out to me that if I don't enjoy popular culture, I'm missing out on things that lots of people get pleasure from, and whose loss is that? That's as may be, but I guess there are compensations. And I don't like La Rambla, not one little bit.

Hop on, hop off - Monday 12 March
I wake into the bleary morning, and the first thing I notice is my head is still pounding. What the hell am I doing here, in this tacky tourist trap, with its 'unmissable' deals and rip-off paella suppers? And what am I going to do for the next two days? Get out my laptop and open it to check my emails – terrific, the battery's dead. There must be a spare socket? Nope, I'll have to unplug the bedside lamp – the only light in the room – and sit on the bed, crouching over with the keyboard balanced on my knees. I try to write:

'Maite [Edu's girlfriend] said, on Saturday evening:
"I hope you find what you're looking for".
I wish I knew what I was looking for.'

Good question. What the hell am I looking for? I squint at the screen in the gloomy room, then put the thing down on the bed, get up and walk over to the window. A few moments fiddling with the blind allows in some thin strips of light, which do little to illuminate the screen - or my thoughts. I twist and turn the laptop, and bend the screen forward and back to find the best angle, then have to sit to one side of it so as not to block the light again. I resume typing:

'But I guess it's better, on Monday morning and alone, to be here rather than alone on a Monday morning at home – wherever "home" is.'

I stop typing again, clasp my hands together and reach up and back to stretch my shoulders. This is ridiculous. Better go find some breakfast. There's a kitchen in the apartment where I'm staying, and I was planning to buy something yesterday - coffee, fruit, pastries, whatever – but I didn't pass any food shops, and I was too tired to go looking for the grocer's that Erik had assured me was 'just downstairs'.

Well, no point staying here, I might as well go out. Down the road

I spot 'La Boulangerie' on a corner on the opposite side of the street. I navigate my way across the road, and push the door open into a cosy, narrow space redolent with fresh coffee and tempting cakes. I smile and point at a sticky pastry, ask the smiling lady for *café con leche, por favor,* settle myself down and get out my pen and note book:

'I'm in a comfy chair in the corner, the sun is shining, I'm off to explore Barcelona, what can possibly be wrong with that?'

As the sweetness of the pastry and dark richness of the coffee hit my system, I remember that feeling I had on Monday morning three weeks ago in Paris, of a world taking itself off to work while I had nothing to do and no one to answer to but myself.

I set off to find the tourist bus. On my ticket it says *'Descuento: PACK HOTEL 201'* – looks like the pack that Erik sold me for €3 was supplied to hotels to give to their clients. Still, I've been specialising, on this trip (and arguably, life in general) in aimless, unplanned, you might even say pointless rambles – turning up in a place, and wandering off somewhere with no clear idea of what I'm doing or why. Sometimes, this leads to wonderful discoveries, and sometimes it leads to wasted time and energy, and disappointment. So, why not, for one day, do something organised, and planned, set out for me by somebody else?

There are two routes, the Red (western) route and the Green (eastern) route, and you can do both as many times as you like in the day for which your ticket is valid. I get on the Red bus, buy my ticket from the smiling guide, climb up to the top (open air) deck, plug in my little headphones, set the channel to 3 (English), dutifully listen to the commentary. I've often seen those buses in London and Cambridge and wondered about taking one some day. I'm only here for two days, for goodness sake, so why not?

The bus stops on Montjuïc hill, and on a whim I hop off, to walk through lush, eclectic gardens: maritime pines, rhododendron, agaves, birds of paradise – the floral kind – and the springtime song of more prosaic feathered varieties. I keep walking through the bright afternoon, one more path, then another, just to get a bit higher, to see the next view. Just a bit more.

Below me, through crystalline light, the city floats white and grey between the blue of the Mediterranean and the blue of the sky. Towers and harbour, the curve of the bay, and around me, the green and cream spikes of agave and red tropical flowers under the bare branches of northern winter trees.

Maybe I could stop for a coffee? I passed a café a little way back. I keep walking under the wires for the funicular railway, the little cars rumbling over my head, between the hill and the harbour. It would be fun to ride on that - seems pointless to ride down after making the effort to climb up, though. Maybe I'll do the upward journey tomorrow.

At the top, two German couples ask if I will take a photo of them all together on their camera, and afterwards they say *'Gracias'*, which is funny because my German is a lot better than my Spanish. The Spanish think I'm French and the Germans think I'm Spanish, but never mind. Smiles and pointing get you a long way sometimes.

I walk back down wondering how long it will take me to get to the next bus stop. There's the café – it doesn't look great, the sort of place where everything for sale is shown in a garish colour photo. Not a good sign. My problem is, I don't want to eat in the tourist traps, but if they show any sign of elegance I think they must be too expensive, and if they look too local I worry that I'll stand out too much. This place has a picture of a hot dog, and suddenly I really want a hot dog - how sad is that?

'Uno hot dog y agua, por favor' I say hesitantly.

The guy hands me a bottle of water and a hot dog and says: 'the ketchup's on the table' in English. 'Oh, okay, thanks!' Tasted pretty good, for a hot dog.

I catch the bus back to the stop on the Passeig de Gràcia where you can swap between the buses. I get off again and go in search of the green bus, but all the ones that pass are the same orange-red colour. I try two different stops, but it's the same story. Eventually it dawns on me that all the buses are identical in colour, but some say *'Ruta Verde'* (Green Route) on the destination board, and some *'Ruta Roja'* (Red Route). The next time I see a *'Ruta Verde'* bus, I jump on.

The Green route, if anything, seems more interesting, but it's getting a bit late for hopping, so I make mental notes of places to go for a proper look tomorrow. After all my moaning, it's been quite a fun day after all.

When we get back again to the Passeig de Gràcia, it's 6 o'clock, and I'm tired. Time to call it a day. I walk back to the apartment, checking out various cafés. I go into one and ask for the *'Menu de Dias'*, but they've stopped serving. Another place just has tired-looking leftover tapas.

Near the apartment there's a Lidl, where I buy a potato tortilla, bread, butter, cheese, chocolate, water, jam, salad, rioja... I'm looking for something with a screwtop, but they all have corks.

While the tortilla is heating in the microwave, I find my emergency cork screw, the one I packed back in the flat in Bedford, then break the cork trying to get it out and have to do it again with the second half.

The rioja is raw but it hits the spot. I'm tired, maybe just the one glass will be enough - but I can't get either of the remnants of the shattered cork back into the bottle. I'll just decant the rest of the wine into my water bottle... Oh - there's a bit left over. Might as well drink it.

Parc Güell – Tuesday 13 March

I'm walking along the Passeig de Sant Joan - Catalan for 'the street of Saint John' rather than the female version of the name. It's uphill, which wasn't so obvious in the tourist bus yesterday. The two lanes of traffic are separated by a broad park, which is divided by the intersecting junctions, alternating one-way. This morning, the crossing lights are managed by police with whistles. I wait for a signal that it's safe to cross, till I realise the best way to do it is to follow the crowd.

The park (or parks) are full of playgrounds, fountains, benches, cycle/running tracks, and at one point, three *boules* courts, levelled, staggered in height (because of the gradient) and marked out by low metal walls. It's a continental version of bowls, less manicured and more casual than the English one – although the courts here are more organised than I saw in the Tuileries in Paris, where I watched the old men playing it on an unmarked patch of level grass. It looks like there's a tournament, with games on all three courts, or maybe it's just the over-70s Tuesday morning league.

A pigeon sips from the green water of an inactive fountain.

A woman of about my age and build watches her grandchildren in one of the playgrounds. She is wearing horizontally striped, skin tight leggings, and a non-matching, horizontally striped top. Her hair is puce-coloured, with a silver quiff over her forehead. It takes all sorts I suppose – not that I'm in any position to criticise anyone else's fashion sense, in my travel-worn jeans and tee-shirt.

A small black curly haired dog straggles along on the end of a lead pulled by a middle-aged bald man. I can't see whether the dog is actually in pain or just doesn't want to go. The man keeps pulling on the lead, then looks up and catches my eye, watching. I look away.

The walk is further and higher than I was expecting. I realise that I haven't brought either a bottle of water or any of the bananas I bought in Lidl yesterday. There are a fair few coffee shops along here but I had breakfast at the flat, so I really ought to keep going.

I'm heading for Parc Güell, the brainchild of the Catalan architect, Antoni Gaudi. I don't know much about Gaudi, other than that my friend Douglas is a fan, and that he was, to say the least, unconventional. I picked up more information from my guide book and the bus tour yesterday, enough to lead me to expect something bizarre and surreal. I keep trudging up the hill, which gets steeper the closer I get, the sun is warm, the crowds of pilgrims grow thicker, and I wonder whatever possessed me to walk all this way. I hope the destination will be worth the effort.

A green and blue mosaic lizard, 'the dragon', welcomes visitors by the entrance. Lush tropical gardens, white steps up to a columned plaza and roof terrace set into the slope of the hill, with staggering views across the city. Lots of ceramic tiles, blue and white on roofs and spires, multi-coloured mosaics on walls, fountains and benches. Biscuit-coloured buildings which seem to have been constructed from part-baked cookie dough, with white icing roofs. Elegant palm trees, and columns which echo their shape. Lots and lots of tourists. The whole thing is impressive in a way, I have to admit, but a bit too Disneyland for my taste.

At least the walk back is downhill. I stop at one of the coffee shops and try my usual trick of ordering 'Café con leche' and pointing at the cake that takes my fancy. The lady asks something about the cake and, not having a clue what she's saying, I smile, nod and say 'Si!' She looks a bit startled, and the next thing I know she has put it in the microwave. It's a kind of oversized éclair without the chocolate but filled with cream. When I bite into it, the cream at the end is soft, but not actually warm, and a little icy in the middle, so I guess it was frozen on the display, and she's just defrosted it. I eat it anyway. It's fine.

I walk on, past Gaudi's monstrous cathedral, Sagrada Família, still incomplete 85 years after his death, and surrounded by scaffolding and parties of American students. Past the Arc de Triomf, through the park and to the harbour.

All the lonely people

My last evening in Barcelona. Moving on tomorrow, back to France. I've checked the map and the train timetables and booked a hotel for one night in Perpignan, just over the border.

By the harbour I pass two buskers, with guitar and keyboard. There aren't many people around and they seem to be playing to amuse themselves, riffing around a tune which sounds terribly familiar but at first I can't quite place it. I walk along the harbour looking at the sculptures, with the tune still in my head, then walk back and sit alone on a bench within earshot of the musicians. That's when the lyrics come to me, and I realise they're playing 'Eleanor Rigby' - I wonder if they're directing it at me, as it seems to have tuned into my thoughts.

I walk back up La Rambla, and confirm that the pavement is actually flat, so I obviously wasn't feeling at all well on Sunday afternoon. I pass a poster describing it as 'the most exciting street in the world'. Hmmm.

On the Passieg de Gràcia, men with drills are digging up the beautiful paving stones – maybe to replace them because they're getting worn. I think about Orwell and his comrades digging up the cobblestones to build barricades.

Maybe some of that spirit still survives, if the graffiti I spot, *'Mort a capital'*, is anything to go by. And in the Plaça de Catalunya there seems to be some kind of demonstration, police vans and people with banners, stopping the traffic enough to make crossing the road easy.

I take the Metro to the railway station, to see if I can buy my ticket. As I found when trying to book my ticket from Brussels to Paris, it's not possible to book tickets into France online. The station has a complicated system of queues, involving numbered tickets. I get as far as producing my credit card, when the booking clerk asks for ID. I haven't got my passport, or enough Euros to pay cash for my ticket, so I return to the apartment empty handed, but at least I now know the time of the train.

I book my next accommodation before bedtime, under the influence of that other half bottle of rioja. A seaside town, Sète, near Montpellier, that Edu recommended to me. I find rather a nice - but not too pricey - hotel, and I book for two nights.

Chapter 7 - Barcelona

Adiós Barcelona - **Wednesday 14 March**

My train doesn't leave till 16.30. There's a park near the station, they told us about it on the tourist bus, so the plan is to get to the station, buy my ticket, put the Wardrobe into left luggage and spend a couple of hours or so exploring the park, or just sitting and reading or writing.

I have to think about what to leave and what to take of the food I've bought. I wanted to make a sandwich to eat on the train, but I've misjudged the bread, I can either eat it with jam for breakfast or fill it with cheese and bring it along. Might as well eat it now. I leave the rest of the cheese, jam and butter in the fridge, along with half a pack of salad, and take a banana, two small bottles of water, some biscuits and two half eaten bars of chocolate (two because I've found another one in my backpack from Sunday).

I haven't worn my leather jacket since I got to Barcelona. Wonder if I'm going to need it again before I get to Norway? Still, it's easier to wear than to shove in the Wardrobe. I've got a great substitute, a grey corduroy waistcoat, which also has loads of pockets, handy for money, credit cards, phones, tickets etc. This is what I've been wearing the last few days. Laura tried to talk me out of bringing it, but I'm so glad I did. It's one of those things that when you're packing, you can't decide about, then you throw it in anyway, and it turns out to be one of the best things you've got. Unlike those other things that also get thrown in at the last minute and never get used. Or the ones you decide to leave that you then really miss. Trouble is, you never can tell which is going to be which.

I leave the flat wearing jeans, boots, a thin tee shirt, waistcoat and leather jacket. The Wardrobe seems to have got heavier again, though I don't know why as I haven't put anything extra in there (apart from a jar of hot chocolate powder).

At the station, first priority is the left luggage lockers. There have to be some, but I wander around for a while looking. Then I find the sign – now I remember seeing it yesterday, because it says: '*Consigna*', which reminded me of the short-lived rebranding of Royal Mail as 'Consignia'.

There are three sizes of lockers, small, large and extra large (rather like chain-shop coffees). 'Large' is €5 and extra large €9, and I'm not sure which I need for the Wardrobe. While I'm dithering, the man on the x-ray machine gets quite irritated with me. I hoik the Wardrobe up onto the conveyor, then he gestures at the backpack.

'This isn't going in, I'm keeping it with me' I try to explain but either he doesn't understand or doesn't care. But he doesn't ask to check my leather jacket, which I do leave in the locker – a large one is big enough, as it happens.

As I walk out of the left luggage area, I spot a cash machine, withdraw €40, head for the ticket window and ask for a ticket to Perpignan.

'When?'

'Yes, one' I reply, not hearing correctly.

'No, when do you want to go?'

'Today.'

'Tickets for today are at desks 21 to 30.'

I curse a little and then go to find desks 21 to 30 and join the queue. It's annoying, but I know there's only one train a day, and it doesn't go till 16.37, so I still have five hours to kill.

There's not much of a queue. I get to the desk and ask again for a ticket to Perpignan. He seems to be making a bit of a meal of it, tapping at the keys and taking much longer than the guy yesterday. I get my credit card ready, and my passport for ID.

'Cash only' he says. This startles me – yesterday I almost succeeded in buying it on my credit card, except for the fact that I hadn't got ID with me. I fish in my waistcoat pocket for the €40 I just got from the Telebank.

'Change at Figueres' he says.

What?

He's given me two tickets, stapled together at the end. One for Barcelona to Figureres, one for Figueres to Perpignan.

And the first train leaves at 12.22. Which is 40 minutes away.

'Gracias' I say, confused but – I'm not complaining.

I wonder whether I'm going to have hours to wait at Figueres and connect with the same train I would have caught anyway, but no, the train is due to get into Perpignan before the one I thought I'd be getting leaves Barcelona.

I find the platform, grab a coffee and a pastry, retrieve the Wardrobe, go back to the cash machine for another €40, and at 12.00 wander over to the check-in desk. There is a baggage check like for the Eurostar, but it moves pretty quickly. My reservation is for coach 1, seat 29, a first class carriage, with a power socket for my laptop and here I am, leaving Barcelona in style and four and a half hours early.

III

Southern France: Languedoc, Camargue, Provence

Perpignan - Sète - Carcassonne - Arles -
Porte-Camargue - Aix-en-Provence - Cannes

Chapter 8 - Perpignan

Leaving Spain – Wednesday 14 March
I'm not sorry about leaving Barcelona behind, but standing on the platform at Figueres waiting for my connection, I feel a bit sad to be leaving Spain. Maybe because this is the first time I've left a country knowing I won't be returning on this trip.

So many things to say, so many words pass through my head, how can I ever capture them? If I write them in my notebook, it may take days before I get round to typing them up, and by that time there are too many other things that need saying as well. Writing down the words as they flow through my head is easy (provided I don't have other things to do, like eat or sleep or book trains and hotels and make plans, or just enjoy being where I am), but to edit them, produce a coherent account which describes something specific, well, that's hard work, it takes time, the brain rebels against it and keeps putting it off and avoiding it.

And I think maybe the only talent I have as a writer is the ability to let all the words out without imposing that filter - of course, you can always do that later, but somehow it's hard to find time for it. I can do a spontaneous splurge but not a thought-through essay.

Perpignan
It's good fun, checking into a small hotel in a new town and then going out to explore. There are patterns to this trip, and that's one of them. My hero, Bill Bryson, makes the same point in 'Neither Here Nor There' about Copenhagen.

At least the hotel isn't hard to find; like the Terminus in Angoulême, with 'Gare TGV' in its name it wasn't going to be far from the station.

But which way out of the station? There's a sign pointing down into the Passage de Salvador Dalí, which doesn't instil confidence – maybe, like a Dalí painting, it leads into the bowels of the earth, and I could find myself winding perpetually round some labyrinthine intestinal pipes. So I take the other exit, but there are no hotels on this side of the tracks. Back in the station, I grasp my courage in both hands and plunge down the steps into the Passage de Salvador Dalí - which turns out be just a tunnel under the tracks that comes out in the middle of some construction work.

Of course, the railway station is never in the best part of town. Looking out of the bedroom window and seeing the 'Hotel Paris-Barcelone' opposite – *quel romance!* I should be staying there! – is one thing, but then you start walking down the road and the next shop is a tattoo parlour with a notice in the window saying *'armes de défense'*, and your nostrils pick up that sweet smoky smell - well, at least I'm only here for one night.

In fact, I'm lucky to have an afternoon here. It's only because the man at the station in Barcelona gave me an earlier ticket. By rights I should still be in Barcelona - and does it sound perverse to say I'd rather be here in Perpignan, sitting in the sun with a coffee on the Place d'Arago? I guess not many people come to this town for its own sake, but hey, a deep sense of well-being comes over me.

I really need to get some sunglasses. I think the magnetic clip-ons for my reading glasses got dumped in the bag I left at my sister's, and that's annoying. Even in misty Brittany, I should have realised it was stupid. I knew that I would be heading south and meeting the spring coming towards me, and that's just what's happened.

I drain my coffee and set off trying to find the interesting bits of Perpignan, with a map from the Tourist Information Office. Should I head for the river or the Palace of the Kings of Mallorca? Somehow I get distracted in the maze of little streets and double back on myself. I come across a lovely park, but why does it have so many statues of naked girls? The inscription on one says it's the town's tribute to Pablo Casals, which seems a bit gratuitous.

There's a lovely fountain, and the giant inverted red funnel is intriguing. Apparently it represents issues of sexuality and gender, symbolising androgyny and hermaphroditic tendencies in its combination of convexity and concavity... makes sense.

I don't want to spend too long wandering about because I need to get something to eat and I don't fancy walking back to the hotel too late in the evening. There's the pizzeria La Roma, which advertises an English menu, near where I had coffee on the Place d'Arago. But when I get there, although it isn't exactly closed, I can't see anyone sitting either outside or in, which doesn't look promising.

I sit down at a table outside one of the other cafés on the square. The waitress (blonde, middle aged) bustles over in a very friendly way, but when I ask for the menu seems as shocked as if I'd asked her to sacrifice her first-born grandchild, and keeps pointing to her mouth and asking *'Manger? Manger?'* in horrified tones.

'C'est okay?' I ask nervously.

'English? Pizza?' she says. She takes my hand and pats it reassuringly. 'Pizza, *oui?* Is okay, is okay!'

She disappears inside and comes back with the menu.

'Pizza *dix minutes'* she says, holding up both hands with splayed digits. 'Okay?'

'Okay!' I agree, relieved that it seems I'm going to be fed after all.

'Très bon! Very good!' she nods with a smile.

The pizza is indeed very good. I eat it in the growing chill of the approaching evening. When I turn and look over my shoulder through the window behind me, I notice that the tables inside are being set for dinner. Maybe it was just the fact that I wanted to eat outside that she had a problem with. I do seem to want to eat at the wrong times, always too late for lunch and early for dinner. I expect I'll adapt.

I think briefly about walking along the canal to have a look at the river, but it's probably best to get back to the hotel by the route I came. It doesn't take long, and the place isn't as intimidating as I thought. That's first impressions for you.

Perpignan- Sète - Notes on a journey – Thursday 15 March
I guess I didn't really see the best of Perpignan. I never made it to the river, just a rather green and sluggish canal. Nor did I find the Palace of the Kings of Mallorca, come to that

My train just crossed over the river (a river, anyway). By the looks of it, I didn't miss much.

It's misty outside, and the train windows are dirty. We've stopped at a station and I can't tell whether the white streaks I can see on the horizon are clouds or hills. Ah, I think they're either seams of limestone or quarry workings on the hillside. Wind farm; vineyard. Now a white industrial plant out in the middle of nowhere, looks like it could be a cement factory, which given the limestone and/or quarries makes perfect sense. Cypress trees, red-roofed villages, trees with blossom, pink and white.

This is a stopping train, every little town. Well, I'm in no hurry.

Suddenly, randomly, outside the window, a mediaeval castle. Quite a small one, just one main tower with surrounding walls and battlements, but still - not what I was expecting to see. Then a three (or four?) pronged metal arch on the hillside, some kind of modern sculpture?

And we're picking up speed.

White rocky hillsides dotted with pines. Big lorries on the motorway (*autoroute?*) running parallel with us, getting left behind.

The man in the seat in front is looking out with rapt attention – what at? I can't see anything – oh, maybe he's just asleep with his head propped against the window.

Another small town, football pitches. Boggy ground, riddled with ponds and ditches. A mere with water fowl - it would be attractive if it wasn't so murky.

Now a wide, flat area of wetlands on either side of the train. How close are we to the sea? I don't know, but it should be to the right of the train (we are heading east) and I'm sitting on the left. The hills are still there behind the marshes, not so far away, and not very high.

More cement factories and round squat cooling towers on the right hand side. We stop for another station, Port-la-Nouvelle, according to the SNCF sign.

And now we're travelling directly over the marsh. Low, flat islands, barely out of the water, but one has buildings on it. The sun comes out and bounces off the wind-raised ripples.

Flamingos standing in water so shallow it scarcely reaches their knees. One opens its wings to the sunshine. Storks and a grey heron.

Back on dry land, vineyards, cypresses, houses on the low hills, another station: Narbonne.

The stump of a tree, every branch pollarded off, looks like a life sized sculpture of an embracing couple.

The vines have been cut back hard, but the thickness of their gnarled, stunted trunks speaks of age and continuity. In the next field, a new spring-green crop of some cereal, then younger vines, then some that haven't been pruned yet, their twigs elongated and unruly, wrapping around each other like teenagers out on the town and looking for fun.

And then some cordoned along horizontal wires, holding hands, waiting for the music to begin, to dance the circle dance of Catalonia.

A castle on a hill, a river: Beziers.

Between the shopping centre and the tracks, a rubbish skip filled with red and white artificial Christmas trees. The land by the railway tracks is no-man's-land. No one notices what happens there.

Suddenly, I realise.

What I'm doing, this whole journey, is wonderful, unbelievable. I feel so privileged to be here, travelling through this everyday yet utterly unfamiliar landscape.

Sete

Chapter 9 - Sète

Bienvenue à Sète - **Thursday 15 March**
Nobody said this trip would be easy - and I guess I wouldn't want it to be boring. Boring it never is. Always one extreme or the other. So after writing lots of lovely gushy stuff in my notebook on the train here, I find myself sitting outside le Brasserie Victor Hugo, wondering where the hell my hotel is.

But am I *misérable?*
Pas du tout!
The train from Perpignan pulls into Sète station about 1 o'clock. I've got the name and address of the hotel in my notebook, and the directions read:

'By Public Transport: From the train station, catch the bus center that will leave you 200m from the hotel.' Pretty straightforward, I'm sure the 'bus center' will be easy to recognise.

What about that bus waiting outside the station? The destination board says '3 Centre Malraux' – wonder if that's the Centre I want? Worth a try. The driver, a stocky middle-aged woman with a blonde pony-tail, is standing outside having a smoke, so I show her the address written in my book.

'Avez-vous des bagages?'
'Oui.'
'Beaucoup?'
'Une seule, mais c'est très grande.' I gesture at the Wardrobe.
She calls her office, and I hear the word 'Monoprix'. Then she looks at me and points to a blue minibus parked behind the bus.

There's a young woman standing next to it. I show her the address in my notebook and she frowns.

'C'est un restaurant?'

'Non, hôtel', I say, and the name of the hotel, *'L'Orque Bleue'*, but this doesn't seem to get through. She looks at the address again and talks to the bus driver. She picks up on the *'Bleue'*, but still looks confused. Maybe she can't read the name of the hotel? I wrote the address out in capitals, but not the name of the hotel because I knew I'd remember that.

I fish in my bag for a pen and start to write it out again, legibly. As soon as she sees I'm writing *'l'Orque'* her eyes light up and she says to the driver: *'C'est l'Orque Bleue'*.

She turns back to me and says: *'vous êtes en face'*.

En face? What does that mean?

'All I know is, the lady on the other bus said the blue minibus' I say pathetically, in English.

After repeating *'en face!'* several times, she gets into the minibus with the driver and they drive off.

Maybe she was saying 'you're facing it', in other words, that it's in walking distance and hence I don't need to take the bus? That fits in with the other driver asking if I had much luggage.

There's a map on the station wall. The town is built on a network of canals. Immediately outside the station there's a bridge going over a canal. The roads alongside the canals are all called *'Quai'* something or other, and I'm looking for 10, Quai Aspirant Herber. From the map, it looks as though I need to cross the first bridge, turn right, cross another bridge at right angles, turn right again and keep going along one *Quai* and onto the last one.

Of course, there's no indication of scale on the map, but it's good to have a plan, so I set off enthusiastically, dragging the Wardrobe behind me, over the first bridge and right along the edge of the canal.

The Wardrobe starts to drag against the pavement. That's the problem with wheeling it any distance - it's not rigid, and when things settle to the bottom it scrapes along the ground. I try holding both handles, the pulling handle and the carrying handle, which helps a bit, but it takes concentration and I'm worried about tearing the bottom.

Right, there's another bridge, where to now? Shoot – I've been so busy thinking about the Wardrobe, I've got no idea where I am – but it looks like there's another map on a post, just over the bridge. Okay, there's the

Avenue Victor Hugo, in the middle of a square island surrounded by canals, and some of the Quais, but not the one I want. Still, I know I'm on the Ave Victor Hugo, that's something. It's a big square, could be the town centre, and I needed the bus for the centre, so I guess I'm on the right lines.

What I need is somewhere to stop and get out the laptop, so I can see the map I downloaded. I carry on along the avenue, looking out for a café. I'm about half way across the island when I get a horrible sinking feeling that the bridge I'm heading for is the one that leads back to the station.

There's the Brasserie Victor Hugo - I order a coffee, pull out the laptop from my backpack and set it up. Don't expect there'll be wifi, but at least I can look at my saved map. Right, looks like I need to turn around 180 degrees, go back along Victor Hugo and off the bridge at the other end, turn right at the other side of the canal, and follow the quay round the edge of the island till I come to the end.

Sorted. Now where's the waiter, I need to pay for the coffee – oh, there he is, inside the cafe, talking to the barman and another man who's drinking at the bar. I think I've caught his eye – no, now he's gone out to the back. I check the menu, and coffee is €1.40. Damn, I can't make it exactly, I'll have to leave €1.50, not that he's earned a tip, not even 10 centimes.

As I walk away, I turn to look - he's come out pretty smartish to pick up the money when he realised I was going.

By the time I get to the hotel, it's about a quarter to three; talking to the bus drivers, walking round the first island, stopping for coffee, checking the map, waiting to pay and then walking back in the right direction has taken an hour and three quarters. And yes, I should have got a taxi, but I was so sure from the directions and the conversations with the two bus drivers that it was an easy walk.

Why did the lady on the blue minibus keep saying '*en face*' if it didn't mean 'facing'? Unless... oh crap, doesn't it means 'opposite'? – she was trying to tell me that they were going in the opposite direction to the one I needed.

All this under a rather grey and miserable sky. I don't think much to this place. Wish I hadn't booked two nights here.

ഔൽ

Sète

My mood improves a bit when I'm in my room, which is nice enough, and even has a bath. It's good just to be here, somewhere to leave the Wardrobe, a bed for tonight, and I don't have anywhere to rush to for a couple of days. So after a quick freshen-up, I head out for a walk.

Sète is actually rather a sweet little town. It's intriguing, with its grid of canals between the open sea and lagoon, the buildings strung out along the quays (hence the 'street' names). Across the canal from my hotel there's a strip of seafood restaurants, and the tourist information office, where I pick up a map and go looking for a café, to sit and study it over a *café crème*. I walk past a *crêperie*, open to the promenade, with a man cooking crêpes almost out on the street. How could I resist? I order crêpe with *marrons* (chestnut puree) and extra *chantilly* (whipped cream) and a *chocolat chaud*, and take a seat inside, away from the chilly drizzle.

I have an English friend who used to live round here. I text him to tell him where I am, and it turns out that he knows Sète well, and my hotel.

'I know where that is. There's a string of seafood restaurants on the other side of the canal. Try the fish soup. And visit some of the Cathar castles while you're in the Languedoc.'

I check out the fish restaurants. One of them, Le Grand Bleu, has a 3 course deal for €13, with fish soup for starter and a seafood pasty for main course. Sounds good for dinner - later. I follow the road out to the headland. The wind blows chilly from the harbour, under a grey blanket of sky. There are signs pointing up the hill for 'St Claire'. According to my map, there are buses that go that way, so bus up and walk back seems like a good idea – but not now, as the rain is getting heavier. Back at the harbour, a sign by the tourist boat says it will be going out on *Vendredi* at 15 *heures*, adults €10. That's my plan for tomorrow sorted.

Forward plans

Back in my hotel room and out of the rain, I fire up the laptop and start researching where to go next. This is the priority when I'm not actually moving - I have to know where I'm going and when. I get engrossed with trying to sort out hotels, distances from railway stations, connections, attractions, routes, bookings etc. It takes hours, and is always stressful.

I'm trying to find out more about the Cathar castles, because of what my friend said. I can't travel round too much because I'm dependent on public transport, but I've found a bed and breakfast in Carcassonne, which seems like a good compromise, because it has a mediaeval castle - its main claim to fame. I'll go there next, Saturday and Sunday nights.

I need to plan ahead while I have wifi, because I won't in Carcassonne. Arles was always on the fantasy route that would take me from Barcelona to Italy. For three years, I had on the wall of my flat a framed print of Van Gogh's 'Terrace of the Café Forum at Night'. I bought it in a charity shop when I was in the process of leaving my husband and moving to my flat, because I've always liked the picture, and even before then the idea of going there one day had been at the back of my mind. But when I was talking to Eduardo he suggested Sète instead. The online reviews about how touristy the whole Van Gogh thing is have rather put me off. Still, I might as well have an overnight stop in Arles, after Carcassonne.

Apart from Arles, I've never given much thought to how I would get through the south of France. My original plan was to leave France through the Alps and start my tour of Italy staying with my friend Ilze in Turin. But Ilze can't put me up till the end of April, so I decided to take the coastal route instead. Another friend, Irina, lives in Terni, Umbria, and I'm planning to see her at the end of March. So I have about a fortnight to get from Barcelona to Terni. How to do it?

Since my sight of flamingos from the train on Thursday, I've been thinking of staying in the Camargue. I have a look at the area on Google Maps, hunting for places that are accessible by train and have relatively affordable hotels. I've found a place in Port Camargue which looks really intriguing, but how do I get there? Would I need to rent a car? I don't want to do that. I just can't make up my mind, and I'm getting hungry. Right, I'll take the easy option, find a (relatively) cheap hotel in Cannes and book that for Tuesday, then go out for my fish soup and pasty at Le Grand Bleu and come back for a bath and bed.

A day at the seaside - Friday 16 March

Lying in bed, listening to the rain, I've been thinking about that place at Port Camargue. It does look really good. I get up and go online. Yes, I can get a train there, why did I think this wasn't going to work? It'll be fine, I'll just book a room for two nights and cancel the one in Cannes.

By the time I get to the café I have in mind, they've stopped serving breakfast, so I go next door, to the place where I had coffee yesterday afternoon. It's just a good place to sit, overlooking the canal, sheltering from the still-wintry weather behind a roll-down weatherproof clear-plastic wall, doing a su doku, reading, writing in my notebook, letting the world go by. It might sound boring, but it's good just to let go of everything for a while. What else am I travelling for, after all?

After breakfast I start walking up the hill and out onto the headland. I'm in a non-touristy area of the town, passing rows of apartments with washing hanging out, schools, garages. There are signs pointing to the *corniche*, the sailors' cemetery and the hill, but they're road signs, not walking signs. The only other people I see walking look like local people going about their normal daily business. I try not to look as out of place as I feel.

I come upon an outlook overlooking the sea, a turn of the road higher than where I got to yesterday afternoon, with a bench, occupied by a woman with a dog. I walk up the road behind the sailors' cemetery, along streets of strangely forbidding white houses, lots of signs saying: *'Propriete privée'* and *'attention chien'*, *'pas de publicité'*, *'pas de la propagande'*, and one I didn't quite understand about no *'services et étrangers'*. It all seems a bit heavy handed. They're nice houses, with beautiful views, but I wouldn't want to live there, with all this paranoia (or maybe they actually are constantly being pestered by propaganda, services and foreigners, which is even more off-putting). Maybe they're holiday homes, empty some of the time. The dogs are real though, and whenever one starts barking they set the others off in a long, intimidating relay.

I keep passing bus stops. I remember I was planning to take the bus up and walk back down, but I haven't seen a bus.

At a cross roads I consult the map, and realise I've somehow taken a wrong turning. Road signs that tell you where you are never seem to be there when you need them, or maybe it's just part of the security, to confuse unwary foreigners and propaganda-mongers.

If I turn here, it should take me back towards where I want to be. My nostrils catch the scent of hot tarmac. Round the bend is a gang of blokes with diggers and levellers and a big heap of black stickiness and a truck with more on the back, and a roller reversing towards me. I dodge back and a friendly workman shows me past the vehicles and round the end of a strip of unlevelled tarmac about a metre wide so I don't have to try and leap over it.

I've been checking the little maps on the bus stops as I pass, and I can see I'm getting close to the chapel of St Claire. One more stop to go. Still no sign of a bus. There's a sign for public conveniences, which surely means there's something of interest around here, and the next I know I'm at the panorama point, reading a notice from the town council about how this area has been restored to its natural conditions, rocks and scrub and wild flowers starting to peep through.

Through the drizzle and mist, I gaze down over the network of canals and streets and pick out my hotel, the harbour and the growling sea beyond. I turn to look the other way, across the bay and far away in the lagoon I can see black grids laid out in the sea. They must be oyster tables – I recognise them because my brother-in-law pointed them out in Brittany. I saw oysters on the menu in Le Grand Bleu last night.

I get out my map and look for ways to go back down again. There are a couple of paths marked with parallel lines going across, which seem quite intriguing. I wonder how long it will take me to get back to the harbour? I want to do the boat ride at 3 o'clock, and I probably should try to get some lunch, or at least a drink. I guess it makes sense to go back the way I came – but I'll just go and see if the parallel lines mean steps. Yes, I was right – might as well walk down them, now I'm here. A long, long set of steps, down into a part of town I haven't been to before. Not attractive - a residential area of blocks of flats, not even shops, just the odd plumber's or home improvement business. A whole block of the road is being worked on and even the footpaths aren't open.

I'm back at the harbour in plenty of time for the boat ride. Views *'sous la mer'* through the glass bottom were advertised, but only if the water is clear enough to see anything, which it definitely isn't. The captain hands me a headset with an English version of the commentary, which I listen to every time there's an announcement over the tannoy. There's a group of Russian youngsters who seem to be having a lot of fun, and when we get out of the harbour the sea bucks and heaves which causes lots of hilarity. Perhaps it seems like a mad thing to do, on a chilly March day, but I feel happy just to be here, following wherever the day leads me, doing things on a whim, in a place I've never been to before and maybe will never see again.

After the boat docks, I have another look at the seafood restaurants, and find one advertising paella and sangria, which seems a good plan for dinner. Everywhere is very quiet and the restaurants are competing for the few prospective clients.

The only other occupants are two ladies sitting together. The one facing me asks in a North American accent:

'Where are you from?' And when I say 'Bedford, it's just north of London', her friend turns round to look at me and says: 'I'm from Gloucestershire!'

The first lady is Canadian rather than American, 'from Ottawa'. We get talking, and I tell them about my trip. When I say that I'm funding it from my divorce settlement, the Gloucestershire lady says: 'Yes!' and raises her fists in a gesture of approval.

'You're doing it on your own?' she asks while her friend is in the ladies. 'Don't you ever feel threatened?'

'Not really.'

It's just about being sensible, isn't it? Not putting yourself into situations where you're likely to be at risk. If I ever feel uncomfortable, I just act as though I know exactly what I'm doing and where I'm going. But on the whole, middle-aged women tend to blend into the background. I remember once attending a conference on risk perceptions where one of the speakers, an eminent expert and self-styled little old lady, pointed out that all the statistics show that little old ladies are the demographic group least likely to be victims of nastiness.

'But you have to pay the single supplement everywhere.'

'Well, I always go for the cheap on-line deals.'

'Yes, so do we, but even so...'

I suppose she's right. I haven't thought about it that way before, I just accepted that I pay the cheapest rate available without thinking that two people sharing would pay the same or little more. It's just one of those things.

But I can't imagine doing this with anyone else. For a start, obviously, there's no one I could do it with. Maybe if there was someone, I wouldn't want to, wouldn't feel the need. But to put it in a subtly different way, I wouldn't want to do it with anyone else anyway. This is my journey, for better or worse, and I'll do exactly what I decide, with no one to argue or to complain when it doesn't work out according to plan, without having to justify my choices, without worrying if it's not what they want, without feeling I'm being judged. What's not to like?

Chapter 10 - Carcassonne

Bienvenue à Carcassonne - **Saturday 17 March**
There's something raucous going on further down the platform, maybe the French version of a hen party, people in brightly coloured curly wigs making loud screechy noises. Outside the station, entrance roads are cordoned off, lots of police standing around, and police cars. Then I see a banner with the word *'Carnaval'* on it, and today's date.

I dodge out of the way of the reversing police van, and realise I'm standing at the taxi rank – exactly what I want. After the farce in Sète I'm not taking any more chances with buses.

A taxi pulls up and I show the driver my notebook with the address, neatly written in block capitals. He frowns and shakes his head. Pulls out a map and starts opening it, folding it, unfolding it, studying it. Takes my notebook and stares hard at it, then throws it down on the passenger seat, shaking his head some more. Turns the map upside down and looks at it again. Speaks into his radio mic, then puts it back.

'They'll call me in 5 minutes.'

'You're a taxi driver, for goodness sake!' I want to shout at him. 'Don't you know your own city?'

He picks up the notebook again and holds it against the map, then takes the mic and speaks into it some more. At last he nods, smiles, hangs up, passes me back my notebook.

'It's okay! It's okay! We go!'

On the radio someone is talking in excited tones, it sounds like a sports commentary, and I hear the word *'Angleterre'*, then voices singing *La Marseillaise*. Can't help humming along – wait a minute, maybe it's a rugby match, England versus France. Mid-March, time for the Six

Nations. From the singing, it doesn't sound too good for our lads.

Within 10 minutes we've reached the mediaeval city walls. There's a barrier across the road, the sort that lifts up to let the traffic through. We stop.

'It's in there' he gestures through the gate. 'Place de Saint-Jean.'

'What?' That's as far as he's taking me?

He points up the cobbled street, then at the meter.

I walk past the barrier, through the crowds of tourists around the gate. What if it's like Mont Saint-Michel, all those steps? My heart sinks.

I pass a one-man band, in cod-mediaeval costume and with his nose painted red, sitting in an alcove. Narrow cobbled streets, the Wardrobe bumping and grumbling behind me. Alleys lead off in all directions, no signposts, I just keep going, with no idea where to. Past cafés and tourist-tat shops, a set of stocks with a dummy in a shabby wig, a well, a haunted house. Looking for Le Logis des Remperts, 3, rue du Moulin D'Avar.

At the Place de Saint-Jean, I can't see any signs. I double back on myself, and in the next street, outside the Haunted House, there's a map. The Rue du Moulin is in the opposite corner of the square, a narrow alleyway, and on the left, a sign reading 'Le Logis des Remparts'. A gate leads into a small courtyard, with loungers, plant pots, table and chairs, and a door in the wall. I knock, but there's no response.

I get the laptop out of the bag and set it up on the table, looking for the details. No luck. I must not have saved it. And I can't get online to recheck the email. But there's a phone number, so I call.

'There should be somebody there but maybe they didn't hear you.' The nice lady gives me the security code for the key pad. 'I think you're in room 1.'

I tap in the code, and open the door. Inside, Room 1 is to my left, on the ground floor mercifully, and the key is in the lock. I open the door and let myself in.

Bare stone walls, a double bed, sofa, table, microwave, fridge and sink in the corner. Tea, coffee and instant hot chocolate. Milk, butter and orange juice in the fridge.

Outside, I take a few steps down the street, turn left and find myself out on the city walls. A chilly wind blows over my face in the drizzly afternoon, up here on the hillside. Past the cream stone blocks and crenellations, I look down on the red-roofed white apartment blocks and churches of the modern town, dotted with bare winter trees and dark evergreens, the river snaking through its valley, and in the distance the white-speckled grey pyramids of the mountains, under low grey clouds.

Wandering around the old town, it's hard to keep my bearings - too many little winding streets, full of cafés, restaurants, *crêperies*, shops selling jewellery, wine, local delicacies, post cards, arts and crafts, toys, books and so on and on. That looks like a good café, must pop back later for a hot chocolate. Which way now? What's round this corner? Oh – I'm pretty sure I saw that shop window with the twee fairy figurines half an hour ago – how did I get back here? And where's that café?

I'm back at the Rue du Moulin again. Might as well pop in and see if someone's turned up. They didn't say I was supposed to wait for them, did they? I used my credit card to book the room online, I guess that's good enough.

There's a leaflet of events on the hall table, with a list of amazing acts performing in the Carnaval. Never mind the mediaeval city, I really must have fallen into a time-warp: Johnny Halliday (is he really still alive? Or is it some kind of character franchise, like Dr Who or James Bond?); The Alan Parsons Project; Duran Duran.

The crowds are thinning out now, but I'm still walking. Back at the drawbridge the one-man-band is still in his niche. There's something particularly tuneless and irritating about his efforts, but he seems happy enough.

I follow the sound of much more tuneful and interesting music. A group in mediaeval costumes are performing, dancing, juggling, all very festive, but no sign of Johnny Halliday.

The *crêperies* and shops are starting to close, outside displays being taken in, shutters closing over windows. I get my *chocolat chaud*, but almost have the table cleared away under me.

I walk onto the ramparts and watch the changing colours of the clouds, from grey to pink, purple and red. As the sun sinks the world turns chilly, but somewhere a blackbird is singing. My phone has run out of battery, but after all, no camera can really capture that feeling of watching a beautiful sunset.

Time for dinner, at a restaurant on Place de Saint-Jean: warm goat's cheese salad followed by *cassoulet*. This is one of the first proper dishes

I learnt to cook, years ago from an international cookery book, but I've never before tasted it in its natural habitat.

Le Chateau - **Sunday 18 March**
I should really do something other than just wander round the city stopping every now and then for coffee or chocolate. I buy a ticket to go into the castle, but don't join the guided tour, I just follow the signs and leaflet and read the information on the walls. The castle was originally built in the 13th century, but the buildings that stand today were restored in the 19th. I want to get out onto the ramparts because there's a section you can only reach from here. I keep retracing my steps because I think I've missed the entrance, but in fact you only get to it at the end of the tour. Now I'm out here, it's started to rain, and the wind is blowing. But it's worth it, because from here you get a better idea of the city as a whole: the church, the walls and courtyards and the round towers with their grey conical roofs. And down there – yes! The restaurant where I had dinner last night, and the courtyard of the Logis des Remparts.

I find a café for lunch, but when I've finished it's still raining, so I go back to my room to write. There's a tap on the door, and I open it to a smiling lady holding a mop.

'*Pardon*, I come back later.'

'Wait a moment please. You're the first person I've met here and I haven't paid yet. Do you...?'

She shakes her head.

'You pay online?'

'Yes, is that okay?' Usually the credit card details are only to reserve the room, and I have to pay the venue directly.

'Then they have your card details, I think that will be okay.'

She shows me how to work the coffee machine and tells me about the bus service for the railway station.

The rain has stopped, so I go out again, checking out my route to the entrance to catch the bus in the morning. I walk round the ramparts I can reach - not all of them are open. On the side away from the city, there are orchards in the valley, white blossom against the green and grey winter fields. I walk down to a church on the edge of town, and back up the path leading round the mound, coming in close to my lodgings.

Apart from the castle tour, there isn't much else to do, as I have no interest in the haunted house, torture museum and shops. But I'm glad I booked two nights and had a whole day to explore. Being here in the evening and early morning when there are no crowds feels like a special privilege, as though I belong in a way the day trippers don't.

Dawn thoughts - Monday 19 March

I start things and never finish them... and then when I have internet access I don't post them, because they're not finished, and there are new things to write about, or I need to sort out my finances or my travel plans or sometimes deal with emails. I write in my notebook and never get round to typing it up, and when I write it's mostly about writing, or feelings, or travel hassles, and not the places I've and things I've done.

And here I am at five thirty in the morning listening to the blackbird outside my room, and thinking yet again about how birds sing with different accents in different places. It's recognisably a blackbird, the one birdsong I know really well, but it sounds different here from blackbirds at home, or in Brittany, or Spain, although now I've been away so long I hardly know whether that's true, because I've got used to hearing them all.

Yesterday when I woke at six I thought I should get up and look at the sunrise, but I stayed in bed brooding and didn't get up till about 7.30, by which time the sun was well up. So today I've got up, but I'm just writing this, not really telling you anything about where I am or what I'm doing.

No surprises there, this is how my life is, and although I hoped this trip would change things, inside I am still the same me. Doesn't matter where I go, I'm as chaotic as always, can't run away from myself, but at least here there's no one to let down and no one to see how hopeless I am.

It's about 6.30 now. I twitch the curtain and the sky is already light. I pull on jeans and a sweater, the minimum I need to be warm and decent, and run outside, towards the ramparts. The blackbird is still singing as I climb up onto the wall at its lowest point, avoiding the very bright street lamp so I can get a picture of the strip of pink sky along the horizon.

I look out for the last time over the still drowsy town, the river, the vineyards and fields, the headlights of cars on the Monday morning commute. A few drops of rain sting my face as I walk back towards shower, breakfast and packing. Another day, another journey.

ഇൽ

Chapter 11 – Arles en Provence

Arles - Monday 19 March

Once I'm over the drawbridge and out into the modern world, the bus stop is right there, and a ticket to the station costs €1. It's a lot easier to find a bus to the station in a town you've been in for a few days than from the station in a strange town when all you have is an address and maybe some directions scribbled down from the internet.

At the station in Arles, I show the address in my notebook to the taxi driver, and after a quick conflab with his colleague, we're away. We pass through dull suburbs to a business park on the edge of town, and with a smirk he deposits me outside a motel and relieves me of €10. I point out that the meter shows €6.80.

'For the luggage' he says, and whisks off.

It's part of the same chain as the hotel in Perpignan, but this is a motel, laid out around a car park, surrounded by distribution depots. It's exactly the sort of place I'd go for if I was driving, but I'm dependent on walking and public transport. Here I am, stuck on the edge of a strange town, with evening approaching, and a few hours of daylight to locate, never mind see, whatever sights it has to offer.

At least there's free wifi, so I spend some time on the laptop trying to locate the Café Forum (now renamed the 'Café Van Gogh'), find out how long it will take to walk there (twenty minutes according to Google maps) and if there's a bus. I refuse to pay for another taxi.

I start walking, across the car park, behind the distribution depot and the DIY hypermarket, out onto a main road leading into the town centre. I pass under a railway bridge, and after about fifteen minutes come to a roundabout with a Monoprix supermarket on one side, which looks like one I rode around in the taxi.

To my right there's a small park, a bus station, and an embankment by a large river, which has to be the Rhône. This at least looks attractive, so I walk along the path till I come to a bridge, where there are signs for the old town. I cross over while the evening commuter traffic flashes by in a flurry of headlights glinting on wet roads. Oh yes, did I say it was raining? Not too bad, just drizzle, but enough to add to the chilly atmosphere.

The old town seems nice enough, but nothing special - maybe I'm a little jaded after Carcassonne. The arches of the Roman amphitheatre loom with shadows in the drizzly dusk, surely the Forum must be somewhere round here? There are plenty of cafés, but I'm wary as usual of that walk back in the dark. Motels usually have a cluster of chain restaurants nearby, which will do me fine.

The rain falls, the shadows deepen, and there's no sign of the bright lights of the Café Van Gogh spilling out onto the greasy pavement, nor of the stars behind the heavy clouds. I start to walk back. Every now and then a bus passes me, but I never seem close enough to a stop to catch one. Okay, where's the nearest restaurant to the hotel? There's a *boulangerie*, but it's just closed. Across two dual carriageways there's a Lidl supermarket, where I buy bread and cheese and take it back to my room.

Au Revoir Arles - Tuesday 20 March

I'm more than grateful for the hotel breakfast: juice, scrambled eggs, bacon, toast, croissants and lots and lots of coffee. If I can get a bus to take me back to the town centre and get off at the roundabout by the Monoprix, I should be pretty close to the railway station. As far as I could see from the online train timetables, I can get a train to Le Grau-du-Roi at 11.00. At 10.50 I'm at the station and in the queue.

When I get to the desk, I ask for a ticket to Le Grau-du-Roi. It takes me a couple of attempts at pronunciation before the lady manages to decipher what I want, and then she reacts with the same kind of shock as the waitress in Perpignan.

'Grau-du-Roi? Grau-du-Roi?' The words: 'why on earth would you want to go to that god-forsaken hole?' hang in the air as she bashes the letters into her computer.

Single to Sirkeci

'Seventeen thirty five.'

'What?' Panic sets in and I try to slow my breath. I look at the clock behind her. It says 10.55, the 11.00 must have left early. I have to stay here till evening? And what time will I get there?

'Or you can take the bus.'

'Bus?'

'The eleven o'clock bus.'

'Where do I catch it from?'

'There.' She points over my shoulder.

I turn and look out of the window. There's a bus parked outside the station entrance.

She's printing out a clutch of tickets, and hands them over one by one.

'Take the bus to Tarascon. Then the train from Tarascon to Nîmes. Then another bus from Nîmes to Le Grau–du–Roi.'

This must be the journey I found online. I just didn't read it carefully enough to notice the connections, and the fact that two of the sections were by bus.

I say goodbye to Arles without regrets. The sun is shining, I'm on the move, I have a bed booked for the night and all seems well again.

At Tarascon, I get off the bus outside a building with the word *'Gare'* on it, an entrance into a gloomy corridor and a flight of stairs, but neither lift nor escalator. Leaving the Wardrobe in the corridor I climb the stairs halfway, and at the top of the second flight I can see a ticket booth (closed) and signs for 'Nîmes', 'Avignon' and *'Billets.'*

Maybe there's another entrance? I go back down to look and at the bottom of the stairs meet a middle aged man, the only other living soul around. He's as confused as I am. We both shrug.

There seems no option but to drag the Wardrobe up the stairs. At the top is a door into the outside world. I'm on top of a viaduct looking down over Tarascon. It's twenty minutes till my train's due, so I take a book from my backpack and sit in the sun to wait.

At Nîmes, the bus is waiting outside the station again. It's not a long journey, but a leisurely one, winding through country which isn't exactly the Camargue of my imagination, but pretty enough: low flat agricultural land, villages burgeoning with new-build estates. I've been longing to see flamingos, but no luck here. The bus arrives at Le Grau-du-Roi railway station not long after 14.00. This is as deserted as the station at Tarascon.

No taxis, just a notice with a number to call. I've got the address for my lodgings: 45, Quai Lapérouse, Port-Camargue. At the bus stop, there's a timetable for local buses, I've missed the 13.35 bus for Port-Camargue, but the next one's due at 14.35. About half an hour to wait – no problem, as long as I've got somewhere to sit and something to read.

The time comes and goes, but the bus doesn't. I'm not the only one waiting, there are two youngsters, but they get on a bus heading back towards Aigues-Mortes, the last town I came through. Where's the one for Port-Camargue?

Carcassonne

Chapter 12 – Port-Camargue

Bienvenue à Port-Camargue - **Tuesday 20 March**
Better have another look at the timetable. What are these letters over the columns of times? At the top of the 13.35 and 16.30 columns it says: *'LàV'*, and over the 14.35, *'Mer'*. Okay, that sounds like *'Lundi à Vendredi'* (Monday to Friday) and *'Mercredi'* (Wednesday). Oh, shoot. The 14.35 only runs on Wednesdays. Today is Tuesday.

I could wait another hour and a half for the next bus. Or call the number for the taxi company and hope the person on the other end speaks good English.

Or find a café and ask there. And get some lunch at the same time.

The street opposite the station looks as deserted as the station itself, but across the road there's a fish restaurant. I take a seat at a table outside. The menu looks wonderful, but too much and too pricey – I only want a snack.

A waiter bustles out and speaks rapidly.

'Café crème s'il vous plait' I say, when I can get a word in edgeways.

He stares.

'You want to order madame?'

'Just a drink please'. Then, in the face of his blank and frosty stare: *'buver?'*

'You want to drink?' He makes it sound as though I'd tried to order a jug of neat vodka with a meths chaser.

'Just coffee please' I add hastily *'Café Crème*. Cappuccino?' Whatever. He sniffs and straightens his spine.

'This is a restaurant, madame. To drink "Coffee"' (he spits the word out like illegal gut rot) 'you must go to a café.'

'Oh!' Will I ever get my head round these niceties?

'The café, madame, is there!' He points to the building next door.

'Oh, *merci.*' Gathering together my luggage - and my confusion - I head that way, hoping for a warmer welcome, but the two men sitting at the only occupied table look up and stare. I deposit my stuff and myself at a table on the opposite side of the room, which seems almost palatial for a café.

The middle-aged man behind the bar comes over and smiles ingratiatingly.

'Can I have a lunch menu?' I ask.

'This is a café, madame. For lunch, you must go to the restaurant.' He points back the way I've come. At least he's smiling – well, if 'smile' is the correct word for the oily grin that smears itself across his features.

'Oh. Just a coffee then please. And can you tell me where I can get a taxi?'

'Where do you want to go madame?'

'Port-Camargue.'

'I can take you myself, madame! Don't worry!'

Somehow, the second phrase of that sentence doesn't seem to follow naturally from the first, but I try to feel reassured, and while he gets my coffee I pull out my notebook to show him the address.

'Quai Laperouse? Where on Quai Laperouse?'

'It says 35' I point out, reasonably.

He opens his arms wide.

'Is long, very long. Like, you go to Paris, you say, "Champs Elysees", is a big, big long road. You need to know where, which end.'

'Well, that's all the information I have.'

'Wait, madame, wait!' he smiles again. I'm feeling less reassured by the minute. He consults in rapid French with the clients on the other table, who have been watching us with considerable and disturbing interest.

He returns triumphant.

'I will take you madame, do not worry. Drink your coffee and we go.'

Le Saphir

We drive through the town and along the canals. Outside the marina office, he stops the car. There's a barrier across the road.

'Quai Laperouse, it is there. Only open to traffic in the morning. '

Behind the barrier, the quay stretches away, water to the right, and a forest of masts. I pull a €10 note from my purse, he snatches it, gets back into the driver's seat and drives away.

Here we go again.

Along the harbour, there are numbers on the concrete in front of the berths. I walk along the waterfront, past apartments, a *boules* court with an intense game in progress, a pizzeria. It's quite a walk, the harbour curves around, with more apartments and a row of offices on my left. There's number 35.

Le Saphir. I was so excited to find it on the booking site. A stationary yacht, with cabins to let. The narrow gangplank leads into an unzipped opening in the tarpaulin covering the front of the boat. I leave the Wardrobe standing on the dock and walk up and in.

'*Bonjour?*' I call hesitantly. There's no reply.

I push through the entrance and onto the boat. On a chair to my left is a sleeping cat, a dainty tortoiseshell, curled into a neat circle. The cabin door is open, and again I stick my head inside and call.

I can't help thinking of the Marie Celeste as I walk cautiously into the cabin. Bench seats either side, a table in the middle attached to the floor, television, cupboard in the corner. Another door, a stove and sink, boat stuff, and steps down.

Where is the owner, and how do I get hold of him? Vague recollections of a phone number in the email, but I can't get online to find it. And how the hell am I going to get the Wardrobe over that gangplank and down those steps?

I walk back through the main cabin and deck, pausing to scratch the cat's head. She wakes, stares at me haughtily, jumps down and pauses by the top of the gangplank to look around, then trots away along the marina. A lady walking a dog is passing in the opposite direction. She smiles, I smile back.

'*Excusez-moi, parlez-vous Anglais?*' I ask politely.

Unfortunately, she doesn't. But she is very friendly and eager to help. In garbled French I try to ask whether she knows the owner of the Saphir, but either she doesn't or she doesn't understand the question. She hails another lady, and they have a minor conflab. They think one of the gentlemen playing *boules* might be able to help, so off we go, me dragging the Wardrobe.

Chapter 12 – Port-Camargue

'Armand!' the lady with the dog calls, and an elderly Frenchman comes over. I start my explanation, this time mainly in English, but he doesn't know whose boat it is, and has no idea how to help. A woman comes over and talks rapidly to him – I guess he's holding up the game. Before she drags him away, he says:

'The lady who sells boats. Maybe she can help you.'

Opposite the Saphir's berth is a low row of offices – estate agency, chandlery, boat sales office. A lady in her 40s with a long black pony tail is talking to someone outside. My new friends have hailed her and explain again about this crazy Englishwoman looking for the owner of the Saphir.

As I catch up with them, she smiles and holds out her hand.

'Hello' she says 'I'm Sabine'.

'Linda' I say smiling back and taking her hand.

'Come into my office and I'll see what I can do to help'.

Her English is perfect, thank goodness. I go through the story again, about how I have a room booked for two nights on the Saphir but no way of contacting the owner.

'I don't know his name' she says regretfully. 'But I see him around sometimes. He has a very beautiful cat, *hein?*'

'Gorgeous!' I agree with a smile. 'She was on the boat, I saw her.'

'Her name is Charlotte. I don't know the man's name, but I know the cat!'

We both laugh. It is the international sisterhood of Crazy Cat Ladies. It's amazing how we find one another, I've often thought it's a bit like the Masons, as soon as you know, it's an instant bond.

'That cat needs lots of… what do you say? Caresses?' she moves her hand in a stroking motion.

'Stroking' I say with a smile. But 'caresses' sounds so much more French. And feline.

We get off the subject of cats and back to my problem of contacting my host to establish if I've got a bed for the night, and how to get my luggage on board.

'Could I leave my big bag in here overnight, if I can't take it on the boat?' I ask. It is a plan B I've been concocting since I saw the gang plank – to take out my overnight stuff and leave the Wardrobe somewhere safe on land.

'I don't think so. This office is not very secure.' I can see what she means. It's quite small, and the front wall is all glass.

Suddenly, Sabine walks to the front window and picks up a narrow flyer from a display of tourist leaflets. It has a picture of the Saphir, and on the back, description of the accommodation.

'The tourist office gave me these' she says. 'Here's his mobile number. I'll call it for you, it may be easier.'

She dials, then speaks into the phone in French.

'I've left a message and asked him to call me back.'

We sit and chat, about cats again, my trip, my divorce, the reasons why I'm here. Like old friends.

'Maybe I can sell you a boat?' she says, indicating the photos around the walls. 'It's my husband's business.' The estate agency next door is hers, selling and renting holiday apartments, and the boat business is his. But she's managing both offices today.

'I'd love one, if I could afford it' I reply, not adding that I'd need a sailor to go with it.

Then the phone rings and Sabine answers.

'His name is Sebastien' she tells me after she's hung up. 'He is working in Montpellier today and will be back about six thirty. There's no problem, he's expecting you. His friend Alain will come and help you with your luggage and show you your cabin.' Then she adds: 'Don't worry about Alain. He works outdoors. He's much stronger than he looks.'

When he arrives, I see what she means. The word is 'wiry' – probably about my age, without a gram of spare weight anywhere, with a floppy hat and friendly grin.

He blenches a little at the Wardrobe, but smiles and hefts it up, striding over the gangplank to my admiration and amazement. He even manages to get it downstairs.

'Do you know which cabin?' he asks. There are four doors. One is locked. Another has an unmade single bunk – he closes that one hastily – 'ah *non*, not there!' with a grin and a wink. That's Sebastien's cabin. The third one is made up, with a single bunk and en suite bathroom – or rather, shower with built in toilet and basin.

We get the Wardrobe into the cabin next to the bunk. 'Sebastien will meet you here at 6 o'clock.' Alain smiles, and is gone.

I go back up the stairs, through the cabin and deck and out on to the dock. Charlotte has made herself scarce again. The sun is still shining, though it has turned chilly. I'm looking for a café, somewhere for a coffee and maybe dinner, but it's the off season, and everything is closed. The harbour curves round towards the right. So many boats, a forest of masts, this place must be very busy in the summer, but now it is quiet, almost deserted.

I turn and take a path going off between the blocks of holiday apartments. Through the dunes, and here's the beach, wide and flat and curving. Waves so small, just ripples stroking the damp sand, but with a delicate line of bubbles, like *chantilly* on top of chocolate. I hear them whispering, surprisingly loud for so little water, stage whispers.

I take off my boots and socks, feel the dry sand cool against my bare feet. It is 20 March - the spring Equinox, a day earlier than usual because this is a Leap Year. Three months, I think, looking out at the sea and a huge statue, a stylised bird's head with out-stretched wings and wicked beak, catching the afternoon sunlight at the end of the spur of land that separates the beach from the Marina. Three months till the Summer Solstice. Three months to get to Norway, from the Mediterranean to the Atlantic. Put like that, it seems like a deadline. I don't seem to have got very far.

Looking out along the beach, away from the Marina, there are wading birds pecking along the shoreline. I strain my eyes for flamingos. Something catches my eye on the beach near my feet. It's a feather. I bend down and pick it up. A pink feather. I put it in my pocket.

I walk along the beach a little way, but I don't want to go too far because I must be back at the Saphir by six to meet Sebastian. There's another path between the dunes, and I put my socks and boots back on against the cold concrete. I pass a children's playground, deserted, and another *boules* court, which is not. Don't these people ever do anything but play *boules?*

Then I think - you know what? I could do that. Play *boules*, and walk on the beach. Listen to the waves and watch the seabirds. Take photos of boats, and photos of sunsets, and of boats in the sunset. Pop into Sabine's office for a coffee and a chat about cats.

I know now. It's obvious. When I get home, wherever 'home' is, I need to find somewhere by the sea. Maybe that's what happens when you get older. That'll be why seaside towns, the nice ones, are renowned for being full of older people. I think about the *boules* players. Maybe it's a deep ancestral thing, a lemming thing, a longing to return to somewhere womb-like. Am I ready for that?

Well, maybe not yet. But it's very appealing.

Sebastien

When I get back to the Saphir, just after six, it's still empty. I feel a little awkward going into the cabin, and sit on the deck under the tarpaulin. It has turned misty and rather drizzly as afternoon blends into evening.

Charlotte appears and stares meaningfully at her empty food bowl, then back at me. She's accepted me then.

There's a man in a black three piece suit on the dock, talking to Alain. He looks pretty official. If he comes on board, what will I say? As he walks up the gangplank, I stand up.

His head appears through the zipped door in the tarpaulin, along with an extended hand.

'Bonsoir. Je m'appelle Sebastien. Bienvenue!'

Younger than me, early to mid-forties, medium height, stocky with incipient middle-age-spread, dark French looks slightly spoilt by a rather round, chubby face. Something rather camp about his mannerisms.

But very friendly. His English is only slightly better than my French, and we communicate in a version of Franglais, which is rather fun.

'I am sorry I wasn't here, I had to go to my other job' he explains. 'I think the English word is – "funeral"?'

'Oh okay', I say, smiling and nodding. Not sure if that's really the most appropriate response. So he's a funeral director – or a part-time funeral director's assistant.

'That is why...' he sweeps an outstretched hand down his body from head to foot, indicating the suit, and grimaces. I laugh, and relax.

'I will change.'

He disappears down to his cabin, emerging a few minutes later in jeans and a jumper, much more sailor-like, by which time Charlotte has also returned, sensing, as cats do, the chance of food.

'Would you like to have a drink with me?' asks Sebastien. 'Aperitif?'

'Er – yes please.'

'Alcohol or no-alcohol?'

'Oh, alcohol please!'

He delves into a box in the corner of the cabin, pulling out bottles.
'I have muscatel – you know muscatel?' I nod '...or whiskey, or a drink I make myself with rum and lime juice – that's what I will have – you want to try?'

'Yes please' I say. 'Sounds good.'

It seems to involve a lot of preparation, squeezing limes, and rapid stirring to dissolve sugar, and various ingredients that I don't recognise, but it is indeed very good.

I wonder quite where this is going – if anywhere – dinner perhaps? Sebastien explains that there's a couple staying in the other cabin. They're sharing a boat with another couple, but it only has sleeping capacity for two, so they come back here at night. They're leaving tomorrow.

'If you go right along the edge of the marina, there's a restaurant ' he says. 'I think you can get dinner there.'

Well that clears that up. I walk round the marina, in the damp, chilly evening air. By the time I've finished dinner, the rain is coming down hard, and I'm glad of my umbrella for the walk back to the Saphir.

Sebastien is watching the sport channel when I get back.

'You want to watch TV?' he asks. 'A movie?' There's quite a selection of DVDs.

'*Non merci*' I say. '*Je suis très fatiguée*' I put my hands together and mime resting my head on them. He grins politely.

'What time would you like breakfast in the morning? Eight thirty? Nine? Ten?'

'Eight thirty will be fine. *Bonne nuit.*'

'Good night.'

I go down to my cabin. It's been an eventful day.

Le Grau-du-Roi – Wednesday 23 March

I wake as usual in the early hours, but the gentle rocking of the boat feels comforting and cosy, and the next thing I know it's eight o'clock. I dress quickly and climb up to the deck, where Sebastien is just leaving.

'I'm going to get the breakfast. You want anything special? Croissants, bread, *pain au chocolat?*'

'Anything will be fine, *merci.*'

The other guests have already left, sailing further along the coast with their friends.

The box of cat food is on the table with the breakfast things. When Sebastien gets back from the *boulangerie* Charlotte is sitting to attention, and he teases her before filling her bowl.

'She has to wait.'

I can't help smiling as I watch him playing with her and talking to her. He catches my eye.

'*Mon chat, c'est ma femme*' he says, slightly embarrassed.

'*Pas le bateau?*'

He seems confused, and I'm not sure whether it's my accent, my syntax or the concept that's the problem.

'*Le bateau n'est pas votre femme?*' Isn't the boat your wife?

Light dawns.

'Ah.' He fondles the cat and tumbles her over. '*Elle est ma fille, peut-être.*' Maybe she's my daughter.

We talk about the boat over breakfast, and I ask if he ever sails it anywhere. The answer's no, because of the cost of the diesel.

'Sometimes, just round the harbour. But it is too expensive now.'

It seems sad, that he has his boat, presumably a lifetime dream, but now he can't take it anywhere. I ask if he lives on it all the time, and the answer's yes, he doesn't have a home on land, just his boat.

'My home and my work – my business' he says.

I wonder about his life history. Divorced, maybe? Or a 'confirmed bachelor', as they used to say? I can't quite make him out.

It's raining again, but I can't stay on the boat all day.

'Like home for you, eh?'

'It's not like this all the time' I assure him, as I leave with my umbrella.

I want to find the lagoon with the flamingos. I think it must be on the other side of the apartments, but when I follow the path through, I come to a road with still more apartments, which doesn't seem to be leading me anywhere. I go back to the beach and round the bay, heading for the town.

I'm not here to sail, or to fish, to sunbathe, or to birdwatch (only in a desultory, incidental way). Wherever I am, I'm here to be here, and I'm never anywhere long enough to feel compelled to do anything to justify my presence.

I used to worry about finding what I'm looking for, because I didn't know what I was looking for. I was told I needed to have a dream, a goal, a plan, and my soul rebelled, I didn't want a dream, dreams let you down. And insofar as I had a dream it was just this, to make this journey.

Finding what I'm looking for isn't important. Knowing what I'm looking for isn't important. Enjoying what I find is what matters.

In Port-Camargue, everything is closed, with the unnatural quiet of an out of season seaside town. Le Grau-du-Roi, about twenty minutes walk along the beach, is more lively. It's very like Sète, with canals and a lifting bridge to allow boats from the sea to the lagoon. Groups of brightly coloured kayaks pass through at irregular intervals, their crews wrapped up in kaguls with the hoods tightly drawn around their faces against the constant rain.

I walk alongside the canal away from the open sea. Surely this must be the way to get to the lagoon? The weather is brightening, but the canal here is less picturesque and more businesslike. Past the railway station the path becomes a road, and then a dual carriageway, heading out of town by the side of the lagoon. There's no pavement, so I slip and slide along the muddy verge, but it's worth it because I've found the flamingos at last, feeding in the distance in shallow, pinkish lakes, divided by low strips of muddy ground.

Dinner on Le Saphir

When I get back to the boat, the radio's on, but there's no response to my *'bonjour'*. Sebastien must be down below - I hope this doesn't mean anything awkward. When I pass his cabin on the way to mine, the door is open and it's empty. However, when I come back up on deck, there he is, looking suspiciously cheerful.

'Can I invite you to have dinner with me and my friend Dominique?'

'Oh yes, of course, *merci beaucoup.*'

His 'friend' Dominique, eh? Hmm. That's a name that can go either way. I'm still wondering.

I go back to my cabin, and this time when I return, a woman has mysteriously appeared on deck. Maybe they were in the double cabin vacated by the departed couple?

'Linda, this is Dominique.'

'Bonjour.' We shake hands. Well, that answers a few questions.

She is petite, very French, not slim, but well turned out, in a short skirt and tight jumper. I feel decidedly shabby. I haven't washed my hair, finding the hand-held shower in my cabin a bit of a challenge. It hangs in greasy rat's tails around my face, and it's been too long since I saw a hairdresser.

Her English isn't as good as Sebastien's, but she's friendly. The three of us go to the supermarket together to buy food for dinner.

When we get back to the marina, there's a man standing at the end of the Saphir's gang-plank, with a big belly and a bushy nautical beard. Not at all my type. He and Sebastien slap each other on the back and talk animatedly in French, far too fast for me to follow, then Sebastien turns to me and says:

'Linda, this is my friend François.'

'Oh lordy', I think as we shake hands, 'please don't say Sebastien and Dominique are trying to set me up with this guy.' How awkward would that be? He talks to me about Manchester, a place he apparently knows well and I know not at all, and he has never heard of Bedford.

Sebastien pours out the special rum aperitifs, and the conversation lapses back into French. I drink mine a bit too quickly and start to cough, but by the time the refills come round I'm feeling more relaxed. François tells a rather raunchy joke, which he then repeats in English for my benefit. I'm drifting into a reverie where a fling with a twinkly Frenchman, albeit a podgy, beardy one, seems like rather a nice idea, when he downs his drink, makes his excuses and leaves.

Oh – why isn't he staying for dinner? Was he just here to check me out and decided he didn't like what he saw? So what's wrong with me? I feel quite affronted.

Ah well. It doesn't spoil dinner: spaghetti bolognaise, chocolate mousse, fruit and cheese to follow, plenty of red wine. Afterwards we sit in the main cabin, Dominique checking something online from her laptop. The news channel is on the telly, there are regular updates about a fire or a prison escape or something exciting going on in Marseille.

'I have to pack' I say 'Nice to have met you'. I go to shake hands with Dominique, but she pecks me on the cheek. *'Bonsoir.'*

Le Grau-du-Roi to Aix-en-Provence – Thursday 22 March
Sebastien is very kindly driving me to the station. As we pass the lagoon, I ask him about the red colour of the water.

'It's because of the salt' he says. Salt pans, of course – that makes sense of the banks between the pools.

I'm looking out for the flamingos, when I see the train coming across the marsh.

'There it is' says Sebastien, braking for the level crossing. I check my watch as the train crawls towards us.

'*La gare est là*' he continues, pointing to the far side of the level crossing gate.

We say our farewells, and for the first time in three days, the station door is open.

The clouds are gathering over Le Grau-du-Roi, after a brilliant sunny morning – but that's okay. It's time to move on.

La Belle Charlotte

Chapter 13 Aix-en-Provence

***Bienvenue en Aix* – Thursday 22 March**

At the hotel in Aix, there's a nasty moment when I pull out my credit card and the receptionist says: 'it says clearly on the site, cash only!'

I feign ignorance. 'I'm sorry, this is all I have.'

'Very well madame, you can pay on check-out, but please make sure you have cash' he sniffs, and gives me the key. 'Room 22, second floor'.

I look at him, and at the Wardrobe.

'Is there a...' I begin.

'No' he says gleefully. 'Stairs. Just outside reception, on your left.'

I start dragging the Wardrobe up one stair at a time. I'm getting used to this, and he was exaggerating – it's not really two flights, there are only a few stairs between the first and second floors. I think he was just saying it to wind me up and get his own back for the credit card.

It's after six o'clock and I want to get out, explore the city and find some dinner. At least I'm close to the historical centre. I look in reception for a map - there are lots of tourist leaflets in various languages - and a gap where the English version should be.

Still, I'm not worried. On the corner near the hotel is a map showing the centre. I locate the hotel and the railway station, almost diametrically opposite each other. Wherever I see one of those maps I'll be able to work out how to get back to the hotel.

The roads are quite quiet, and through a window to my left I see the words: *'Sciences Po'*. Looks like I'm in a university area. The two young men coming towards me could easily be students

Further in, the place is heaving in the early evening sunlight, lots of pavement cafés, little narrow cobbled streets opening into pretty squares with fountains and statues. Can't take many photos as the battery is low on my phone - never mind, I'll just walk and enjoy the atmosphere. I follow the signs for the Hôtel de Ville and as I walk into the square in front of the City Hall, I notice a good looking man sitting on his own at a café table – reading something so intently that he's shovelling the food into his mouth almost without noticing – clearly an academic. Another exceptionally good looking man is walking towards me and meets my gaze – or was he just staring at the young blonde in front of me when I walked into his sightline? *C'est la vie.*

Following a few more twists and turns, I come out into a wide street full of cafés. I'm happy people-watching. In the trees there are large numbers of starlings, flocking and squawking. The ruckus makes it feel almost like a winter's evening.

There are plenty of places to eat, I just need to confirm the way back to the hotel and choose somewhere close so it's not too much of a walk back afterwards. So – which way is it?

I always assume it's going to be possible to retrace my steps. I mean, I know roughly the direction I came from, don't I? I don't have to go back exactly the same way, this way is more or less parallel, isn't it? It'll take me approximately the right way, won't it? Except – I don't remember that church – I don't remember any of it. So where the hell am I?

I try a corner, and I try another corner, and – I'm not going to panic. Not really. Ah, look, there's a sign for the Hôtel de Ville – yes, I can find that. And I'm still observing, still noticing things: the woman begging outside the church; the toy shop; the *crêperie* with the man in the floppy chef's hat making his crêpes and chatting to the passers-by, pulling in the punters. There's a young man in the doorway playing an instrument that looks like a drum but makes lovely, tinkling music.

Now I'm in the square by the Hôtel de Ville, so which of the entrances did I come in by before? I remember the man eating alone, the one I guessed was an academic, can I visualise which way the tables were laid out and spot which café it is? Not really, they're starting to close, and the staff are packing the tables away.

Well, that one looks most promising. I walk up the road leading out of the square that way and – yes! – I'm sure I recognise that shop! I've definitely walked this way – aah – there's that tinkly music again, and the toy shop, the church and the beggar. I'm going round in circles – I must be, because half an hour later I see that same street again, from the opposite direction. I look for maps, but there aren't any, just historical markers with notes about landmarks.

At last I come out of the old city into a large square with a fountain, which looks like the place where I caught the taxi from the station. There's traffic here, and bus shelters, which have maps. I try to read one, but it's a bus map, showing the routes but very difficult to read the names of streets in the dim light. I can see that I have to go right through the old city and out the other side, but it's impossible to recognise names of streets that might be helpful.

I work my way back yet again to the Hôtel de Ville. Because of the winding nature of the streets, it's impossible to keep the orientation clear in my head. I keep passing landmarks that I recognise, but can't be sure how many times I've seen them.

Then in one corner of the square I see painted on the wall the words 'Chat Rêveur'. I remember this because I tried to work out if it meant 'dreaming cat'. It was over a shop that was just closing, and I walked down the street to one side.

I remember seeing it across the square but from which direction? I go up the street diametrically opposite, and things slowly start to click into place: a signpost for the tapestry museum; a Vietnamese take-away, with a couple talking to the owner. When I emerge from the street, I can see the hotel.

So now I know how to get back, and I'm starving. I aim for the Vietnamese take away, but as I approach a man walks out of the side door carrying some boxes of rubbish. His shop is closed up with a grille over the entrance. I look at my watch. It's 20.45. All the cafés are closed, and the few bars open in the side streets aren't serving food.

Back in the square, a row of restaurants are open for the dinner traffic. But all I want now is something quick and cheap. Maybe the crêpe man's still working? I set off across the square, and see a sign for the Topkapi. I noticed it earlier, because it got me thinking about Istanbul. It's tucked away in the corner, a bog-standard kebab shop that could have been anywhere, a doner sandwich and a bottle of water for €6. Perfect! I sit at one of the outside tables to eat, then walk back to the hotel, stopping at a late night supermarket for a pack of four chocolate creamy desserts, and eat two at my desk while typing.

Chapter 14 Cannes

Aix-en-Provence to Cannes – Friday 23 March 2012

I've got time after breakfast to walk to some of the places I saw last night. Just passing through. Another of those towns to be chalked up on the list. Outside a handsome old church I pass a group of art students, sketching away. A wedding has just finished and guests are spilling out onto the square, photos being taken, cars arriving to take them away. What is it about weddings that attracts so much attention from passers-by who have no connection to the central couple? I don't like weddings, whether that is cynicism or just sour grapes, I wouldn't like to say. But I snap the mayhem anyway, the mixture of artists, guests and gawping onlookers.

The journey goes smoothly for once, and the hotel really is in easy walking distance of the station. The receptionist is very camp.

'The reception will be closed from t'ree till seven t'irty. To get into the building between those times you will have to press the intercom button, which will put you through to my colleague at the other 'otel across the street. You must tell 'im your room number and last name, and 'e will open the door and let you in.'

'How do I get on to the wifi?'

'It isn't working madame, but they 'ave it at the coffee shop.' He waves his hand vaguely to the left. The tiny lobby holds no room for anything but the desk and lift - no sign of a coffee shop. He means one down the street, but which one, I wonder?

Bienvenue a Cannes - **Friday 23 March 2012**

Why did I decide to come to Cannes? We had a family holiday here in 1998. This is the first place I've been to on the trip that I've only been to before with my ex-husband. Maybe that's why I feel so uncomfortable here. Walking along the Croisette in the drizzly evening, hunched inside my coat against the chilly wind coming off the sea, I feel very detached from it all, the glamour and the excess, the designer shops and the handprints in the pavement. I can't even walk on the beach, because it's privatised, partitioned off, claimed by the restaurants and hotels. Even the sand looks fake - I'm sure it's been shipped in because I remember it being pebbly, not sandy. I can't see the attraction. Port-Camargue was much more my kind of place.

I should've gone to Antibes, or Nice, rather than here. I remember Antibes, the lovely little square and the narrow streets. And Nice has the flower market and the Matisse museum. But I booked a hotel in Cannes, because, when I was thinking of how to get from A (Barcelona) to B (Terni) it was the first place I thought of. And the hotel seemed so reasonable and convenient, it beat anything else in the area.

I try a few coffee shops, but I can't find one with free wifi. I start to panic - I need to sort out my onward travel. Then I spot the familiar golden arches of McDonald's. It's noisy with youngsters of all nationalities and permeated with the usual smell of greasy food and sweaty adolescents, but it's out of the rain.

Italy is next on my itinerary, and I'll be staying there for almost a month. I have two friends I'm planning to stay with, neither of them Italian: Irina from Romania and now living in Terni, in Umbria, and Ilze from Latvia, who lives in Turin.

My original plan was to go from France through the Alps to Turin, and after that to work my way south. Both my friends are busy in early April, but Irina can put me up the last week of March. So I changed my plan to go to her first, and then spend a couple of weeks exploring Italy on my own. That part's pretty vague, but I've got it in my head that I should go to Rome, Florence and possibly Venice.

My priority is to find the best route for getting to Terni. Looking at the distance, I need two overnight stops. I email Irina to ask whether she can meet me on Tuesday, then start jumping between Google maps and the French and Italian train company sites. I'm not sure what Irina will say, I feel a bit guilty, I haven't been in touch since I left England, and this is quite short notice. What if she can't or doesn't want to put me up after all? I try to focus on checking the connections, looking for journeys without too many changes, and places which might have some inherent interest. Genoa seems a logical choice, the first place I can think of across the border in Italy, and I can get there in one day from Cannes. For Terni, I'll need to get a local train from Rome, so what's a good staging post between there and Genoa? How about Bologna?

My email pings and it's Irina – yes, that's fine, she can meet me on Tuesday. What time? I haven't got a clue yet – but at least that's one worry sorted.

I rub my aching eyes and glance at the time. It's gone 9 o'clock, I've been here in McDonald's for over two hours and I'm exhausted. So much for the glamour of the Riviera. At least it's stopped raining, and it's only a 10 minute walk back to the hotel. I go straight to my room and collapse into bed.

Cannes - Saturday 24 March 2012
I'm back in McDonald's for breakfast, still stressed and irritable, cursing myself for lying in bed awake and not getting up and writing. Checking out trains for Genoa, Genoa to Bologna, Bologna to Rome, Rome to Terni – and of course, hotels as well. All that lot takes me another two hours, and then I can email Irina with my ETA, take the laptop back to the hotel and set off to spend my day in Cannes, still feeling rather fretful and unenthusiastic. Maybe I can take a bus to somewhere more appealing.

At least the rain has gone and it's starting to warm up. There's an antique market on the square, full of crowded stalls and browsing tourists between the bare stubbly trunks of pollarded plane trees. It reminds me of the Saturday antiques market on the Place du Grand Sablon in Brussels. I love to wander round and just look. It's like being in a museum, because I have no intention of buying. I guess I could get something small, jewellery perhaps, certainly not that huge and ugly green porcelain soup tureen which catches my eye because it's so repulsive it's almost fascinating. There's a rather nice-looking man selling model cars and trains, but then, would you really want a man who was that into model cars and trains? Even if it's his business, there's something a bit obsessive about it.

On the other side of the market is the bus station. I'm surprised the buses take so long: an hour to Antibes and 90 minutes to Nice. And I've only got one full day here in Cannes. There must be something to do.

I keep walking, but there's a lot of redevelopment going on at the western end of the harbour, roads closed off and big equipment, and those ugly orange barriers that funnel you into narrow corridors, where you have to step to one side for families with buggies and children on scooters. Then at the end of the headland, the old town, another promenade, and a public beach, rocky breakwaters, children on the sand and swimmers – one or two – in the waves.

I lean on the rail and watch. At least here everything seems open, there are no restaurants hogging the beach. To my left is a breakwater with rocks piled up, and below me the blue of the Med rattling over the pebbles. I could swim, but can I be bothered to go back to the hotel for my swimsuit and towel?

I walk to the end of the breakwater. There's a middle aged couple sitting with their backs leaning against each other. Makes me think of that holiday - we didn't spend much time in Cannes, it was just a base - my memories are of Antibes, Nice, Monte Carlo and Grasse.

Along the promenade I stop at a café, but the outside tables are already serving lunch. The waiter says I can have coffee if I sit inside, but I get up and move on. A couple of doors down there's a *crêperie* where they don't mind serving me outside. Maybe I'll have a swim this afternoon and come back here for crêpes.

Further on there's a green square, a park with trees around a pond and a children's playground. I cross it diagonally, and come out the other side away from the sea and opposite a multi-story car park. Next to the entrance there's a narrow path with steps, leading upwards to a rather ordinary street between blocks of flats. Looks like I've done my usual thing of finding the less attractive parts of town, but the road leads up and I climb in the sunshine.

The zig-zagging streets soon bring me to the top of the hill, the *'Castre'* and a white stone clock tower. It's just struck 12, and carries on striking notes for a while, so that when I reach the lookout, I can see the bell's still moving. There's a man with a grey pony tail, alone and taking photos; some families with children, and a young couple. A cluster of people with cameras are gathered around a seagull on a wall. I think to myself: 'Come to Cannes, where even the gulls are poseurs', and take one myself. When I look up the grey pony-tail man is watching me. How touristy and naff of me, to photograph a seagull.

There's a church and museum, with a sign outside. A succession of people read it, then go down the hill. I walk over to see what it says. Entry is €6 and it's closed between 13.00 and 14.00. It is now 12.20, which is probably why no one's going in. There's a bench behind it, in a sheltered corner between the white clock tower and a statue of a rather knowing Virgin and child, under the green branches of the maritime pines and the blue Mediterranean sky. Seems like a good place for a picnic. I rummage in my bag and pull out a bar of dark chocolate with hazelnuts and a bottle of water. The bitter chocolate melts deliciously against my tongue, as I sit in the sunshine enjoying the peace of the moment, the sound of birdsong and the distant roar of traffic.

Sur la plage

Back at the hotel, I change into my swimsuit, with my clothes over the top, and head down to the beach I passed earlier. It's a beautiful day, warm enough to strip off. Some English girls are chatting nearby - so near that it's hard to avoid overhearing their conversation. A couple of French families with children running around in swimsuits are enjoying the sunshine, and a few people are swimming. I walk self-consciously down to the water's edge. The water is chilly over my feet and ankles, but I paddle a little further, out to the rocks. Now I'm in it up to my waist, and I pull myself up to sit on the rocks, wondering if I'm brave enough to put the top half of my body under too - always the biggest challenge. And it's still only March, after all.

Feels as though everyone must be watching me, this crazy woman who can't quite make up her mind whether she's going to swim or not. And I've left my purse with my pile of clothes. That's one of the problems with being on your own, having to leave your stuff unattended sometimes. I can sort of keep my eye on it, but not all the time.

I must be mad, and anyone who sees me must think I'm mad. I could just wade back to the beach, of course, dry myself off, and that would be it. Not really such a big deal. Except that I'd know I'd chickened out – and so would everyone who saw me. Does that matter? Well, yes, it does. It always does.

So I plunge into the water, over my shoulders, even though it takes my breath away, and start to swim. And as always happens, after the first shock, it's okay. I swim out almost to the end of the breakwater, where a young couple are looking down into the water. It's surprising, once you get going, how far you go without realising it; you turn round and look back and the beach seems miles away, the people sitting on it so small. It's far enough. Honour is satisfied.

Back at the beach I wrap myself in my towel, but the sun is surprisingly warm. My blood is rushing, and my body tingling. I'm glad I did it and I'm glad it's over.

The English girls have been watching me. One walks towards the water's edge.

'It's pretty cold' I call out to her. She turns and looks, perhaps a little surprised at my English accent. Then she plunges in and screams:

'It's bloody freezing!' Her friends laugh.

I sit in the sun for a while to dry out my damp swimsuit, then put my jeans, tee-shirt and jumper back on. I've swum in the sea in the last week of March. Not bad. As long as I don't catch hypothermia. And I've earned my crêpe.

Au revoir Cannes - Sunday 25 March 2012

Two weeks today since I left San Sebastián. Six weeks today since I left the flat. Is that right? It seems much longer, a different life - I feel very detached from everything that went before. Never even think about those days – this is my life now, travelling from place to place.

Two weeks since I left Eduardo's. That's three days travelling to and being in Barcelona, then ten days drifting, wandering through the Languedoc and Provence. I'm not sure where one ends and the other begins, or whether the Languedoc is a subregion of Provence. Anyway, today I leave France, and that's that, I won't be coming back, not this trip anyway. Into Italy, which is new territory for me. The only time I've spent in Italy up to now is three days at a workshop in Rome. I was longer with Eduardo than I anticipated. I won't stay more than a week with Irina, that seems too much to expect. But Ilze is busy till the third week of April. Which is – what? Three weeks from now? So, a week with Irina and then a fortnight of moving around, and maybe a week in Turin with Ilze and then – on to Istanbul. I need a target – to be there by the end of April, Budapest by early May. Prague mid-May. A month to get across the continent to Kristiansund. That should be okay – as long as the money doesn't run out. But let's not think about that.

ഇരുജ

IV

Italy

Genoa - Bologna - Terni - Naples - Sorrento - Rome - Florence - Turin - Venice

Chapter 15 – Genoa

Cannes to Genoa – Sunday 25 March

The Riviera drifts by the window in the sunshine. It's beautiful in the highly polished fashion of a film starlet, a celebrity. It palls easily. The colours - vivid greens and blues of the sea and sky, white of the cliffs and little houses, red roofs, deep green of the pine trees and yellow beaches – seem clichéd. My overall impression is of a film set, a neatly manicured landscape studded with big, expensive hotels and shiny cars, designer-labelled to serve as a backdrop for the power plays and intrigues of the rich and famous.

Into a tunnel – one of many as the track weaves through the mountains. Darkness, then a flash of blue sea and green headlands, then darkness again.

This tunnel becomes the brightness of a station. The announcer says 'Monte Carlo'. The train comes to rest, and the carriage empties, but I'm staying on till the end of the line. Booking the ticket confused me – Vintimille or Ventimiglia? The name seemed to keep changing. But of course, it's the same place – with both French and Italian names.

I'm still not altogether sure where it is until I get there, but it's Italy all right. I have fifteen minutes to change trains, and I can't see an electronic display to tell me where my connection goes from. Try to breathe slowly and stay calm as people push past me, piling down the staircases.

There's a noticeboard with a printed timetable. It shows only two trains between 14.00 and 15.00.

'Milano, *signora?*' says a man's voice behind me.

'Genova.'

'*Quattro*' he says, just as I spot Genoa on the list of stations for the

Milan train. He has the Wardrobe and is taking it down the stairs.

'Grazie' I say feebly as I follow him through the tunnel and up to platform 4. He stops and asks me something. I pull my ticket from my coat pocket and show it to him. He reads the carriage number and sets off up the platform.

It occurs to me that he isn't just being helpful to a stranger. But how should I react?

I follow him to carriage 7, where he lifts the Wardrobe on the train and starts pulling it down the corridor. It's a compartment train, must be at least 20 years since I saw one of those.

The man goes into an empty compartment and points to a window seat. There are two overhead racks, but he looks meaningfully at the Wardrobe. It's about as wide as the space between the two rows of seats, but there's no way he's going to lift it to the rack.

He stands in the compartment entrance while I extract my purse from my waistcoat pocket. The first coin I pull out is a euro. I offer it, but he's still standing there. I find a second euro coin. He takes that as well, mutters something dark and angry, and leaves.

Well, I didn't ask him to take my bag, did I? He didn't give me any choice. The smallest note I've got is €10 - why should I feel obliged to give him that? My first experience of Italy leaves rather a sour taste.

I put my coat in the overhead rack, the backpack on the seat beside me, and sit down with the Wardrobe standing next to the seat, blocking me into my corner.

I've got the compartment to myself for a couple of stations, then an elderly couple get in, glare at me and let loose a torrent of Italian. I hoist the backpack into the rack and try lifting the Wardrobe onto the seat, but this obviously isn't good enough. They carry on speaking rapidly to me, but all I can do is shrug. Another couple of similar age come in, and the second man takes the Wardrobe from me and stands it out in the corridor, where it takes up about a third of the space.

They talk constantly, occasionally they say *'Signora'* and look at me meaningfully. It begins to rain, driving against the roof and window as I stare out.

I hear the sound of a bicycle bell, but think nothing of it until the door opens and a man sticks his head through. He's passing down the corridor with a trolley selling drinks and biscuits, but can't get past my case. I stand up, very shame-faced, and pull it into the compartment, avoiding the feet of the grumbling senior citizens, until he passes, then push it out again.

I have a sinking feeling that this might all be an omen for my stay in Italy.

Genoa

I have very clear directions for finding the hotel in Genoa – 50m from the station, on the left, after the pharmacy. There's the pharmacy, on the corner of a small square set into the hillside. I check in then go back out into the chilly Sunday evening. Which way to go? Head for the seafront – usually a good place for tourist stuff, and easy to find as it's always downhill. I stroll round the harbour taking photos of the sunset, find a kiosk and order a cappuccino.

'For here?' the man asks in English, tapping his hand on the counter between us.

'*Si.*'

'Eighty cents.' That seems remarkably cheap. I hand over the money and take my coffee to one of the tables.

'No' he says. 'Special price is to drink at the bar. Drink at tables is service, the price is €2.'

Oh. I hand over the extra €1.20.

Back near the hotel, as darkness settles over the city, I find a pizzeria, where I order pizza and a glass of red, all excellent. It's a very small place, feels like it's used more by locals than tourists. The man on the next table eats his pizza very slowly, cutting it into tiny pieces with his knife and fork. I finish mine and have a look at the dessert menu. The proprietor comes over.

'You like some fruit salad *Signora?*'

The desserts are in a glass case, and the tiramisu looks very tempting.

'*Tiramisù, per favore?*'

'The fruit salad is very good, *Signora*'.

I try again, but he's not going to be moved, so I give in to the inevitable and take the fruit salad. He's right, it is very good.

But I return to my hotel with the sneaking suspicion that the Italians are going to run rings around me.

C3༄

Chapter 15 – Genoa

Breakfast in Genoa – Monday 26 March

Bedlam in the coffee shop. People milling around. Pastries on the counter and in the cabinet. Blokes at the bar knocking back the espresso – I assume it's only espresso at this time in the morning. Girl with a dark pony tail on the coffee machine.

And one confused Englishwoman in the middle of it all.

I let a couple of other people pass me by as I scan the pastry cabinet, and spot something sweet and sticky.

It's my turn, he's speaking to me. I try the technique I perfected in Spain.

'Cappuccino?' with a rising intonation and self effacing smile.

'Cappuccino? *Si*'. At least he picked that up despite my lousy accent.

'*Y*...' I point to my choice in the cabinet. I think '*y*' is right for 'and' – or is that just Spanish?

'Self service' he says as he passes me my change. 'Help yourself.'

'Ah... *grazie*'.

I fiddle with the cabinet door, get it open, grab a napkin and pick up my pastry. The coffee machine girl is shouting and holding several conversations at once, but I can see the milk frothing into the cup. She looks at me.

'Cappuccino?' she says kindly.

'*Oui – er, Si.*'

I take my pastry and coffee outside. There are tables alongside the café, separated from the square by a low cable hanging from a row of posts. A large and noisy family is sitting at the end table blocking the way. They start to shuffle around, but I smile and say 'It's okay' as I climb over the cord.

I sit and sip my coffee, eat my pastry, people-watching and thinking about the breakfasts I've eaten in Caffé Angelo's back in Bedford, about Angelo's Twitter competitions and his bacon butties.

I've already been to the station and bought my ticket from a machine. I finish breakfast, and I still have three quarters of an hour to kill. At the back of the square, where it meets the hillside there are steps up, and a sign saying '*Ascensore*'.

A lift up the hillside? That might be interesting, just to go up, have a look at the view, and come back. The Wardrobe is still at the hotel and it won't take long to pick it up on the way to the station.

The sign points to a door, and behind it is a bare room like a lobby built into the hillside. There's a ticket machine with a sign saying what coins it takes but no indication of the price. While I'm wondering what to do, the lift appears at the back, the doors open and a group of maybe half a dozen people get out. Through the glass walls I can see rails leading away for quite a distance behind it.

I push a few buttons on the ticket machine, enough to find out that a single fare is 80 cents. I buy a single ticket - I'll ride up and come back down the stairs next to the entrance.

It's a cross between a large glass sided lift and a small underground train. There's a shelf along the back and red fold down seats. How do I make it go? I can't see anywhere to put the ticket in, or any buttons to press.

Two young women come in and ask:

'Does this go to Albert's Castle?'

'I'm not sure' I shrug. 'You have to buy a ticket' I indicate the machine 'but I don't know how to make it go.'

'It's leaving in three minutes.'

'How do you know?'

They point up. I step outside, and over the top of the entrance is an electronic display with a rolling sign indicating *3 minuti per partenza.*

I sit down on one of the seats while the girls get their tickets. A man is talking to them and showing them how the machine works. I clearly hear him say *'cinque minuti'*, but whether that's the frequency or length of time of the journey, I can't tell.

The doors start closing while the girls are still talking to him, so I'm on my own in the car when it starts moving. I can see the track quite clearly, leading ahead and slightly upwards through the tunnel. It comes to a corner, turns to the right and stops. Through the glass I can see that another car has just come down. At first it seems empty, but through the gloom I make out another woman sitting down inside. The mechanism clanks, and the other car moves off down the corridor. Then I start going upwards.

I was hoping for a view out over the town as we rose, but it's inside a shaft. After a couple of minutes it stops and the door opens again into a lobby, much smaller than the one at the bottom.

I walk out blinking into bright sun. On the other side of the road is the

Castello Alberti, a museum *'del culturas del mondo'*. I walk to the corner and look out over the city, through a chain link fence.

Whereabouts are the steps? They could be anywhere – so going back down that way isn't an option when I've got a train to catch. Given the distance I've just travelled through the mountain, I have no idea where I am relative to the station.

Back at the lift, I buy another ticket to go down. A couple are just loading in a set of suitcases, and a pregnant lady gets in with a backpack larger than mine. We all sit, the doors close and we ride back down to the road by the station.

The harbour in Genoa

Chapter 16 – Bologna

Genoa to Bologna - Monday 26 March

The first part of the trip is via Milan. It's in a compartment train again, but I'm ready for it this time: I'll move the Wardrobe into the compartment while people are passing up and down the corridor. Put the backpack on the seat beside mine, knowing it can't stay there. Go through coat pockets and backpack for anything I might need on the journey and put them in my waistcoat pockets. Zip up backpack and put it and my coat on the rack. Then, when we are moving, the Wardrobe goes out in the corridor.

Genoa seen from the train (and perhaps in other ways), is like Marseille, the city squeezed onto the mountain sides and into the valleys, lasting for longer than seems possible, endless grubby suburbs.

The man with the trolley arrives and I get up to move the Wardrobe out of his way, but he is more skilful (or more obliging) than the guy on the Ventimglia to Genoa line, he moves his trolley past and leaves it in the corridor further down.

The passing scene, a clock tower, an orchard, viaduct, valley. Tiny trickle of a river between high, wide concrete banks.

Viaducts and tunnels – they look as though they should be exciting, but when you're in or on them, you don't notice anything. Especially tunnels. Well, maybe viaducts are pretty spectacular, but you don't think of being on them when you're on them, just looking at the view.

Then comes the ticket inspector. Take coat down from the rack and get ticket out of the inside pocket.

And suddenly, unexpectedly, a flat landscape, fields and roads, lorries and cars, the mountains lost in the grey haze along the horizon.

How did that happen? While I wasn't looking, all my attention on my notebook, someone took the mountains away.

At Milan, there should be half an hour to make the connection – 12.50 to 13.20. We get in at 13.05. As I walk the length of the platform, a small Asian man with a big smile and a luggage trolley makes eye contact. I shake my head. Not again – anyway, I have no money and no idea how far I have to go. It might just be the opposite side of the platform.

I stop to read the overhead display, find the 13.20 for Bologna departing from platform 18. Eighteen? Good god, where the hell is that? Now I'm craning to see that the platform on my right is 20, the one I just got off is 21. I get to the end, turn right, there it is, with the train already waiting. But I need money. I go through the coins in my pocket. Two Euro, one euro, two fifties. Four euros. I had a tenner this morning – handed it over for breakfast and took the change without looking at it. Then €1.60 for lift tickets. I guess that works out.

No sign of a cash machine, and when I check my watch to find it's gone quarter past. So no lunch then.

On the train, I'm up and down, endlessly, I need this, I need that. Is it here? No, look, in there. What? Oh, there it was all along. I lose my pencil. I wouldn't mind but it's the one I bought in San Sebastian. Look under the seat. Go through the bags, the pockets again. The lady opposite looks concerned. I feel embarrassed – she's not to know it's only a pencil. When I've given up looking, I see it, neatly balanced along the hinge of the bin.

This is my life. Constantly messing about, expending energy, never getting anything done, never achieving anything, always moving, up and down, look in here, look in there, sit down, try this, get up again. Never sitting still. Or rather, too much sitting still, too much lying in bed awake. If I sit still, everything piles up behind me, it doesn't stop, it goes on and on and I am further behind than ever.

What's the point of running away? I can't run away from myself. I will always be there, messing everything up, tripping over my own feet, faffing about. Nothing ever changes.

Bologna
We get into Bologna some time after four. I've got directions in my notebook.

Single to Sirkeci

'On foot or by bus from the station once you exit the station go left until you reach Via Indipendenza and follow direction city centre until you reach Via Bertiera (after the statue of Garibaldi on horse, the second on the left). Turn into Via Bertiera: Vicolo Cattani is the second street on your right. Bus shuttle service "C" (stop in Augusto Righi).'

I turn left out of the station, past the waiting taxis. There are two exits, the one I just came from is on the right hand side of a semi-circle, with the second in the centre. I walk towards the left hand end of the semi circle, where there's a McDonald's on the corner, then along the road leading left from the station. After a short distance, there's a major junction, a multi-lane dual carriageway across the city. I can't see any road signs, but I'm guessing this isn't the way to the hotel.

Okay, I'll pop into McDonald's, get online and have a look at the map. I buy a coffee out of my remaining meagre cash, set up the laptop and settle myself down. Try and fail to get online - then I see a notice on the wall, telling me (once I decipher it) that in order to use the free wifi, I need to supply an Italian mobile number, and the logon details will be texted to me.

This is a disaster. I'm depending on McDonald's to supply me with free wifi. If the same rule applies everywhere in Italy, I could well find myself with a problem. Quite apart from the immediate one of finding my hotel for tonight.

There's a bus map outside McDonald's, but it doesn't tell me anything helpful – nor can I find the shuttle service 'C'.

OK, I'll get a taxi. But first I need a cash machine. I didn't see any sign of one along the road past McDonald's, so I cross over in front of the station again and walk the other way down the street – right from the station, in my understanding, but maybe there's some subtle Italian way in which it's actually left? I look out for Via Indipendenza just in case. But I don't find either that or a cash machine. I cross to the other side of the road, which, dragging the Wardrobe, is a challenge in itself. Still drawing a blank, I walk back up until I'm standing opposite the station entrance.

There's a small park, and the dual carriageway has become a flyover. The sign suggests that it's Indipendenza, but I'm not going to climb up there and walk along. There's a road running parallel with it on the ground that leads into a shopping area. I walk some way along there, without finding a cash machine, an equestrian statue or Via Bertaria, turn round and go back.

That's when I call the hotel. I must sound quite demented. The answer I get pretty much repeats what I've got written down.

'Have you seen the statue of Garibaldi? On a horse'.

'I don't know. There's a statue, but I don't know who it is. And he's not on a horse.'

It's a funny thing about giving directions. I hate doing it – giving them, that is. I think when you know somewhere, it's hard to understand how difficult it is for someone who isn't already familiar with the place. You assume that they must be able to find a street, even when there's no sign to say what it's called.

The woman at the hotel convinces me that the road I just walked along is the one I need. So I turn again and keep going, past the place where I turned back last time.

It's 6 o'clock by the time I get there. I check in, and go out looking for a drink. After the confusion of finding the place, the hotel is actually in a very good location, right in the middle of the old city. Although I don't have time to get a really good impression of the place, I have the usual walk through darkening streets past handsome university buildings and ridiculously pricey shops. The feel of the place is very similar to that in Aix-en-Provence. At a bar round the corner from the hotel young office workers are enjoying a post-work drink, something dark gold with ice cubes and orange slices, so I order the same and it comes with a plate of little hors d'oeuvres, very pleasant. Then I move on to a restaurant where I order spaghetti Bolognese - what else?

Chapter 17 – Terni

Irina's Garden – Wednesday 28 March

A day of quiet, in Irina's garden in Terni, Umbria, watching lizards run up and down the white wall behind me. Soon the sun will be on my laptop screen and there won't be enough shade to see it, and then it will be lunchtime…

Irina met me at the station yesterday afternoon with her two little girls, Sofia, who's just coming up to her a second birthday, a week after mine, on the 14th April, and the baby Emma.

It's so great to be in a warm, happy family home. I have a bed downstairs in the family room, which is almost a separate apartment, with a kitchen and bathroom attached. I've met Irina's husband, Lucian, before, at a workshop in Rome in 2005, and once in Brussels. Her parents, Constantin and Cecilia, live here too. They don't speak English, but we manage to communicate pretty well. And then of course there are the girls, and the dog, and the cat, and a stream of Romanian relatives and work colleagues who wander in and out.

I'm being terribly lazy. I should really be getting on with some writing. Telling Irina about Carcassonne, or Port-Camargue and the Saphir, I realise I need to capture the stories before they fade from my memory. And every time I try to help around the house, I'm told: 'you're on holiday! We don't expect our guests to work'. But I've been on 'holiday' for six weeks already and I'm starting to feel a bit of a fraud.

A neighbour walking her dog stops to talk to Irina over the gate, and she introduces me. The friend says something and Irina laughs.

'I told her about your journey, and she said: "why did she come to Terni, of all places?"'

'To see Irina, of course!' I reply.

It is a quiet place, a steel works town, though very different from Scunthorpe, where I was born and grew up, or Bilbao. Perhaps it's the Italian sunshine and translucent blue sky, or the staggeringly beautiful backdrop of the mountains, or the yellow and terracotta painted stucco houses in the backstreets. Maybe it's just that pollution control in the steel industry has moved on from the belching blast furnaces and burning skies of my childhood.

The garden starts to get busy. Constantin is lighting the barbecue. There's some big football match on the television this evening, and Irina's brother and friends are coming round. As the light starts to fade, more and more people turn up, introductions are made, and the men gravitate towards the barbecue till there are six clustered around it, and I can't help thinking there must be a joke somewhere about how many Romanian men does it take to manage a barbecue. It's so enthralling that some of them even miss the start of the match.

The evening ends in my bedroom (the family room, that is) in front of the big-screen TV, with far too much food and red Romanian home-brew wine, until finally the vodka comes out. There's a big Romanian community in Terni, and Lucian has a shop and business importing food and drink from the home country. When the match finishes, the visitors are chased home to give me some peace to get to bed, but the jug of wine is still left on the table after everyone has gone - a terrible temptation.

Day trip to Rome – Friday 30 March
I'm off to Rome today by myself, on the commuter train. Lucian takes me to the station, and buys my ticket. The train's about to leave from the opposite platform, so I rush through the tunnel just in time to catch it.

When the ticket inspector passes through, I hand over my ticket. She inspects it, turns it over, looks at the other side, and says something in Italian.

'Sorry, English' I say with a smile. It usually excuses most things.

She carries on talking to me in Italian. It takes a while, but at last I work out she's telling me I've got to pay again because the ticket hasn't been validated.

Well, no one told me I had to validate it - and I would have missed the train anyway. I try to explain, but if she understands, she's not going to let anything I say change her mind.

I get out my purse. It contains a €20 note and a small amount of change. She shakes her head. It's not enough.

I pull out my credit card. She shakes her head again.

I feel in my pockets, and find an additional €10 note.

She takes the tenner, the twenty, and a €1 coin.

'That's all I've got!' I say 'can't you take my card?'

'No card. Card at station in Rome, but then €50. Here €31 cash.'

I'm not sure whether she means I've to pay another €50 as well when I got to Rome, but I don't want to argue any more. She writes out a receipt for €31, writes the date on my ticket and hands both to me. I pocket them and stare out of the window, cursing myself.

Just before we get to Rome, the train stops at a signal, waiting to get into the station. I wonder if the Carabinieri are about to storm the train, having had word about a dangerous foreign fare-dodger.

The inspector walks back through the carriage, and a middle aged blonde lady sitting on the other side and a few seats in front of me says something to her. I noticed this passenger earlier because she reminds me of the actress Geraldine James. The inspector makes a short reply and carries on, but now the lady starts talking to the other passengers on her side of the train. A younger man, with cropped thinning hair and a goatee, sitting the other side of her seat, turns round and joins in.

The conversation gets more animated, with people throughout the carriage putting in their two penn'orth. I sit quietly minding my own business, hoping no one's going to ask my opinion, as I haven't got a clue what they're talking about.

A man with a beard comes to the seat in front of mine and looks over the back at me.

'They are talking about what the inspector did to you. That lady' he points to Geraldine James 'is saying that she shouldn't have done it because you are a foreigner and didn't understand. She and that man' he points to the one with the goatee 'know her, and they say she is a bad person and will cheat you.'

'Oh, right' I'm rather non-plussed that all this fuss is being made over me. The train starts up again and the man in front of me staggers a little and then braces himself as we chug into the station. The conversation's still going on as people start to gather their belongings prior to leaving the train. I stand up and put my coat on. Geraldine and the young man with the goatee join the queue behind me.

'How much money did the lady take from you?' asks Geraldine.

'Thirty one euros. It was all I had', I add, building up the pathos.

'Did she give you a receipt?' says the young man.

'Yes' I fish in my pocket for it.

'She didn't have to do what she did. We are going to tell the police about her, do you want to come with us?'

'Er – yes.' It would be churlish to do anything else, after all.

We get off the train. Further down the platform there's a police office.

'I have been in London' says the young man. 'I think you don't have to validate the train tickets there, they have the date on already, is that right?'

'Yes. I mean, no, you don't have to validate the tickets. I didn't know I was supposed to'.

We walk into the office, and my two champions explain the situation to the officer at the desk. I hand over my ticket, and the receipt. He asks a question which is interpreted and passed on to me:

'Did you write the date on your ticket, or did she?'

'She did.'

Apparently I could have validated the ticket myself by writing the date on it, but as I hadn't done that, it wasn't valid. The inspector had the discretion to tell me this, but €31 was the officially sanctioned fine, and she had given me the correct receipt, so legally she had done nothing wrong. She hadn't, as my champions implied, taken more than she should have done and pocketed the difference, which they claim they've seen her do in the past. The policeman is sympathetic – and apologetic – but it's out of his hands. She was in the right, legally, and he can't refund the fine. I'm just grateful he hasn't charged me an extra €50.

Rome by tour bus

As I'm only in Rome for the day, I take the tourist bus from the station. I stop first at the Coliseum. Men dressed as gladiators wander around, asking the girls if they want their photo taken with a 'biga boya'. I get in the queue for a ticket (for the Coliseum, not for a photo with the 'biga boyas'), then a guide says: 'if you want to take an audioguide there is no queue' so I go round to the desk for the audioguides, €5.50 on top of the price to get in, then there's a queue to get through the turnstile, then there's another queue to collect your audioguide.

Inside the Coliseum it's pretty much as you would expect, big walls of grey stone blocks and lots of stairs. It's not very clear which way you're supposed to go and I wander around a bit by the entrance and book shop. It's warm and sunny and there's an awful lot of people. Across the centre of the arena, on the reconstructed floor, a bloke in a purple shirt and yellow hard hat is pushing a wheelbarrow. But the views across the city are wonderful.

I've only got limited time, so after doing a circuit of the upper floor I hand in my guide, walk back to the stop and catch the next bus. We drive along by the River Tiber, the plane trees barely breaking into leaf and not obscuring the view of the other bank and Castel Sant' Angelo in the beautiful spring sunshine. We cross over the bridge to the Vatican City, and I leave the bus again in St Peter's Square.

It's exactly a week to Good Friday, and the place is being prepared for the Easter celebrations. I walk around the piazza, looking at the crowds, and the queues. A youngish dark-haired woman in a white shirtwaister dress and dark glasses, and carrying a clip-board, speaks to me in American-accented English:

'Do you want to go into St Peter's?'

'I haven't decided.'

'We've got some spaces left in our group, and if you join us you can get in with no waiting in line.'

The tour is leaving in 10 minutes, it includes the Vatican Museum and the Sistine Chapel, a guided tour with an English-speaking guide... but she still hasn't mentioned the crucial point.

'How much is it?' I finally manage to break into her flow.

'Forty euros.'

'Okay, no thanks' I start walking away.

'It will cost you €30 just to get into the cathedral' she calls after me.

That settles it then. I walk around the square and back to the bus stop.

At the Capitol Hill, I get off the bus again to walk along the edge of the Forum, and buy a pastry from one of the vending vans, then back on the bus to Termini station and the train back to Terni.

So that was my day in Rome. I'm not sure whether I want to go back or not.

Cascades of Marmara – Saturday 31 March

Irina asks if I'd like to visit the Cascades at Marmara. I'm up for anything, but it seems to take a bit of coordination. These artificial waterfalls, beloved by Lord Byron (among others), were first created by the Romans when the water of the River Velino was diverted to improve drainage and for flood control. These days they're used to produce hydro-electricity, but the flow has to be controlled, so the falls are only in operation for certain hours each day.

When we arrive the falls are in full and spectacular flow, filling the valley with moisture and roaring. Irina has to get back to town to do something with the children, but I decide to walk up through the woods to the top, so she leaves me and arranges to come back for me later.

It 's a beautiful day, and even though the water has slowed to a trickle again, it's lovely to be out. There are hiking trails going up all the way, and a café at the top, though it's not open today. I walk through trees and birdsong, quite a treat to be out in the countryside, as for most of the time over the last couple of months I've been staying in cities. I keep passing groups of people, couples, families. I'm the only one walking alone. But there are worse places I could be. I find a shady bench, overlooking a deep gully with the sound of the river somewhere below the trees.

I wonder if I'll ever be ready to settle in one place again? Sometimes I feel that I just want to keep going forever, that I'll never find a place where I want to stay.

Being alone is what I'm used to, even in the times when I wasn't physically alone, there was always that place inside me that never really connected to anyone else. I wonder why? Is it inherent in me or a product of the relationship I was in for such a long time, with someone else who never really shared himself?

Time to move on – Sunday 1 April

I just woke up and realised the date. I've been losing track of it - but suddenly it's less than a week to my birthday. Irina has got other guests coming on Tuesday, and I promised her I'd be gone by then.

It's been very easy to be here and the time has gone really quickly, though yesterday evening when the baby was crying and some intense family conversation was going on and all my offers of help with the bustle were being politely refused – then, I did feel a longing to be somewhere anonymous again, so I could be by myself without feeling I was being unsociable.

I guess it's time to start thinking about moving on, but I haven't got a definite plan. I was wondering about going down south, to Naples or Salerno, for a couple of days, leaving the Wardrobe here and picking it up again on the way back. But that was when it seemed as though I had plenty of time.

I've been thinking of ways to reduce the load in the Wardrobe. I ask Irina if it would be possible to post some things back to England, and she seems happy to do it for me.

'We can get a box from the Post Office' she says.

I start clearing out a pile of stuff that I think I could do without, but I get a little carried away, and when Irina sees the size of the pile she seems much less enthusiastic. Then I Google the Italian postal service, and find rather a lot of reports from people who've tried sending international parcels to and from Italy, only for them never to be delivered, so I've gone off the idea.

I also need to plan how to spend my birthday, and the rest of the Easter weekend. I read online that there are two must-have experiences on the Italian railways – to take the boat-train to and/or from Sicily, and also to take a night train. I could go to Naples on Monday, stay there for three nights (I find and book a hotel near the station), take the train from Naples to Syracuse in Sicily on Thursday, book a hotel there for Thursday night, then on Friday night take the sleeper train back to Rome, arriving on the morning of my birthday – this seems a suitably spectacular way of celebrating it.

It's my last night here. I'm awake in the early hours, and can't get back to sleep. It's important to book the train tickets early to get a good fare. I get online and book the sleeper for Friday night from Syracuse to Rome, with a couchette, for €70, a hotel in Syracuse for Thursday night and one in Rome from Saturday night till Monday.

With that sorted, I put my mind at rest and go back to sleep.

Chapter 18 – Naples

Terni to Naples – Monday 2 April

Mist lying in the valley when we emerge from the tunnel, yet the sun's so bright it bounces back from the white walls of farmhouses and the cars passing on the *Autostrada*. I stand to take my notebook and pen from my bag in the overhead rack, then I'm stranded in darkness as we enter another tunnel.

Monday morning and time to be moving again. It's been lovely to be in the middle of a family, but in some ways I'm ready for the anonymity of a hotel room. It's been a while since I've done any café sitting.

Outside the window, little towns perched on mountaintops, bare mountains behind, towns down in the valley in front, by the railway line. Orchards, orderly rows of trees with pink or white blossoms.

Wetlands, white egrets. A farm with cattle with big horns, like water buffalo. Where did the mountains go? Flat as far as the eye can see. I looked away to read my book while we were in a tunnel, and someone stole the mountains. I could be back in the Camargue. Poplar trees along the ditches. Wide channels with dykes on either side. Roads on stilts. Market gardens and poly-tunnels. Fields with green stalks and yellow flowers opening that look disturbingly like oil seed rape – in the land of the olive?

The mountains have reappeared – grey blue and distant – maybe they were there all along after all.

My phone pings. Text from a friend at home: 'Be careful in Naples, or avoid altogether. Lots of trouble there.'

I've not been keeping up to date with the news, maybe occasionally I pick something up from a television report when I happen to be near a set that's on, or from the Yahoo or MSN headlines when checking my emails (though these always seem to be about 'celebrities' I've never heard of). I wonder what 'trouble' he's referring to? Ah well, I'm committed now, I've booked three nights and then I'll be off.

The hotel is in walking distance from the station, and I've got the directions in my notebook again. I've read so many awful warnings about Neapolitan taxi drivers that this seemed sensible, but of course, when I get there it's not so easy to find my way. Out of the station, cross Piazza Guiseppe Garibaldi, Via Firenze, right on Vico Milano, left on Via Venezia. Two hundred metres. Except that having that in your head doesn't feel so helpful when you're standing on a crazy square with people and traffic coming at you from all sides, dragging the Wardrobe over cobbles and potholed pavements through a mayhem of aggressively canvassing taxi drivers, piles of rubbish and street vendors trying to sell you dodgy mobiles and socks (socks?), road-works, traffic bearing down on you from all directions, keeping your head down, avoiding eye contact, carrying on because you don't want to turn back and make it even more obvious that you haven't got a clue where you're going.

Up a stereotypical Neapolitan backstreet with washing hanging from tenement balconies and angry men in sweaty vests shouting and gesticulating in the street, I see the entrance to my hotel. I'm shown to my room by a lady who may be my age, but looks older and is a lot slighter, while my efforts to drag the Wardrobe up the stairs are ignored by the man on the desk.

Still, the room is clean and cosy with a comfortable bed, en suite bathroom and a view (through window-bars) over the crazy backstreet I've just walked up, and I feel quite secure and glad to be here.

Benvenuti a Napoli

When I've freshened up, I go out to explore my surroundings. First to the station to check out the trains to Syracuse. Remember that wonderful plan to take the boat train from here to Sicily, stay one night, then catch a night train back to Rome, arriving on Saturday morning? At the station, they tell me that every train into Sicily on Thursday is sold out already.

What the hell do I do now? Head for the seafront, find a nice café to sit and mull things over. Except that there's seafront and there's seafront. It might be a nice promenade, maybe with a beach, or a quaint little fishing harbour, or a marina with yachts. All of which often come with nice cafés. Instead, what I find is docks: working docks, commercial docks, container docks, big, mean, industrial looking docks, with chain link fencing and noisy, angry guard dogs and acres of concrete.

I walk along the road for miles, wondering if this is going to get any better. I just want to get out of this town. I'll leave a day early, cancel the last night in the hotel here and get to Sicily as soon as I can.

I come at last to a road on the right and turn up it, inland. There's an equestrian statue in the middle of the road, and as I'm wondering whether I'm ever going to find my nice little café, I spy a red, open-topped City Tours bus pulling up on the far side of the road. I dodge my way across and reach it just before it drives away.

'How much for a ticket?' I ask the guide.

'Twenty two euros, and there are three routes. You've only got time to do two today, but the ticket lasts for 24 hours, so you can do another one tomorrow morning'.

'Great!' I say. I can't see how else I'm going to find the tourist sights, and clearly there must be some somewhere. 'Can you take a credit card?'

'My machine isn't working. But get on anyway, we're nearly at the terminus.'

The terminus is on the Piazza Municipale next to a hulking medieval castle, the Castel Nuovo, or Maschio Angioino, the court of the Angevin kings. Unfortunately the entire piazza is being dug up, in fact the whole city seems to be in a state of turmoil. There's a kiosk on the square for the tour buses, but apparently their credit card machine isn't working either.

'We'll be here for about ten minutes, and there's a cash machine over there if you want to go and get some' the guide tells me. I dodge my way round the building site and through the traffic to the bank and then back to the bus.

Getting online

There are two McDonald's between the station and the hotel. When I get back from the bus tour, I walk to the nearest one, and confirm that there's a sign, as there was in Bologna, to say that in order to use it, you need to supply an Italian mobile phone number.

There are also quite a few mobile phone shops, so I go into one and buy a cheap pay-as-you-go sim card. After all, I'm going to be in Italy for a while, and I can't be sure I'll have wifi everywhere I stay. I put it into my spare phone, send a text to my main phone so I've got the number, send a reply, then take the phone and laptop into McDonald's. I order a burger, get onto the wifi, and enter my new phone number. A message appears to say the passcode has been sent to the phone. So I wait, but neither that nor the message I sent from my other phone appears.

Back at the phone shop, I explain my problem. The two ladies who are serving check it and send a message from their system, which also doesn't appear.

That's when I remember that this phone has a habit of filling up its inbox without telling me, and just not accepting any messages. I try explaining this to the ladies, but they're too busy trying to sort it out. They take out the Sim and try it in another phone, when all the messages start to come through.

'It's a problem with the phone' they say in the end and give it back to me. I knew that, but I thank them and delete some older messages, which solves the problem.

Back in McDonald's, I get onto the Trenitalia website and confirm that there's no way I can get to Sicily on Thursday, and not only that, but the trains for Wednesday are also full, so the plan B of cancelling my last night in Naples and going a day early won't work either. In fact I check through all the possibilities of getting from here to Sicily in the next week, and concluding there aren't any, I give up and go back to the hotel.

Day in Naples – Tuesday 3 April
I need breakfast, but none of the numerous cafés and pastry shops I pass on my way to the tour bus terminus looks welcoming to a confused foreigner. At the terminus there's about twenty minutes before the bus leaves and I spot a couple of places near the bank that might offer breakfast. The first one has a fabulous display of pastries, but doesn't seem to sell coffee. A dark haired middle aged woman steps out of the café next door, and says:
'Breakfast? You want breakfast?'
The pastries aren't very appetising by comparison with the place next door, and there's a long queue for coffee. I don't really like the look of the place, or the woman, who says again, more aggressively this time:
'You want coffee? Breakfast?'

I haven't got much time, and I don't want to get into conversation with her. I walk into the pastry shop and ask if they do coffee, but the answer's no.

When I walk out, the woman's there again.

'Coffee. You come in here. Good coffee.'

'Too many people.' There's a crowd of Japanese tourists at the counter. 'I don't have time' I point to my wrist.

'You want cappuccino? Espresso? Big coffee? Small?'

Looks like this is the only way I'll get any coffee. And if I don't have something now, when will I get another chance?

When I get into a situation like this with an aggressive person, I go quiet. And they keep repeating as though they think I don't understand, whereas I understand what they're saying perfectly well, I'm just trying to think what to say.

'I get it for you. Very quick.'

'Espresso then'. That should be quick at least. She circumvents the Japanese party and comes back with a cup.

While I'm wondering how to get past the queue to pay, she takes the €10 note from between my fingers and returns with a fiver. Five euros for an espresso. That's some tip she helped herself to. As she passes, she taps the packet of sugar in the saucer with the tip of a red-painted fingernail. I'm so intimidated I sugar the coffee even though I haven't had sugar in coffee for years.

She goes back out onto the street looking for fresh victims, and the crowd has thinned out. The man behind the counter seems relatively normal. I ask him for a glass of water, which he passes me with a smile.

I really don't understand about the Italians and espresso. I thought their culinary philosophy was all about taking your time and savouring things, not about knocking them back for a quick fix.

There's still time before the bus goes to buy a pastry from next door and eat it at the stop.

I'm starting to get a bit more of a feel for the city. The views from Capodimonti, and even more from the coast road, are wonderful. But the chaos of the place, the rubbish in the streets, the paint-peeling shabbiness, the constant turmoil of building and/or renovation, the sense that no one cares very much about the monuments that are there, and the dire traffic, all combine to drag it down. It's not exactly the best place for wandering around aimlessly – or sitting watching the world go by. Bill Bryson wasn't at all impressed, so unimpressed in fact that he passed straight through and didn't stay here at all.

Although the tour buses are hop-on, hop-off, I never feel any inclination to get off and walk around, except on top of Capodimonte or a couple of places on the coastal route, and then I'm worried that I might find that my 24 hours worth is up and I'm stranded somewhere far from the hotel. And when I do try to get off, the bus starts up again before I get down the stairs.

Still, the sweep of the Bay of Naples is glorious, and the beautiful colour washed pastel pinks, greens, and vanilla cream of the buildings reminds me of Neapolitan ice cream.

Walking through Naples

Back in McDonald's, I check out how to get to Amalfi tomorrow, which means eating another burger meal. Then I drop off the laptop at the hotel and wonder how to spend the afternoon.

Mostly what I like to do is just walk, or sit in a café or park and read or do a su doku, or people watch. But this neighbourhood of Naples just doesn't feel comfortable for that.

Along the road to the station are quite a few shoe shops. I left home with just my newly-bought black leather boots and an old pair of trainers. The weather for the last week has been so lovely, I'm sure I've left the cold and wet behind now till I reach Scandinavia. I didn't pack any sandals, because I thought I'd buy some. But there's a problem - a familiar one. My feet are an extra wide fitting English size 7, but because of the width I have to have size 8 - continental 42 or 43. Unfortunately, every shop I go into stops selling women's shoes at size 40. Frustrated, I finally buy some men's sandals, beige leather, which fit and don't look too bad.

Crossing the road is almost as much fun as buying shoes. There appear to be no rules at all - if you happen to be born on one side of a street, you're pretty much stuck there unless you want to take your life in your hands. I remember Bill Bryson's advice for crossing the road in Rome – find a nun and cross where she does. In Naples I perfect a technique which doesn't require female members of a religious order, but is summed up as: find somebody who looks like they know what they're doing and stick to them like a shadow. Cars are big and heavy,

I am (relatively) small and light, more manoeuvrable (as long as I don't have the Wardrobe). I can dodge out of the way and break into a run if necessary. This seems to work pretty well – it gets me a few glaring looks and the odd angry Italian comment, but at least I get where I want to go without injuries.

In one place, I pass a bird's wing lying on the pavement, trampled on and over by the passing throng. It looks as though it's from a pigeon, but there's no sign of the bird itself, not even a smear of blood on the pavement – though the place is so grimy, I'm not sure I would've noticed.

According to the map, to the east of my hotel there's a place called the Piazza Nationale and further on, a green area with small brown blocks marked on it. If there's anywhere in walking distance that has parks to sit in, this seems the most promising, so I set off to walk that way.

When I reach Piazza Nazionale, rather than the picturesque square with attractive coffee shops that (against all expectation) I was secretly hoping for, it's a large roundabout, with some benches and a children's playground in the middle. I keep walking towards a large glossy skyscraper up ahead, and suddenly find myself in an area of walkways and raised beds of shrubs in between skyscrapers, with steps leading down into underground car parks - a modern business district. I look round, and behind me is a standard ramshackle Neapolitan neighbourhood of old style tenements. The sudden juxtaposition between the old and new areas is striking and surreal. I keep going, thinking of areas of urban regeneration like the Docklands in London. But it's disturbingly quiet. Where are all the people? The only other human being is an old black man carrying a bag that could contain rubbish or all his worldly possessions – maybe they're one and the same. Are the people all in the offices? Perhaps, but it's getting on for 5 o'clock, won't at least some of them be getting ready to leave, surely there should be a bit more activity?

One of the buildings has large letters attached to the windows, and as I get closer I manage to decipher it – it's advertising offices to let from €600/month. There are large posters on some of the buildings saying 'Welcome Americas Cup', and other posters advertising offices from €150.

It feels like a ghost village, a casualty of the economic bust, all these handsome office buildings, built in bravado in some construction boom, and now standing unwanted.

Single to Sirkeci

In front of me is a tall fence, and behind it a distant view of Vesuvius and the spire of an old church. As I get closer I see that the fences are all covered with graffiti. It's hard to see past them, so I go hunting for a gap, only to find that behind the barrier is another urban wasteland, more scruffy city areas. It brings to mind the Potemkin villages, barriers put up and painted with fake houses to convince the Tsar that his country was flourishing.

I'm pretty sure I've been walking parallel with the railway tracks, so if I turn to my right, I should be going towards the tracks, which will lead me back towards the station and from there to my hotel. Behind the row of glossy offices, I find signs of life again, teenagers playing football between the office buildings and blocks of flats and then, behind them, communal wheelie bins, the rubbish spilling over onto the pavement, even a rather good looking pair of leather sandals, which I'm half tempted to pick up and try on.

No sign of the railway lines, so at the end of the next big block, I turn right, back into the central area. I pass the opening to the underground car park area, and looking down into it, I see piles of black rubbish sacks and windblown litter coming to rest. On the surface are modern metal sculptures, buildings that look like sculptures, a security guard's kiosk and outside it, the security guard's official scooter. In the distance, in the gap between the buildings, a plane taking off.

Teenagers from the flats have invaded the open areas and are standing around as only teenagers can. Small boys kicking a ball. A cluster of young mums sitting on a bench. Near the end, I see the same old black guy with the bag who was hanging around earlier.

Then I'm out of the office buildings and back to the usual filthy bustle. Shops, stalls, all spilling out onto the street, cars parked everywhere, other cars forced to crawl along. People buying, selling, trying to sell, all races, all languages. I wonder if this is Chinatown, but it's more like Everywheresville.

I grab my laptop from the hotel, and retreat to McDonald's, looking for a hotel in Rome, or a nice seaside town between here and Rome, or wherever. Just somewhere to get out of this place.

I spend ages online, but when I follow up places on the coast, most of them seem to be quite industrial. I feel discouraged and disappointed with my experience of Italy, and I've still got almost two weeks to fill before Ilze's expecting me in Turin. I find a hotel in Rome and book it for three nights from Thursday to Sunday. It's not particularly where I want to go, but it seems like the easiest option. And as for the €70 I paid for the train ticket from Sicily on Friday night, there's no way I can recover that, I've just got to write it off.

Circumvesuviana – Wednesday 4 April

To get to Amalfi, I need the Circumvesuviana local train. There are plenty of signs in the Central Station for Garibaldi Station on the Circumvesuviana Railway, mostly pointing downward, but I get the same sensation I had on the Paris and Barcelona metros – that walking through the station takes you half way to where you're going. Maybe the name 'Circumvesuviana' means you have to walk all the way round Vesuvius before you even find the platform. I jump onto a packed, sweaty train that chugs through grimy industrial suburbs and out at last into the countryside. The other passengers gradually disperse, especially when we get to the station for Pompeii.

After Pompeii the train is more comfortable and the scenery much better. Lemon orchards spring up beside the track, pine trees like umbrellas are silhouetted on the edge of the hillside. Buskers get into the carriage at one station: fiddle, accordion and flute, then at the next station they get out and go into the next carriage.

The train terminates at Sorrento, and from there I plan to catch the bus along the coast to Amalfi. I get off the train and walk out of the station building. In front of the station is a little piazza, with small shops and cafés on either side, leading down to a view of the beautiful Bay of Naples shimmering in the sunlight, and I know instantly.

This is the place where I want to spend my birthday.

Amalfi Coast

Suddenly the world is transformed. I catch the bus to Amalfi, winding up and down the mountains, through tunnels and round inlets, with the sea shimmering below. At last, my fantasy expectations of Italy are starting to drift into the reality of experience. When we reach Amalfi itself, I can't believe how unspoilt it seems. I walk along a jetty, sit on a bench, listen to the waves. At the height of the season it must be packed, but on this sunny Wednesday in April it is sleepy and pretty in a way that's just too good to be true. At a seafront restaurant I order lunch and a glass of wine. The menu says the set lunch comes with 'ice cream' – it is pure white, and so sharp with the tang of lemons that with every taste I can see them hanging from the trees.

After lunch I sit on a bench, swapping the Italian pay-as-you-go sim card from my spare phone to my smart phone. I can't wait till I get back to McDonald's and the laptop, I have to do it now. I find a bed and breakfast in Sorrento and book three nights from Thursday to Sunday. I cancel the hotel in Rome, I have to pay for the first night, but I don't care.

Last night in Naples

Back in McDonald's that evening, a small east Asian lady, possibly Thai, is sitting at the next table:

'Excuse me, you are tourist?'

I look up and smile. We go through the usual formalities - where are you from, etc - but there's clearly something she wants to say.

'Be careful, your laptop. There are many bad people, want to snatch it from you. Bad person outside now, waiting to grab your bag.'

I thank her for the warning. Do I really look that naïve? Over her shoulder, I glance out of the window, and see a motorbike parked outside. I don't know if she's saying there's someone specific, or just giving me a generic warning. I've been in the habit of carrying the laptop to and from Mcdonald's in my canvas tote bag, the strap over my right shoulder and the bag tucked between my right arm and the side of my body, with my right hand holding the front of the bag. That way it just looks like a general shopping bag, the way I normally carry it, I don't think it looks particularly obvious.

I stay there, checking emails, sorting things out. After a while I look up again and the motor bike has gone. I pack up and leave. It might have been coincidence, but anyway, I get back to the hotel without incident.

And at least this is going to be my last night.

Chapter 19 - Sorrento

Benvenuti a Sorrento – **Thursday 5 April**

Two things I've learnt on this trip: strange towns never have street signs, especially near the station; and when I get to the seaside, the weather turns grey and rainy.

So here I am sitting with a cappuccino in the café outside the Circumvesuviano station at Sant'Agnello, watching the drizzle, listening to the radio and reflecting on the directions provided by the nice man who served my coffee: 'Turn right, then two, three roads on the right, about 5 minutes.'

I finish my coffee and set off undaunted up the road to the right till I come to Via di Cappuccini. I'm looking for 36, Casa Susy B&B.

The Wardrobe drags and grumbles over the cobbles. The street is narrow, with no distinction between footpath and road, the occasional car or motor bike passing. And then, unexpectedly, I enter an area of perfect quiet except for the sound of birdsong. On my left, number 34, the Hotel Angelo, and then 36. A red security gate, with bells. I press and speak.

'I've got a booking for tonight.' The gate starts to swing open

As I walk up the drive, the smell of oranges reaches me from the orchard on either side of the path. At the entrance, the door is open, and the lift is already on its way. It arrives and a small, smiling lady steps out and speaks to me. I smile back and heft the Wardrobe into the lift. We shake hands.

'I am Susy' she says.

We go through the door into the first apartment, which doubles as reception.

'Do you have your passport?'

I fish it out, and she hands me the paperwork to complete.

'Ah, your birthday, is Saturday, no?' she says with a smile.

She shows me to my room. A big double bed and a sofabed. A huge, beautiful wardrobe, which has four doors, two at the top and two below (I've never seen a double decker wardrobe before) with honey coloured marquetry inlays, like a high-class version of the sort of furniture my grandmother and elderly aunts would have had. Susy opens the bottom right hand door to reveal a space: 'this is for your dresses'. I hope she isn't expecting me to dress for dinner.

The room is full of little feminine touches, pictures of scenery and saints, baskets of pot pourri, fresh flowers, crocheted throws and cross-stitched pillows, fabulous old furniture. I admit, it's not exactly me, but after the last few days, it's a joy and a treat to be in a place where somebody cares.

'Your breakfast, do you want it in your room or in the dining room?'

'Oh, dining room please'.

She smiles again – actually, I don't think she ever stopped - 'ah, you will have breakfast with me!' and I'm glad, I think breakfast with her will be a pleasure, even if the language is tricky.

She gives me a map showing me where to walk into Sorrento. 'You go up here' she draws a pen along the Via Cappuccini, leading away from the station '… you come to a very beautiful church, very beautiful, then here is a view of the sea where the big boats come. And this is the road into Sorrento, very nice there.'

After she leaves, I take the laptop out onto the balcony, fire it up and start to type. The smell from the orange trees in the orchard below is intoxicating. I look out over the town. Is that Vesuvius over there, covered with a white cloud?

Time to stop this and go out to explore.

Walking to Sorrento

In the drive, the windfall oranges lie on the tarmac, some of them crushed under the tyres of passing cars. I turn left, as Susy suggested, towards the sea. There's a sign on the corner for the Ristorante Moonlight Pizzeria - tuck that away in my memory for future reference. Here's the church, rather modern and not as attractive as I expected. But the sea view is as spectacular as Susy said. The drizzle has eased off and sunlight squeezes between the dark clouds to bounce back off the dazzling white of the cruise ships in the Bay of Naples with the brooding cone of Ischia behind.

I can't walk all the way along the coast, it appears; all that land is private, and the roads I follow seem to take me further and further inland. The walk into the town centre is longer and not as picturesque as I hoped, through a residential area with occasional hotels. But when I get there, it's worth it. The central square, Piazza Tasso, is a bustle of outdoor cafés and bars perched at the edge of a deep gash into the vertiginous cliff which drops down to the bay. I lean on the rail and watch people descending the steps to the harbour. Behind the square is a network of cobbled alleyways, just wide enough for tourists, donkeys and motorbikes, and full of small shops and signs for the Marquetry Museum, between villas painted in Neapolitan vanilla and gardens of palm trees and bird-of-paradise flowers.

I make my way down to the harbour, watching the gleaming white cruise ships, chatting with the resident cats, and read the times and prices for boats to Capri. At a restaurant reaching out over the sea, I order pizza and beer. The sun is shining, the food is delicious, I watch the gulls, the boats, the waves, the cats. Life is good.

I start walking back to Sant' Agnello, looking out for buses. I'm on the right road, but every time one passes I'm between stops. It starts to grow dark.

As I approach the centre of Sant'Agnello, near the church, the crowds get thicker, and there's a rumble of anticipation in the conversations around me. At first I keep pushing through the crowds, but as I get nearer to the corner of Via Cappuccini my curiosity gets the better of me, and I stop to see what all the excitement is about.

I can hear the sound of drums approaching from behind the church. Of course, tomorrow's Good Friday – maybe it's something to do with that? But I'm not prepared for the processors when they finally appear, dressed in white gowns and pointed hoods like members of the Ku Klux Klan. People of all ages and sizes pass by dressed like this. Some are carrying crosses, life sized ones, on their shoulders, and various other symbols, including the occasional chicken. There are choristers too, men and women, wearing robes but without the hoods.

I stand for a while watching, but it seems to go on and on. Flaming torches appear from behind the church, and a shiver goes down my spine. I'm sure it's all perfectly harmless, but it's pretty disturbing.

Capri – Friday 6 April

It's Good Friday, and I'm taking the ferry to Capri. The weather is glorious, and the harbour full of small boats, white, yellow and blue, at the feet of the white cliffs and their clusters of shining white buildings. White birds fly across the dark green of trees tumbling down the mountainside.

The ferry docks and I start to walk up the steps to the town. I'm expecting a long haul, and that doesn't bother me particularly, I just keep going, taking breaks every now and again to admire the view.

But what's at the top? Just a square full of tourists and overpriced shops and cafés. Squeezing through crowds to gawp at designer shops is not my idea of fun. It's a repeat of my experience of Cannes, but if anything even worse, maybe because my expectations were higher.

I'm not sure how to fill the time until I need to be back at the harbour to catch the boat. Maybe I can get a bus somewhere, but if so, where from and where to? Anyway, I'd have to make sure I was back in time for the boat. All the cafés are packed, so I join the queue in a snack bar and buy a tasty-looking pastry, but when I come out and look for a place to sit and eat it, there are signs along the road saying 'no picnics'. I make my way back to the main square and join a crowd of other people eating snacks sitting on the steps.

I try walking the other way, along the cliffs, past a bus station stinking of diesel. The view over the sea is undeniably lovely, but I can't see any way up into the hills. I walk back to the harbour and buy an ice cream while waiting for the boat back to the mainland.

Back in Sant' Agnello I head for dinner at the Ristorante Moonlight I saw yesterday. It's on a side street, and seems almost empty: a family with a little girl and a tiny baby at one table, and a couple on another table in the corner. I'm the only foreigner; in fact they all seem to know one another – they could even be related. Passers-by keep coming in to coo over the baby and ask after one another, the chef is called out from the kitchen several times to shake hands and slap backs. I feel a little awkward, but everyone's very friendly. I order *'fritto misto'* for starter, mixed sea food and vegetable fritters, which is wonderful but I'm pretty full before I even start on the main course of farfalle with smoked salmon.

Worse, I almost have to skip dessert, but manage somehow to squeeze in a tiramisu, then the waitress brings me a glass of limoncello 'on the 'ouse!'

I walk back, appropriately under a beautiful full moon, anticipating a lovely day for my birthday tomorrow. Nothing too strenuous, maybe a leisurely swim, or at least a paddle.

Happy birthday – Saturday 7 April

I wake early, to the sound of birdsong. Step out onto the balcony, and the music washes over me, filling the air between here and the mountains, the sort of dawn chorus I haven't heard for three years while I've been living in the middle of town. I'd forgotten how beautiful it can be, or maybe I always took it for granted. The same familiar songs, even thousands of kilometres away from home, blackbirds and song thrushes and many more I can't identify by name, but still recognise.

I go back to bed, and when I wake again, the music has changed to the steady rhythm of falling rain. Clouds over the mountains.

When I walk into the kitchen for breakfast, two girls from New Zealand are sitting at the table. Susy is busy, squeezing oranges and making coffee. Her son, handsome dark-eyed Francesco, comes in from his post on the reception desk for an espresso.

'Like this all day' he pronounces gloomily.

'All day?'

'Cloud all over.' But I'm sure I saw some breaks in it, some differences of colour. This is Italy, for goodness' sake, not known for the sort of persistent, unending, day-long rain that I remember from childhood but haven't seen even in Bedford for years.

Susy says: 'Two hours.' She has maps and vouchers for the City Sightseeing bus. It isn't restricted to Sorrento but goes out around the peninsula, taking in other places as well.

'The buses are open topped' says Francesco. 'No good in the rain.'

I ask Susy if I can stay for an extra night.

'You stay with me in my 'ouse' she says, patting me on the shoulder. 'And it will be sunny tomorrow.'

I go to my room to do some writing while the rain beats relentlessly onto the balcony. It seems silly to sit there all day, but what else to do? I hunt through the Wardrobe for my red beret, used since San Sebastián only for protecting my external hard drive. Finally I wrap myself up in coat, hat and scarf, and walk to the bus stop by the big church.

I need an umbrella - I saw a tourist shop on Thursday selling them for €3, although here in the alleyways, an umbrella would be a nuisance anyway, there are so many of them, jamming against one another. I pass a shop selling them for €5, €8, €20, and a little further on, on my right, the shop I saw before. An American couple are standing outside, testing umbrellas.

'This one goes up' says the husband.

'But does it work the same way as the other one?' asks the wife.

'They all work the same.'

'Do you think I'm going to need one for tomorrow?'

'Yes. This one's OK.'

'But the other one broke. I don't want another one if it's going to break.'

They leave and go back to the other shop, maybe to buy a €20 umbrella. But an umbrella's an umbrella. If it doesn't break, I'll probably leave it somewhere. I pick out a red one and hand €3 to the proprietor.

In Piazza Tasso, the open-air café that takes up the western part of the square is covered with awning, with plastic windows against the rain, and advertising *'Cioccolata calda'*. Fantastic! I sit with my hot chocolate for a while and scribble in my notebook. A man in a cream linen suit walks past, wearing a cream panama hat with a green band - he looks like he should be in a sunny day in the 1930s, stepping onto a yacht.

People around me are ordering lunch. I'm amazed that the waiter isn't hassling me to spend more money, just sitting here over my chocolate. I wonder about lunch. I can't sit here all day.

Protected by my new brolly, I leave the café and head into the old town again. I don't feel like walking down the cliff to the harbour, and I'm beginning to think I'm reaching the limits of what the town has to offer in the rain. I pass the entrance to the cloister of San Francesco. I've already passed this way several times, but it's raining and it looks as though I might find somewhere to shelter.

I walk under the stone arch, and the mood changes. How can I explain? It's small, a quadrangle set around an open space in the middle. The rain drips and blows under the arches, but it is peaceful here. A wisteria hangs scented purple blossoms over the corner.

I brave the rain again. I've been this way before, I think it's the end of the road – I'm sure the path just goes into a hotel – but I guess I could give it a try. Well look at that – it's brought me out the other side, onto a road I don't recognise. The rain is beating down on my umbrella again, but there's nowhere to shelter. The road seems to lead out of town, the opposite side from Sant' Agnello. I'm looking down on a church with a green and gold roof, and a fishing harbour I've never seen before. I feel like an explorer discovering a lost city. The path descends as broad steps between white walls and high gates. I take shelter in an archway, a shrine hollowed into the cliff face, along with a young couple. We stare out as the rain pours past, roaring over the path and the steps like a series of cascades. When it eases a little again, I venture out cautiously, because the path is steep and slick with rain.

I come down to sea level, overlooking the harbour, this isn't where the ferry boats go from, a real fishing harbour, away from the tourists. Kittens are playing on a pile of sails, tarpaulins and other nautical gear. I watch them as the sun appears just above the sea, peering under the clouds as it often does in the evening after a day of hard rain.

On the walk back I'm looking for a good place to have dinner, hoping for something special - it's my birthday, after all. I finally settle on tagliatelle carbonara, but it is overpriced and the service is indifferent by comparison with the Ristorante Moonlight. Still, I had my birthday treat a day early, that's all.

Easter Sunday – 8 April

Awake in the early hours to an intermittently flashing light. Then, faint in the distance, the subsequent rumble.

Step out onto the balcony. The birds are starting to call softly. A grey cat steps along the wall of the orchard. I speak to it, but it is too far away to acknowledge, or perhaps it chooses not to.

The flashes and rumbles are not over the sea, but inland, over the mountains. Not over Vesuvius either, the other way, further inland. I hear the sound of the drops landing on the leathery leaves of the orange trees. The lightning comes in sheets, no forks.

I feel a little unwell. What did I eat? Ah yes, raw eggs. The carbonara was good, with little nuggets of crisp bacon among the pasta, not flaccid ham. But they didn't offer me extra parmesan. And don't order garlic bread again, that must be an English thing. I was intrigued because I hadn't seen it on a menu before, but it was terrible.

Please, no more rain.

Time to go back to bed.

At breakfast, there are chocolate and eggs on the breakfast table.

'*Buona Pasqua!*' says Susy, passing me an Easter egg and indicating the chocolates. 'These for you! Help yourself.'

'*Buona Pasqua*' I reply. '*Grazie.*'

Francesco comes into the kitchen, and gives me two oranges.

'From our orchard.'

He seems in a mood to practise his English. He tells me how to make limoncello. Lemon zest, sugar, alcohol, water. Leave for seven days, then strain it off. He offers to give me a bag of lemons to take home in my suitcase. I imagine carting them all round Europe. 'The limoncello you buy in England, not as good as Sorrento. Made with lemons from Spain' he says dismissively.

He talks about the orchard, not the one outside the flats, but up in the hills, and about going out fishing with his father. I wonder about his father – there seems to be no evidence of him around, and Susy is clearly Catholic. I don't ask.

'I wanted to go to the beach yesterday if the weather wasn't so bad, but all the beaches seem to be private' I say.

'There is a beach here in Sant'Agnello that is open to the public' he tells me. 'The steps go down near the café.'

It's overcast and damp, but not actually raining, maybe the sun will come out later. I walk down towards the sea, where I went the first day. I see the steps that Francesco was talking about, they lead down into what looks like a subway and there is a sign outside.

The rain starts, so I stop at the café, order a cappuccino and take a seat on the covered terrace overlooking the sea, but it gets too chilly even to sit there, and I take refuge inside. All the other customers follow my example, and suddenly the café is packed. I get a sudden flashback to childhood holidays spent staying with relatives on the Isle of Man, sitting in cafés waiting for the rain to stop.

I catch the bus into town. At first the bus crawls so slowly through the traffic that it would have been quicker to walk, and shortly after I get on it the sun tries to shine, though it never actually stops raining.

I'm planning to stay on till the stop beyond Piazza Tasso. But I suddenly realise that I haven't seen Piazza Tasso, and I have no idea where I am. So I get off at the next stop. There are steps leading down to a road, which I walk down, a winding, narrow road, with no pavements, the passing traffic honking at me.

The road goes through a short tunnel, and I close my umbrella. When I come out the other side, the sun is shining, and I can hear church bells. A little further on, another bend in the road, and I see the sun bouncing off the rain-shining gold of the church tower at the harbour I found yesterday evening.

I walk towards the headland, the side of the harbour I didn't get to yesterday, passing a rather swish looking restaurant. The dining area is huge and empty, the waiters hovering. I try not to look too interested. I'm really after a snack bar, but I need somewhere that will take a credit card, because I'm out of cash.

The road leads into a hotel and a footpath with steps up the cliff, with a sign warning of falling rocks and one forbidding pedestrians from going any further.

I turn back and stop again at the big restaurant. The lunchtime special, for €15, is the seafood risotto. The photo shows a heap of prawns in the centre of a pile of rice, and some octopus round the outside. My expectations are – this could either be €15 thrown away or one of those experiences that become a lifetime memory.

The *maître d'hôtel* shows me to the terrace overlooking the sea, where I sit in splendid isolation, outnumbered by waiters by an order of magnitude. Maybe it's a little early for lunch, or maybe everyone but me is eating Easter lunch at home with their families.

I just want the seafood risotto and water. I've given up drinking alcohol at lunchtimes, I try to stay alert in the afternoons as much as possible. The young waiter opens and pours my 'sparkly' water with such a flourish that I wonder whether he is going to wait for me to taste it and pronounce it acceptable.

The risotto arrives – and it is fabulous, far beyond the image conjured by the menu photo. Every species of mollusc to be found in the Gulf of Naples – and a lot of them. If they weren't endangered before, they must be by now. I hope I won't regret this later. The rice is delectable, and it comes with freshly fried little fluffy herb and potato gnocchi.

The restaurant is filling up. Apparently I was just early after all. I am out over the sea so far that the waves are crashing behind me onto the beach, grumbling to themselves in a threatening manner. I watch the boats pulled up onto the beach, the gulls dipping over the water, my fellow diners. I'm glad I'm here, and not catching the train to Rome, as originally planned. Tomorrow will be soon enough.

After lunch I stroll back through the still erratic showers to the town centre. In the Cloister of San Francesco, I can hear a choir singing in the church. The cloister is used as an education centre. In one of the upstairs rooms there is an exhibition of local art, with rather a lot of marquetry. I never did make it to the museum.

I walk back to Sant'Agnello, and find my way to the stairs down to the beach. After a couple of flights down, it goes into a tunnel, a cave in the cliff. It's only half an hour or so before the gate at the top of the steps will be closed for the night. I wonder if I should risk it. When I reach the bottom there are blue beach huts, black sand, a mural of badly copied Disney characters, a closed snack-bar, gulls and waves. Waiting for the season to start.

Arrivederci Sorrento – **Monday 9 April**

Step out onto the balcony, and the peak of Vesuvius is white. A trick of the light? It looks like snow, it seems unlikely, but I've seen the mountain so many times in the last week and I've never seen it like that before.

It must have fallen overnight. There was another thunderstorm just after I went to bed, great curtains of light blowing into the room and vanishing again.

At breakfast, Signora Susy says (amongst discussions about whether it snowed on Vesuvius last night, and whether I'm going home today, and on hearing I'm going to *Roma*, whether I will visit *il Vaticano*):

'The bill, it's change. You pay change.'

They want cash.

'OK, how much is it? I will have to go to the cash machine' I explain to Francesco.

I'm about €180 short.

Affable as always, he tells me where to find the cash machines, near the Circumvesuviana station.

Plenty of time. I was aiming for the 10.39 train to Naples, but I can take the 11.09 if necessary and still have plenty of time to catch the 13.10 to Rome, which I booked a cheap ticket for last night.

Walking to the station, I dodge into the side alleys and find a square with a fountain just casually there, hidden between the buildings, with teenagers playing football. Nothing special, just a cool splash of water.

I am congratulating myself on transferring some money from my English bank to my euro cash card last night online. Otherwise I wouldn't have enough to do this.

I emerge into the street by the petrol station, and have to double back towards the station, but pass the cash machine on the way.

The sun is shining on the screen, making it hard to read. I ask for €200. After the usual sequence of button presses, I get a message saying that the daily limit has been exceeded. I decrease it to €150. Still no luck. And again to €100.

Maybe the message has been translated badly and the machine is actually out of cash.

I see another bank across the street and try there. This one says straight away that it's out of cash. Easter Monday morning, I think, a long weekend of bank holidays.

But now I start to worry. Last time I made a transfer from my account, it went through instantly, but that wasn't on a Sunday evening before a public holiday. Before the transfer there was €97 on my card.

I try again in the original machine, to withdraw €70. It works.

Now I need another €110 to pay my hotel bill, say €150 to give me some spending cash. I've brought debit cards on two UK accounts, and two credit cards.

I check my wallet. All I have in there, apart from my euro debit card, is a credit card. I don't want to withdraw cash on a credit card, nor even a UK debit card, if it can be avoided, but it can't.

So, my debit cards must be in my other handbag, packed away in the Wardrobe. Bad planning. I should always have at least one with me, but today I haven't.

Check the time. It's 10.00. Should only take me five minutes to get back to the hotel. I've got an hour. It'll be fine.

I fantasise about Francesco whisking me back to the station on a *moto*, me sitting demurely side-saddle on the back, Audrey Hepburn style, the skirt of my silk dress flying upwards (but not too far), my right arm clasped around his waist, hair streaming prettily behind me, and the Wardrobe wedged... ah, maybe that's where it falls down.

When I finally get back with the money, he seems almost surly. No question of that *moto* ride, then. Not even a bag of lemons – though that's just as well. I drag the Wardrobe, protesting, over the cobbles. Checking whether I can get between the parked cars. Other pedestrians keep going, but they are more manoeuvrable, don't take up so much space. The third time this morning I've gone this way, how come I didn't notice before that it was uphill?

The harbour in Sorrento

Chapter 20 - Rome

Sorrento to Rome – Monday, 9 April

I've been in one place for too long. Time I was moving again. Even from lovely Sorrento.

This is what I used to fantasise about. After all the stress comes the moment when I get on the train and sit back into that sense of – well, nothing to do now. No need to worry or think about anything at all for the next couple of hours.

'It's better to travel hopefully than arrive...'? No, that's far too focussed on the destination. It's just a metaphor, a rather negative one, about how reality never lives up to expectations. 'Travelling hopefully' suggests thinking about where you're going, not where you're travelling through. Travelling is a process, a moving forward (no, even that sounds a bit 'goal-oriented'). Because it's best if it's just about itself.

There's snow nestling in all the high mountain valleys. I wonder just how high they are? It's hard to get a concept of scale from down here, along the coastal strip. More of those strange big-horned cattle I saw on the way down – I think they really are buffalo, kept for milk, to make mozzarella. White egrets by a brown river, ditches and embankments, willow trees and oil seed rape – it could be East Anglia but for the mountains behind. And there's Vesuvius, so familiar now I can recognise it at a distance.

We're by the sea again, and coming into a town. The announcement comes over the tannoy: 'next stop, Formia'. That was one of the names I picked up last week, when I spent ages online in McDonald's trying to find a seaside town between Naples and Rome. When I Googled them, all the places I found seemed industrial rather than seaside resorts. Funny how the next morning I got on the Circumvesuviana and found Sorrento. After all the hassles, and despite the weather, I had a wonderful birthday.

Benvenuti a Roma – **Monday 9 April**

My accommodation is a room in an apartment with a shared bathroom, rather like the one in Barcelona, although without a kitchen. There are no breakfast facilities, but on check-in they give me three vouchers for breakfast at a café down the road, which consists of a cappuccino and a pastry. The room is on the seventh floor of an old building, not a great part of town, but by comparison with Naples it feels fine. There are swifts calling outside the window and the sun is shining.

I booked online for three nights, and I ask at reception about staying an extra night. They're already fully booked, but recommend a place near the station.

I'm not really sure what I'm going to do, no particular plans. The day I spent in Rome before I went to Naples hasn't left me with any clear impressions of things I want to do. I'm just here because I've got a week to kill before Ilze is expecting me in Turin.

Walking through the neighbourhood, I find the bus stop, metro station, post office and a green square, but there isn't much in the way of cafés and tourist places. It's a cosmopolitan area, all colours of people on the street, but I don't mind that, it doesn't feel threatening like Naples. Lots of repair work is being done on old buildings and streets, scaffolding and blokes in overalls and hard hats shouting to one another.

By the River Tiber, I cross the bridge to a central island. Street entertainers and vendors everywhere, the tail end of the Easter holiday. I watch the water going over a weir into the channel beside the island, plastic waste in multiple colours accumulated and tossed by the current, jammed up against the weir. Alongside the river there are concrete walkways, and with the central island I'm reminded of the Seine in Paris, but that's where the resemblance ends. The water level seems very low, and surely the Parisians wouldn't accept that amount of rubbish in their river?

Still, the late afternoon light sheds a golden glow over everything, as though the air is infused with syrup. I walk along the river bank and back towards the Capitoline Hill, but I'm walking round in circles and can't get through to the other side of the Forum. I take the Metro back to my hotel. It's strangely quiet, although not late, only about 19.30, and the most welcoming place I can find for dinner is a curry house, so I eat there, feeling self conscious and being ignored by the waiters.

First day in Rome – Tuesday 10 April

I've got some cards to post, I bought them when I spent the day here, and started writing them in Sorrento, but they got wet in my bag and stuck together. Still, they're pictures of Rome, so I want to post them in Rome. When I get to the post office there's a complex system of queues and numbered tickets, and by the time I get to the café with my breakfast coupon for coffee and pastry, it's almost lunchtime.

I walk from the apartment to the Spanish Steps. At the top there's an art market which looks interesting, but everything on offer is very much aimed at tourists, slapdash watercolours of the Coliseum or Vatican, and weirdly coloured 3D images. After two months of travelling, I've seen a lot of such places and they're starting to pall.

The Spanish Steps are covered with people so I pick my way down carefully. There's a wedding, with the couple and guests posing for photographs in the middle of it all. In a neighbouring street, I find a snack bar for lunch. The street vendors on the corner are all selling balls which spread out and lose their shape when they land on the floor, looking like brightly coloured ink blots, but when scraped up again they reform into balls. One young man of North African appearance throws the balls listlessly, trying to get the attention of passers-by who've seen it all a million times across the city. In the end he packs them up in a battered attaché case and prepares to move on. I wonder if he was sold them as a sure-fire way of making money, and got caught out.

I head for the Trevi Fountain and then the Basilica of Santa Maria sopra Minerva. I don't visit a lot of churches, but I'm intrigued by the continuity between Minerva and Mary, the taking over of the pagan goddess by the Christian saint. Minerva, or rather the original Greek version, Athena, being the goddess of wisdom, is a figure I feel an affinity for, and anyway, I like owls, so I was pleased to find a statue of the saint showing attributes of the goddess, including an owl.

Behind the Pantheon, according to my guide book, there's a café that sells the best cappuccino in Rome, so I stop there before walking back. Doesn't taste all that great to my jaded palate. Neither does the dinner

I order at a restaurant on the road near the apartment - indifferent food and rude waiters, who try to short-change me.

Another day in Rome – Wednesday 11 April

Queues outside the Coliseum. Brown dead blossom blowing from the trees in the blustery wind.

In the Via dei Fori Imperiali, the top shelf has blown off one of the vending carts, shards of broken plaster Coliseums, the contents of snow domes and scattered fridge magnets lie across the pavement.

At the foot of the statue of Julius Caesar, there's a faded laurel wreath. Maybe it was left there to mark the anniversary of his death, on the fifteenth of last month. Maybe it's a formal thing, done every year, or maybe it was just left by an admirer. It seems a strange gesture, as though his assassination was within living memory. I can't imagine there'll be many tributes left for J F Kennedy 2,000 years hence.

The street sellers who were yesterday peddling squidgy balls and holographic perspex blocks are now trying to persuade me to buy umbrellas. I have one in my bag, the one I bought in Sorrento, but there's no point in putting it up in this wind anyway.

I heard the rumbles at 4.30 this morning, but no signs of lightning, so I hoped the day would be fine like yesterday. Lucky I decided to wear my coat.

I do a lot of walking around, wherever I am, a lot of observing, absorbing, and taking photos. It's never very structured. Sometimes I people-watch, sometimes I just sit and stare, or stand leaning on railings or whatever, lost in my thoughts. Maybe it's a product of being on my own so much, of not having regular conversations with anybody.

Walking through the park not far from the apartment brings me out opposite the Coliseum, where I cross the road and walk through the area around the Forum. The Classical city surrounds me - columns in varying degrees of destruction stand in strange juxtaposition with the souvenir and snack sellers and the snarling traffic. The path leads to the steps of the Capitol, the Piazza Campidoglio, with its elegant stucco palaces, marble and bronze statues, and views over the city.

It's starting to drizzle, and I'm ready for somewhere to sit with a coffee, but it's getting on for 12.30 and most places are serving lunch. I head for the coffee shop I went to yesterday, the one reputed to sell the best cappuccino in Rome. All the seats are outside. It's stopped raining, but given a choice of standing inside or sitting on a wet seat, I decide to pass on the best cappuccino and go elsewhere.

I wander into the backstreets around Piazza Navona, and find somewhere for a crêpe and a coffee. The place is being run single handed by a young girl who can only do one thing at a time, so she can't start on the crêpe till she's finished with the cappuccino. By the time I get round to drinking it, it's already cold.

I head for the Vatican. As I'm following the signs for the Sistine Chapel, there's a massive cloudburst, the rain bouncing up off the pavement, umbrellas bouncing off each other, and the umbrella pedlars looking in vain for someone, anyone, who might still be in need of their wares. Michaelangelo's ceiling loses its appeal, and I dodge into a café called the Dolce Vita, with stills from the classic film on the wall, and a great display of cakes and pastries.

The sun comes out at last as I head back towards the river. In front of the Castel St Angelo, I stop on the top embankment , watching the aerial ballet of sea gulls and swallows.

I see movement near a clump of reeds, a moorhen with one chick. A little further along, before the bridge, there are steps down to the lower embankment by the water's edge. I walk along and down and then back to where I saw the moorhen. A German couple are on the embankment, looking at the water. The man walks towards me and past, but the woman stays watching the river. Suddenly she calls to him:

'Papa! Papa!'

I think she must have seen my moorhen, but when I get closer to see where she's pointing, I notice something furry in the reeds, a few metres out from the edge. It looks like a large guinea pig, almost as big as a cat, and it has a baby.

My first thought is of beavers. And then coypus – are there coypus on mainland Europe? I have no idea what the range is for either of them. Or otters, perhaps? They seem too stocky and not elegant enough for that.

The German man has come back and they are talking in low voices. Then I see one swimming.

'There's another baby' I say 'in the water – *in's Wasser!*'

The lady acknowledges, and I think of how easily German comes to me, by comparison with my stumbling French and non-existent Italian.

Single to Sirkeci

We watch for a while. The swimmer climbs out and joins its siblings. The babies clamber over their mother like kittens. The Germans are counting. *'Fünf!'* says the woman. *'Sechs!'* whispers her companion (Father? Husband? could be either). The mother gets off the island of reeds and swims towards the middle of the river. I wonder if she's trying to distract us. The Germans walk away along the bank. I go a little way and find my moorhen, then spot another chick, and a third. They are quite a distance from her, but all three suddenly swim back to her at the same time, triangulating onto where she is.

I sit on the edge of the embankment, jotting down in my notebook, thinking about the river. There's hardly anybody here, down at this lower level, apart from the odd jogger. Two American girls run past me, and one says:

'Oh my god! Well, it's Italy.'

I look ahead to what they're talking about. A police car is parked a little way ahead, two policemen looking into the water. What can they be looking at? They get in the car and drive past me.

When I draw level with where they were, I can see. Piles of rubbish. There is rubbish all along the bank, bags which have been dumped into the undergrowth just below the embankment, but here it's disgusting.

The Romans clearly don't love their river. It saddens me, I can't imagine anything of the sort in Paris, or London for that matter, or even Bedford, certainly not on this scale.

I approach another bridge. There are sets of steps either side of each bridge leading up to the higher level. The further one seems to have a miniature shanty town built on it, piles of something, I can't see what. I can hear music - a piano? No, that's just too bizarre. It's clearer now – sounds like a saxophone. Not a tune, not exactly scales, but some kind of exercise. I can see the silhouette of the player, far ahead by the next bridge. The noise bounces back from the walls. One of the street musicians practising, he can't expect to make anything from these ones and twos of joggers.

At the bridge, I climb up the stairs to head back. On the bridge there's a shrine of flowers and offerings, with a picture of a small child. There's a typed explanation, little Claudio, aged 16 months, 30th March at 17.00. I remember a news report when I was staying with Irina, her husband Lucian explaining to me that a child's body had been found in the river, he had been missing for months, murdered by his father, as revenge on the mother.

'Italian men are very jealous of their women' Lucian told me.

I wonder if this is why the river is so deserted.

It's a beautiful evening. Up the road towards my lodgings, I find a little trattoria, walk in and ask: are they still serving, can I have a table? There are two young waiters, and a group of people having drinks outside, but no one else inside.

'*Espagnol, Signora?*'

'No, English.' He tells me the offer is one dish from the first course, one from the second, one side dish, for €12. I choose mushroom risotto, sausage with mixed vegetables, potatoes. It's delicious, but I can't eat all the potatoes.

The music is Marvyn Gaye, 'Sexual Healing', then other songs: 'Whiter Shade of Pale', 'Tired of Being Alone', 'My Girl', 'Ain't no Sunshine'. The waiter comes and asks me:

'*Signora,* you like a song by Michael Bolton?'

'This is fine for me!' I say with a smile. 'Marvyn Gaye is fine!' Don't change it for me.

They ask if I want a cappuccino. I ask about dessert. The waiter smiles, but instead of a dessert menu he brings me a plate of shortbread and chocolate biscuits with my coffee.

'This is for you, free!' he says.

And when I go up to pay, they give me a chocolate, 'this free for you'.

I wonder why they were being so nice. Maybe they felt sorry for me, on my own. Maybe I reminded them of their mums.

Hazards of public transport - Thursday 12 April

I'm moving hotels today, to a place near Termini station. I get on the bus expecting to buy a ticket on board, but there's no ticket machine. I stand with my backpack and the Wardrobe and hope the inspector won't get on – it's only a few stops.

At the next stop a few people get off, but still no free seats. I move down the bus to where there's more room. An old boy sitting on one of the single seats catches my eye and points to his seat. I smile and shake my head. 'Termini' I say, to let him know I'm getting off soon. He looks about 80 - I figure he needs to sit more than I do, and it's easier to hang onto the Wardrobe while standing.

He gets up anyway at the next stop, but instead of leaving the bus he comes and stands next to me and a stilted conversation ensues.

'English? You stay here?'

'Yes.'

'Where you live here? In hotel?'

'In a hotel, yes. One more day, then I go to Firenze.'

I'm holding the pole with my right hand. He moves his left hand to cover mine. What a sweet old man, I think, smiling back, though I haven't got a clue what he's saying. It's like having your hand patted by an elderly uncle.

Then the words start to make a bit more sense:

'You might like me too much. Very strong. You understand?'

That's when I realise that his eyes aren't on my face, but a little lower down.

'Ah, no, *grazie*' I say firmly, and move my hand out from under his and down to the lower part of the pillar, below the cross bar. Looking out of the front of the bus, I can see the back of the station buildings.

'Termini?' I say, pointing.

'*Si.*'

The bus is pulling to a stop, and I start to move the Wardrobe.

'Ah no, *proxima,* next stop' he says. 'You have somebody?'

'Yes' I lie, as the bus moves off again, round the station buildings to the rows of bus stops in front.

I wonder if he's noticed I haven't got a ticket, and whether he'll shop me to the driver if I don't give him what he wants. After all, I have form when it comes to fare-dodging.

'Where you staying here? Hotel? *Albergo?*'

'Going to Firenze' I say as I struggle the Wardrobe down the steps to the platform.

'Which hotel? What is address?'

'Goodbye.' Please God, don't let him follow me.

He gets off the bus behind me as I launch myself in the general direction of the station buildings, even though that's not quite where I need to be, dragging the Wardrobe behind me. I daren't look back till I'm on the far side of the bus ranks, by the entrance to the Metro station.

03&0

Trastevere
After escaping the old man and dropping the Wardrobe and backpack at the new hotel, I set off to walk across the river to Trastevere and up the hill at Gianicolo. I'm trying to find a way into the Botanic Gardens, which I'm sure are beautiful, from what I can see through the fence.

Trastevere is lovely, much more like a ramshackle old mediaeval town than the more splendid parts east of the river. I've set myself a goal of the church of Santa Maria in Trastevere, which is alleged to be the site of the first Christian church in Rome, and decorated with friezes, but I end up going in completely the wrong direction and finding myself outside the church of St Francesco and having to go back down the road and twice past the shop with the dried sausages hanging outside and the smell of cheeses.

In the Via de la Cisterna I stop by the water fountain and wash the second of the two oranges Francesco gave me in Sorrento, the ones from his garden, by the drive where the windfalls lay and were crushed under the wheels of passing cars so that the smell was intoxicating. I stay by the cistern so I can wash my hands afterwards. It's impossible to peel, but the peel is so thin I eat right through it, and the flesh is dark, purple-red. I fill my water bottle, drink it and fill it again, and eat dark chocolate with almonds.

When I finally get into the church of Santa Maria, I'm intrigued by a painting which shows a woman wearing the papal crown and with an entourage of women. I can't find out anything about this female pope in references to the church online, although I know that the Papess is associated with the tarot.

In the evening I go looking for a place to have dinner in and around the Piazza della Repubblica, close to my new hotel. I've been looking forward to it, because surely there must be more choice than the place I've been staying? There are certainly more restaurants, but all of them offer the same bog-standard trattoria fare, and I don't really want another pizza or spaghetti carbonara or variation on pasta in thick tomato sauce. In England, even in a provincial town like Bedford you can find foods from a whole range of different cuisines from all over the world, but the Italians, creators of one of the greatest food cultures, seem quite happy to rest on their laurels. And although I've had some wonderful meals, mediocre Italian food can be pretty mediocre indeed, and it's not easy to tell from appearance or price whether you're going to get something fabulous for a pittance or be ripped off.

I agonise over which restaurant to try, but end up yet again with so-so food and lousy service. The waiters are Indian, and combine the worst of both Italian and Indian cultural attitudes to women - I might as well not be here. I was hoping to stay for a coffee and Amaro after a sumptuous dessert, but I can't get out of there fast enough.

Things to love about Rome:

The man-hole covers have 'SPQR' on them, as though they were put there by the Legions.

The number 8 tram goes to Argentina.

Calendars (on sale everywhere) with a black and white picture of a beguiling young priest on the front. I mean, what is the target market for monthly photos of handsome men in clerical garb? 'Get a load of Padre Agosto.' The mind boggles.

Two dogs bonking vigorously in a park, while their owners carry on a conversation, rather than frantically trying to pull them apart. Three schoolgirls sitting on the grass watch with interest. Very educational.

In another park, a protected colony of feral cats, behind railings which the cats can get through, but which keep them safe from dogs and humans. Penalties (enforced by city statute) for disturbing, persecuting or molesting them include terms of 3 months to 1 year in prison and fines of several thousand euros.

Chapter 21 - Florence

Benvenuti a Firenze – **Friday 13 April**

Press the intercom button on the door of a cream-stuccoed apartment building in a narrow, slightly grubby back street of Florence. The door opens into a dark hallway with a staircase. Here we go again - the *pensione* is on the fourth floor, and there's no lift. I start to drag the Wardrobe up the stairs, one at a time. When I reach the second floor, a face appears at the top of the stairwell. A woman about my own age, with an expression that could curdle milk. She grunts and grimaces, then disappears. When I reach the top of the stairs, she's holding the door to the apartment open for me.

We go through the formalities, and she shows me my room. It's comfortable enough, probably one of the nicer ones I've had.

'How long you in Italy?' she asks.

'Four weeks.' She looks meaningfully at the Wardrobe, and curls her lip. It's a stupid amount of luggage for a four week stay. I don't try to explain, it's not worth it.

Then she takes me back into the office and over to the window, to point out the café on the corner where I can exchange my breakfast coupons. Just beyond it is the Cathedral of Santa Maria del Fiore, the Duomo, black and white and red like a painting from Leonardo's sketch book, or a Disney reconstruction, not a real building at all. I catch my breath.

A room with a view indeed. Even if the view from my room is of a dreary grey street.

CXE)

Santa Felicita

I walk through the warren of back streets, from the Duomo to the Piazza della Signoria. The yellow bricks and arched windows of the Uffizzi stare down at us visitors, huddled into coats and scarves on the rain-slicked grey pavement, as we navigate around the white marble statues of gods and heroes.

I'm heading for the river - always down to the water or up to the hills, wherever I go. The neat white facade of the Ponte Vecchio stretches across the river. Slate roofs and square windows on the upper storey, and underneath, higgledy-piggledy yellow-painted buildings squeezing together and bulging out over the water. People jammed into the middle of the bridge as tightly as the shops on either side. I lean over the central arch to catch that last burst of sunlight when the setting sun sneaks under the blanket of clouds. A solitary white egret stalks along the water's edge, then takes off and flies across the river and maybe under the bridge, though I've lost sight of it behind the jewellers' shops. I don't think anyone noticed it but me. Crowds everywhere, clustering around the shops, pushing in and out. Why are people so obsessed with having their own photograph taken in famous places? I can't look anywhere without some grinning idiot in the shot. I fantasise about a photographic neutron bomb, which will remove people from the view, but leave the buildings standing.

Over the bridge I walk through the Piazza Santa Felicita, and smile because it reminds me of little Felicity. A waitress wiping tables outside a restaurant catches my eye and smiles back.

'Are you looking for dinner?' she calls, 'come and look at the menu.'

'Maybe later.'

In the square there's a push bike parked with a cat basket fixed on the back. That's what I need. Will need. When I have a home again. And a kitten I can raise to love travelling as much as I do.

I walk through the streets of the old town. It's one of those places where just walking around is joyful enough. Outside a dress shop my eye is caught by a top in peach coloured lace, with a matching vest, hanging from a rack. It's marked as half price. I'm not buying clothes, partly because I'm watching my budget, but mainly because it would be stupid to add to the burden of the Wardrobe, and anyway, I don't need any more clothes. But there is something about it.

On the way back to the bridge I pass the Santa Felicita again. I stop to look at the menu, then go inside. The waitress recognises me and smiles. 'You came back!'

The head waiter comes to meet me.

'Ah, my lady, welcome! You are English? Come, please.'

He shows me to a table, produces the menu and pours the wine. About my age, balding and paunchy, but oozing classic Italian charm as he chats to me.

'Anything you want, please ask the boys and girls, we are here to serve you. For me, it is all about a good experience for you. If you are happy, you tell your friends, yes? That is how it works. That is what we are here for, to make sure you have a good time.'

The *gnocchi* are wonderful, the wine is wonderful, the 'boys and girls' are smiling and friendly. There is something about this place.

Two couples on the table to my right, the younger from Italy, the older from Mexico, talking in English. They've only just met, in the city for a conference. The youngsters are talking about wedding plans, trying to decide where to go for their honeymoon.

'Cancun is the place' the Mexican man is saying 'or Acapulco. Depends what you are looking for. But I can promise you good weather. This weather here, I can't believe it, this is like winter, it should be spring!'

They are talking about Florence.

'Living in Florence' says the Italian woman 'it's like living in a fairy tale, not a city. Being in Rome is more like living in a legend, it's a real city.'

'Although Florence is a city as well, of course' adds her fiancé 'but it's very special.'

The head waiter is showing a new recruit how to clear a table. Deftly his hands move over the crockery, the cutlery, stacking them in the crook of his left arm. For some reason, he is talking in English too. Maybe the new waiter isn't Italian, so they too are using the twenty-first century *lingua franca.*

'Our job is to make sure the customer is happy, that is the most important thing of all.' He looks over at me and smiles. 'Ask my lady! My lady knows!' He winks. I smile back.

After dessert, the waiter asks if I would like coffee and anything else? I order Amaro, and then am flummoxed when they ask me to be more specific. I thought it was a brand, not a generic term. They bring out a bottle, a local product, they explain. It tastes of sweet sunshine and bitter herbs, and warms its way down into my heart as I sip it alternately with the rich dark coffee. The bill comes, then more coffee, then the head waiter returns with the Amaro bottle and tops up my glass.

When I leave, he takes my hand and kisses it with a flourish.

'My lady, come back and see me again.'

There's something about this place that encourages extravagance.

The Duomo – Saturday 14 April

It's raining as I head for breakfast. When I come out, it's raining even harder. I join the queue outside the Duomo. At least in there I'll be out of the rain. I sign up for the guided tour, which includes going up inside the dome, and outside. We walk around a gallery along the edge of the roof, huddling under umbrellas. Look up at the dome proper, and right at the top, there's another gallery around the central spire, and what looks like umbrellas moving around. Surely we're not going up there?

Back inside, more steps. Now we are inside the dome, with its mural of the Day of Judgement. I'm looking for any female figures, still searching for Minerva, Sophia, the holy wisdom. I can't hear the guide, she's too far ahead. It's a narrow passage, single file. You're not supposed to stop, but people do, and others squeeze past them. More steps, another door, wait your turn, squeeze out onto the gallery, not afraid of heights, are you? I seem to have lost the guide altogether. Stairs down now, and they are slick from the passage of wet feet. Be careful.

It's a relief to get back to ground level, but not to find myself back outside in the rain, wondering what to do with the rest of this miserable day. I head towards the Uffizzi, and *en route* find a snack bar for a coffee and the dress shop where I saw the peach top. At least, it looks like it, but of course the rail isn't outside today. I go inside, find my top, try it on. There is a matching peach scarf that comes with the outfit, but the smiling Chinese assistant persuades me into another one as well, which has an abstract pattern with turquoise, yellow and blue as well as the peach. What was I saying about encouraging extravagance?

At the Uffizzi, the queues are confusing. I get into one, and then find that when I get near the front, only people with special permits are being allowed in. The sign says that, in honour of national culture week, gallery entry is free. The free queue goes in another door, or rather it doesn't, it ends at another door, but it isn't moving. No one seems able or willing to explain to me which queue I should join. Although entry is free, you can buy a timed reservation for €4, which entitles you to join the shorter queue and be let in at the appropriate time. To buy a reservation you have to join another queue, which is at least inside the building and therefore dry.

At last I get in and wander through the galleries, but what interests me most are the ceilings, covered with quirky, grotesque images of people, animals, plants. I notice a bare-breasted woman sitting at a dining table with a man-sized heron eyeing her lasciviously.

Back outside, I am on a mission – to buy toothpaste. In the old town there are no normal shops, no supermarkets, nowhere to buy the simple necessities. I am looking too, incidentally, for somewhere for dinner. I'm sure that earlier I passed a place offering pizza and sangria for €7. At last I find a pharmacy, ask for toothpaste and am charged €9. Now I'm looking for my pizzeria, in an effort to rebalance the budget after last night's blow-out at the Santa Felicita (not to mention the toothpaste). I retrace my steps onto the Piazza del Duomo and out via a different exit, cross the river and back, and find a pizzeria, just not the one I had in mind.

Back at the *pensione,* I get into a text chat with a friend from home who happens to mention watching the Old Grey Whistle Test. I have a very clear memory of watching Joni Mitchell on TOGW singing 'California' from her 'Blue' album, in about 1970. At that time, as a young teenager, I knew Joni Mitchell's name, but didn't really know anything about her music. But I heard this song and it seemed like magic, and it still does.

As I'm chatting to my friend, I'm suddenly struck by the lyrics. This is a song about homesickness – but it's also a song about being in exotic places – Paris, the Greek islands, Spain – and thinking about home from a distance. And I remember how wonderfully, impossibly glamorous it seemed to me then, to be able to travel like that – right across Europe. To sit in a park in Paris reading the news from home; to buy a ticket and go to Spain, just for a week or two.

It's funny, isn't it, what sets the patterns of our lives? Who knows where our inspiration comes from – buried so deep, we don't recognise it ourselves till it kicks us in the face.

I always wanted to look and sing like Chrissie Hinde – but I wanted to live and write like Joni Mitchell.

Etruscan echoes – Sunday 15 April

When I wake, it's still grey and drizzly, but not actually pouring any more as I head out for breakfast. I walk to the archaeological museum, marvelling at the displays of Etruscan artefacts. I follow an American couple around, eavesdropping on their conversation. A stone lion, which I swear I recognise from the cover of a book on nineteenth century archaeologists which I read thirty years ago. A bronze brooch, maybe three inches long, but etched with an exquisitely intricate pattern of tiny ducks and a barking dog. We all comment on this, and the American man says to me: 'Get your husband to buy you one' which makes me bridle, at his casual assumptions both that I have a husband, and that I can't admire something beautiful without wanting to own it myself.

I'm looking for the entrance to the botanic gardens. I have my guide book with me, and pass the wall, but can't find the way in. I'm also trying to find a café, but they seem surprisingly scarce. A little further on I come to a dual carriageway, and I can see a café on the other side of the road, but when I've crossed past the whizzing traffic, I find it's closed.

It feels as though I've stepped out of the fairy tale and back into the modern world. I cross back, and into the comforting arms of the old city. Zig-zagging left and right through little streets, I come to the other side of the botanic gardens and the entrance. Entry to the garden is free, but there's a dinosaur exhibition at the moment, and it's impossible to get into the gardens without paying to see the dinosaurs. I did enough of that kind of thing when the kids were small, so out of bloody-mindedness I head back towards the heart of the old city.

I need to get my boots repaired. I've been wearing these boots just about constantly since I left England, and the heels are worn down. Not only that, but the quick-polish sponge that I brought with me is pretty much empty, and they look shabby. I've got a lot further to go and don't want to ruin them completely. Florence is full of leather shops, the smell sometimes oozing out onto the streets, but none that obviously do repairs, and I'm too ashamed to walk in in my scruffy boots and ask.

In the Piazza della Signoria, I walk through the open-air gallery of the Loggia dei Lanzi, and stop before the statue of the captured barbarian princess Thusnelda, standing thoughtful with legs and arms crossed and her chin resting on her hand. I feel an affinity with her - I too am a Barbarian, far from the country of my birth, but unlike this lady I'm not a captive – except, perhaps, of my dreams and thoughts - a wanderer across this wide, wonderful, frustrating, enchanting continent, from West to South, East, and North.

I want to go to the Boboli Gardens, and I know they're on the other side of the river, but somehow I can't quite find out how to get there. I climb a hill to the Piazzale Michaelangelo, where I marvel over the city in the valley, creamy yellow buildings, red terracotta domes and blue hills behind. But the atmosphere is spoilt by the crowds clustered around the ice cream stand, waiting to have their photo taken next to an oversized copy of Michelangelo's David. There's a City Sightseeing Tours bus, but to me this is a city best explored on foot.

On the way up I passed signs for 'the Gardens of the Rose', a somewhat quirky translation. Too early in the year for the roses, but I enter this garden on my way down and fall in love with the place, laid out over the hillside. The sun comes out at last as I walk the little paths, and sit on a bench. Two olive trees. A pergola, grown over with yellow blossoms, like tiny roses, perfect miniature yellow roses in clusters like May blossom. I read the label: *'Banksiae Lutea'*. In the distance, the Duomo, down in the valley, and further still, the mountains of Tuscany. Daisies in the grass. A tabby cat stalking. Birdsong. Florence at my feet. Sunshine and cypress trees. Quirky statues in bronze, the reading man sitting on a bench, the cat-bird, but best of all the fish-man, standing by the pond where goldfish swim. The sculptor, Jean-Michel Folon, was born in Brussels and married an Italian woman, who after his death persuaded the City Council to display them in this beautiful park. It's easily the nicest place I've found so far during my stay in Florence.

Boboli – Monday 16 April

Now I know why I couldn't find the Boboli gardens yesterday - the entrance is through the Pitti Palace, entry free again due to the generosity of the Italian government. The rain is heavier than ever as I walk into the central courtyard of the Palace. How do I get out to the gardens, and what am I going to do there in the pouring rain? The exit is at the other side of the courtyard, pointing up some stairs. Not obvious till you know.

A series of terraces, under my umbrella. At the top, the museum of porcelain, a good place to shelter. There's a milk jug shaped like a cow, which reminds me of an Etruscan lamp, also cow-shaped, which I saw in the archaeology museum yesterday. Outside, a formal rose garden, with few blooms this early in the season, and without the charm of the 'Gardens of the Rose'.

I follow signs pointing through an exit to the Villa Bardini. This is on a smaller scale and much more attractive. There's a café terrace where a lady in a kiosk sells me a cappuccino. A middle-aged English couple pass by, admiring the vertiginous view. 'I always think the Italian landscape has so much character' says the woman.

Back in the Boboli, I walk aimlessly along the terraces and through the wooded areas, coming at last to the Oceanus fountain with its central island. The causeway to the island is closed by workmen with a truck full of trees in pots, but a heron stands unconcerned, watching the fish.

Arrivederci Firenze - Tuesday 17 April

Predictably, on my last morning in Florence, the weather turns at last. I check out of my lodgings, drag the Wardrobe to the station and put it in a left-luggage locker.

Ilze can't meet me at the station in Turin until after she finishes work, so I've booked an afternoon train, which means I've got another morning to spend. I'll head back to the Boboli and take a few photos in the sunshine.

As I'm leaving the station, an elderly American lady stops me to ask for directions.

'I'll try' I answer cheerfully, 'but I'm not from round here myself!'

'Via Venezia' she says carefully, 'Vay-ee-en-ee-zee-i-ay'.

I shake my head 'sorry, I don't know it' I say. She thanks me anyway, we wish each other a good day and that's that. But why did she say 'vay' instead of 'vee'? I know Americans say 'zee' instead of 'zed', but I didn't think they pronounced the other letters any differently. Maybe she assumed I was Italian? I'm quite flattered. I noticed in Spain that I was surrounded by people who looked like me in terms of hair and eye colour, but it never really occurred to me before that my looks are not the normal run of the mill for an English person.

On the Arno, between the Ponte Vecchio and the Ponte Santa Trinita, a bloke in a boat, white boat, white hat, green jacket, not moving, not sailing, not fishing, just sitting. In the middle of the river, in the middle of the city, in the middle of the Tuesday morning sunshine.

And me, watching.

Three youngsters, two girls and a boy, perfectly dressed, together with their backs to the river holding a camera in front of their faces, to make a record of their perfection.

On one of the supporting pillars of the Ponte Santa Trinita, a girl. She takes off her jacket, underneath she is wearing a sleeveless vest top, and sits down on the broad stone, her back pressed against the wall of the bridge. Unlike the man on the boat, she seems purposeful, settling herself, rummaging in her bag. How did she get there? Just climbed over the wall from the bridge, I guess.

And now she is comfortable at last, she pulls out a book. She has a purpose. To read her book and work on her tan, arms and shoulders at least.

The man on the boat is standing, has moved at last, looking at the girl, perhaps. He bends down and pulls at the motor, it kicks into life. He moves to the front of the boat and pulls something from the water. The motor dies again. He has moved perhaps a boat length, a couple of metres.

Something flashes through the air, a line of silver, drawn by a nib so fine you could use it to write on a rice grain. Then it's gone. Not idle at all; he's fishing.

I walk onto the bridge, trying to catch a glimpse of the girl, but from the bridge itself she is invisible, hidden behind the wall and the cluster of youngsters leaning on it and chatting.

I lean on the wall further across, nearer the middle of the stream. Something underneath the bridge is causing ripples, maybe just the water squeezed and confined between the bridge supports and hurrying to get out into the open again.

Where they catch the sunlight, the ripples twinkle on the surface of the river – it sounds corny to say 'like stars' or 'diamonds', but that is how I feel. It brings back memories of all the hours I've spent standing on the Bedford Town Bridge, over the Great Ouse, and watching the same effect. Standing on bridges and watching rivers seems to take over my life.

I watch the man fishing from the boat. I wonder if he's noticed me. Maybe he's part of my story, maybe I'm part of his – the woman on the bridge. A small part, admittedly, of a small story.

I walk past the church of Santa Felicita and feel drawn to go in, if only so I can tell my grand-daughter I've been in her church. The golden light through the stained glass windows falls on a display of azaleas beside the altar. There's a sign at the entrance forbidding photography, then another one inside saying 'no flash'. It seems ambivalent, and I'm moved by the light and the beauty to sneakily take one anyway, but it's so badly distorted by camera shake that I guess someone up there disapproves.

It's time to leave Florence.

Room with a view - the *Duomo* in the rain

Chapter 22 - Turin

Benvenuto a Torino – **Wednesday 18 April**

Step out onto the balcony and look towards the mountains. The trees are perfectly still, not the slightest movement in the damp, chilly air. Sounds of traffic along the road, and blackbirds making their clacking, warning sound, but no song.

The forecast for today is heavy rain, but it's not raining at the moment, just grey and gloomy like yesterday. I swear I've seen more rain in the last two months than I have for years back home in Bedford. I'm getting tired of people saying to me: 'must be like home for you, eh?' and not believing me when I say: 'no, where I live we don't get this much rain'.

It's taking me a while to warm to Turin. It's lovely being with Ilze, but the city itself doesn't seem to want me here.

Ilze's at work, leaving me with breakfast, a book of walking tours, and a bus timetable. I read the descriptions and my mind goes fuzzy, so in the end I just take the bus into town and dutifully follow the prescribed itinerary, admire significant buildings, take photos. The city seems an odd mixture. The most positive word I can think of at first acquaintance is 'handsome', with its elegant arcades and posh cafés. It strikes me as a *Mitteleuropean* city, like Vienna or Budapest, that's somehow also Italian. Not wanting to follow the guide book too obviously, I keep missing turnings and losing my way, doubling back on myself. I trudge around the historic 'Farthingales' district, hoping and failing to find the charm of Florence. This clearly isn't a tourist town, I tell myself, and I mustn't judge it on those terms. It stays grey and gloomy, but I keep to the streets, saving the museums and palazzos for the wetter days that I'm convinced will come later in the week.

Single to Sirkeci

In the afternoon my phone buzzes with a text from Ilze, suggesting we meet after she finishes work, about 18.30, and have dinner in town. 'Sorry the weather's not very welcoming' she says, and I think: 'at least it's not raining', then: 'I'd better not say that because it will start' and within ten minutes or so it does.

I pass a café advertising hot chocolate and go in out of the rain. *'Cioccolata calda, per favore.'*

My carefully pronounced request is greeted with a scowl and *'Hunh?'*

'Chocolate' I repeat, very distinctly, in English. I've found this often works better than my feeble attempts at speaking the local language.

'Hunh?' The scowl deepens, and with a shrug she turns to someone propping up the bar, who explains in Italian that I'm trying to order chocolate, which must have been really hard to guess, given that it's their speciality.

My hot chocolate, when I get it, is okay, but I'm not convinced it's worth the ritual humiliation. At least I'm out of the rain.

I need the toilet, but there's no sign of one in the café, and I'd rather pee on the floor than ask the proprietress. After a lengthy search, I come across a self-cleaning one in a secluded piazza. It's occupied, but the door opens, rather disturbingly, while the occupant is still titivating himself in front of the mirror. Should I sneak in before the door closes after him, to save my 50 cents? Lucky I didn't try, because after he's gone, I hear a strange, gurgling, burping noise coming from inside the structure, and then the gushing of water as the self-cleaning goes into action. When the display indicates that it's ready to accept my money, and the door opens to admit me, the floor and everywhere is glistening. My innate honesty has saved me from an impromptu shower.

Ilze's suggested meeting place is in the Piazza Vittorio Veneto, near the river, which is where I'm heading anyway. At last, the sun is starting to come out, as I walk along the Via Po, the main shopping street, through Piazza Vittorio and down to the bridge, where I stand and watch the river for a while, then return to the Piazza and find a café still open for a cappuccino. When I finish my coffee, Ilze still hasn't arrived, so I move out to one of the stone benches in the square and read my Kindle till she turns up.

The table's booked for 19.30, so we walk around for a while, over the bridge to the Gran Madre church, where we climb the steps and take photos of the rain-washed city glistening in evening sunshine. Ilze shows me around the back streets by the film museum and the university. I'm telling her the story of the self-cleaning toilet when we walk into a square which looks vaguely familiar: '…and if I'm not mistaken, it's just here.'

'Here?'

'Yes, there it is, look!' I say gleefully.

'That's incredible!' We've stopped outside a trattoria on the opposite side of the square, while I point out the toilet. 'This is the restaurant!'

We have a lovely meal, and a happy evening, and after the first half-hour my eyes stop straying towards the self-cleaning toilet.

And, after an inauspicious start, I feel my love affair with Torino begin.

Growing on me - Thursday 19 – Saturday 21 April
Back on the bus into the city centre again with my trusty guide book, I start another of the walks. When the rain gets really hard, I head for the cinema museum. The building itself is spectacular, originally built to be a synagogue and with a tower and spire, the Mole Antonelliana, which is a symbol of the city. The film museum is pretty special too, its central hall with giant screens and lounge seats, surrounded by smaller rooms and displays showing themed film clips from all genres of film and decades of the last century. All the films are in Italian – the foreign films dubbed in Italian, not sub-titled – but I'm mesmerised, watching them all regardless. I completely lose track of the time, and when I pull my phone out to check, it's gone six and there are two missed calls and a sequence of increasingly panicky texts from Ilze about arrangements for the evening. And I still haven't been up the lift to the tower.

I call her and apologise, agreeing to meet later, then climb into the lift to take a few photos in the gloom. Looking to the west side of the city, I'm startled to see that the sun is peering through a v-shaped crack which must be a valley between the mountains. It's been so overcast and gloomy since I got here that this is the first time I've been aware of the mountains, let alone that they're visible from within the city.

Next morning, the sun is shining at last. In the Parco Valentino, by the river Po, the trees have been pruned back to their main branches, and leaves are sprouting directly from the trunks. Youngsters pass by screeching, racing in four-wheeled buggies with four sets of pedals, like two tandem bikes side by side with a roof.

Sometimes all you can see is what's in your heart, and what's around you, however lively, doesn't really matter. Even I get lonely sometimes, walking through crowds of strangers. But the city is growing on me.

On Saturday, Ilze and I take the bus to Venaria Reale, a gorgeous royal palace of the Kings of Savoy, in the mountains, with its formal Versailles-style gardens and amazing multi-media projections directed by Peter Greenaway. The idea is that the inhabitants of the Palace, in their original costumes, are projected into the rooms so that visitors are privy to their conversations and thoughts - which is a little lost on me as it's all in Italian. This is the only full day the two of us have together, but the weather and the setting are wonderful, and we laugh, walk, talk and share a lovely day.

We are following the horizon, trying to get close to the mountains, through the vast gardens, but the closer we get the further they retreat, as mountains do. At the end of the garden, we climb the bank which forms the boundary, for a better view, and find an arable field on the other side. As the day wears on, the clouds gather, making, strange, surreal shapes, a suitable background for the sculpture garden. The rain comes down just before we reach the bus stop, huddling under our umbrellas.

Sunshine on the Po – Sunday 22 April
Walking through a shower of blossom.

Sitting on planks over the river drinking a coffee.

Sunday morning market along the Murrazzi.

Two sparrows squabbling, making enough noise for an army.

White lion guarding the base of Garibaldi's statue.

Light glinting off the river.

Car horns on the bridge, boats on the river.

Ducks swimming and a bloom of brown blossom petals on the surface.

A couple slow dancing under the arches of a bridge, the woman softly crooning.

A black crow perches on a white log in the river, pecking at something invisible.

Everything is good. Sun on my face. The river, purposeful yet calm, unhurried.

I cross the river, and catch the bus to Sassi, then the old rack railway up the mountain to Superga. On the train from Florence, before we reached the city, I noticed this white Baroque church, perched on the top of a mountain, with no apparent reason for being there. When I reach it, I can do nothing but marvel and point my camera. Round central tower in yellow stucco, surrounded by classical white pillars and porticoes, topped with a grey dome housing the bell. However high I am, I'm always driven to go higher, so in the yellow church I climb the steps up to the top of the tower and look down on the terracotta roof of the nave. The white peaks of the mountains surround and mesmerise me.

Notes from a mountain - Monday 23 April
Ilze's back at work today.

'Why not take the train into the mountains? she suggests. 'It takes 29 minutes to get to Avigliana and 1 hour 22 minutes to Bandonecchia.'

I get out at Avigliana and walk around the town. There doesn't seem much to see and I'm not sure what I'm looking for. I walk towards a church, past some pretty old buildings, along a road out of the town and up a hill. A path through woods leads to a small stone tower, with views over the valley and towards the bigger mountains. I've brought a picnic of bits and pieces, a salad of cherry tomatoes and mozzarella left over from last night's dinner, a packet of Tuc biscuits bought from the trolley-man on a train somewhere (Rome to Florence, I think, or Florence to Turin), a Bounty, an apple and a Ritter sport with nuts. A feast, and a good place to eat it.

Sometimes I find myself in a place, and I don't really know why I'm there or what to do there or where I am exactly. Most often, it's in a city. Today it's on the side of a mountain. Not a big, glamorous mountain, I don't know its name, maybe it doesn't have one. It's just part of the great chain of mountains, I guess, a fractal part of something bigger, where does it end and where does the something else begin?

In the valley below me is a house with a balcony and steps up to a terrace. Earlier I saw a person and then an animal, probably a cat, walking across the terrace. The Latin words for the cat family, *Felis*, and for happiness or good fortune, *felicitas*, are so similar, and it seems appropriate. I wonder if it's coincidence, or is there some connection deep in the roots of language?

There's someone on the balcony, leaning on the rail, but they haven't moved for a while. Maybe they're thinking: 'there's a person up there, sitting on a rock on the side of the mountain.'

Now there's a car moving away from the house. I can hear birds all around, and distant traffic, an intermittent sound that could be humming if it was more regular, maybe someone chopping logs with a circular saw. A plane. Sounds that could be thunder in the mountains but hopefully is just other planes.

Into the soundscape comes a train. I wonder if it is going towards Bardonecchia or Turin. Whichever, I've missed it now.

Making plans - Monday 23 April

Ilze and I are huddled together over her computer, searching for accommodation and trains between Turin and Venice. I've not been able to get online, trying not to worry about it too much, although I know that the next stage, Venice and then leaving Italy and heading East, will need a lot of research and planning.

Ilze prints out pages of advice for me on what to do at the train station: a warning that I might have to pay for an extra ticket on the water bus if the luggage is particularly heavy, a list of fares, a map of services (which is a good idea, but in practice not that useful as it's in black and white – imagine a London tube map printed in black and white, and you'll see what I mean); top ten things to avoid for first time visitors to Venice, etc.

After a month in Italy, it's almost time to leave. And although I haven't really fallen for the country in the way I expected, I've grown used to it, and I'm not sure I'm ready to strike out towards Istanbul, or how the hell I'm going to get there - unless I find a magic carpet.

Notes from a Piazza - Tuesday 24 April

On my last day in Turin I climb the Monte dei Cappuccini to the church of Santa Maria del Monte, lower than Superga, but I have been looking at it and drawing it from the other side of the river for a week. I walk back down into the city and find a seat, people watching.

Young buck in jeans and a snug, black-and-green striped tee-shirt, prowls a balcony on the first floor of a building overlooking the Piazza Carlo Alberto. Smoking a cigarette, he paces, like a caged animal, watching the square, and then is gone.

Kids playing in the Piazza, forming a line, starting from the lamp post, foot to foot, legs akimbo. The girl in the bright pink track suit does the splits perfectly. Now they've switched to hide-and-seek. A boy leans against the lamp post, arms folded, head on the arms, while the rest run away. Three teachers, one man and two women, are supervising. The man is taking photos. I am in the background. Am I part of their story? The girl in pink hides two of her friends in line behind her. The teachers shepherd them round the Egyptian statue for a group photo.

A woman with glasses, leaflets and a clipboard asks me for a contribution. I wave her away. Am I part of her story?

The square is quiet now the children are round the statue. A middle aged man with long grey curls cycles across the centre. I turn to watch him go and notice the bald spot among the curls. An older man in a duffle coat walks across the other way, carrying an armful of books. Academics, they have to be.

Smooth looking man with well groomed silky silver hair, dark blue suit, silk scarf and sunglasses walks past me and behind me, arms swinging easily.

I head back to the tourist shops along the Via Po. Ever since the journey started, I've avoided buying things, souvenirs and presents, because of the weight and watching my budget. But fridge magnets are light and cheap and make good souvenirs. I buy one with a quote from Proust, translated into Italian. My Italian isn't great, but I think I've deciphered it:

'The true voyage of discovery consists not of searching for new lands, but of seeing with new eyes.'

I meet Ilze, and we sip *aperitivi* and nibble *hors d'ouevres* (an Italian habit which I first came across in Bologna and of which I thoroughly approve) in the Art Nouveau elegance of a classic café.

Chapter 23 - Venice

Benvenuto a Venezia – **Wednesday 25 April**

Usual stress at the station. At least I don't have to pay extra for the Wardrobe on the water bus, and the people at the ticket office are quite helpful and clear: 'number 2, on the right'. Sounds straightforward enough, but it seems the number 2 to San Marco goes from two different docks – which one do I need? I let one go, then get on the second one in a panic, and find it's going the wrong way. But it really doesn't matter, it's a circular route and I just get a longer ride across the lagoon.

Who decided to make the roof tiles of the Campanile the same turquoise colour as the canals? The chilly wind whips up the water into my face as I drink in the perfect colour scheme, the white and terracotta churches with their domes and towers emerging from the water, the sunshine, the brilliance, the boats, the busyness.

The dire warnings on Google about heavy wheeled luggage and stepped bridges are laughable – I cross one, and it's nothing compared with dragging the Wardrobe up four flights of stairs. The hotel is a terrific bargain, right in the heart of the city, five minutes walk from Piazza San Marco. The description says: 'Our staff will be happy to provide you with everything you need for your most romantic vacation ever...'

'Romance', eh? Maybe I should dress up a bit, forget the jeans and wear leggings and the new top I bought in Florence. It's the perfect peach colour to match the brickwork illuminated by the afternoon sun, and I'm wearing the scarf which has not only Venetian peach but Laguna turquoise as well.

I want to text Ilze and tell her I'm sipping an *aperitivo* in Piazza San Marco. But the cheapest prices are €11 for Campari and soda or €18 for

Aperol spritzer. I left my credit cards in my waistcoat pocket, and I've got about €40 cash – I'm not going to blow almost half my budget for dinner on a drink.

I want to watch the sunset over the water, but the buildings crowd so closely it's impossible to see anything. I think this way should lead me to the lagoon, or at least the Grand Canal.

In a gloomy alleyway alongside a canal, with water lapping against the steps, and a bell tower silhouetted against the fading light in the narrow space up ahead, I have to acknowledge that I'm hopelessly lost. And I can feel that my leggings are starting to work their way down my hips, not, I'm sure, because I've lost weight, but because the elastic has been stretched so far it's given up in despair. Which is pretty much how I'm feeling. Like all those other times, like in Arles, and Aix-en-Provence, when I got lost and had to find my way back to the hotel. And I have to keep stopping to try and pull my bloody leggings up discreetly. What an idiot I am, getting lost, and not wearing my waistcoat and not bringing enough money with me.

I've got a map, but even when I see the names of the streets I'm walking through, I can't pick them out. I keep walking. Somehow it always feels more comforting to be moving, even though I have no idea where I'm walking to, and could indeed be going in completely the wrong direction, through busy piazzas, past bright bars and cafés, over bridges, into mazy little alleyways, as the evening grows darker, and the alleyways emptier. Now there are fewer bars and cafés, fewer people. Another bridge, a dead end, dark buildings, iron balconies.

Retrace my steps? Easier said than done, all those alleyways, all those false turnings, all those paths between the buildings that end with the moody waters of a small canal, entrances visible along the banks, but no path and no bridge, so the only way is to turn back and find a way between the buildings, until you come out again, at another watery dead end, looking across the water to where you were ten minutes earlier.

Surely sooner or later I must find either the Grand Canal or the Lagoon, which would give me a chance to find my bearings? Wouldn't it?

I enter a square and see a family of four, two parents, a boy and girl in or nearly in the early teens. They're too far away to speak to, but I follow them through an exit on the other side, then a few minutes later I meet them coming back. They're German, but they speak to me in English, the international language, and ask me for directions. They're as lost as me, but it's oddly comforting to know I'm not the only one.

At last I find myself in a square that seems vaguely familiar, and realise I'm back in the area near my hotel. As happened in Aix, by this time most of the pizzerias and tourist trattorias are closing down. I've been walking for four hours, I've had nothing to eat, but I'm back in my room, and I'm safe.

Water bus – Thursday 26 April
This morning I'm in search of a decent guide book. There's a book shop near the jetty where the water-buses (aka *vaporetti*) dock, and I spend a happy hour or so browsing among the vast range of books that have been inspired by Venice. Wait a minute, I'm actually here - maybe I should go out and make the most of it.

The weather is glorious again. Should I get in the queue for St Marks and/or the Doge's Palace? Or skip the big attractions and just explore by myself? The *vaporetto* I caught yesterday from the station is on a circular route – how about taking it again in the opposite direction, through the Grand Canal rather than the Lagoon?

Everything is wonderful. People-watching my fellow passengers, eaves-dropping on conversations. Passing under bridges, and past the entrances to small canals, line up the camera because you never know what vista you might catch between the buildings, so it's best to be prepared. Boats loaded with crates of bottles, delivering to the bars, and others full of vegetables, washing machines, boxes of groceries, anything. The colour and the light and the sunshine. Not many gardens, but sometimes window boxes, pots on the balconies, vivid red of geraniums, a burst of purple wisteria on a wall, boats full of cut flowers, blue, yellow, orange.

Back on my feet, on dry land, exploring the alleys again in vivid daylight. An ice cream on one side of the Rialto, and later, an Aperol spritzer on the other side. That was the aperitif I had that night in Bologna, I finally identified it in Turin, with Ilze's help. Watching the water. And the gondoliers.

I've always thought there were something a bit too Gilbert and Sullivan about gondoliers, too camp for words, in their beribboned straw hats and striped jerseys. Seeing them in the flesh, so to speak, is a revelation.

I've never really thought before about just how tough a job it is, how fit and sinewy they have to be. Not just the ridiculously sexy young bucks with the tight black jeans, dark eyes and bouncing, Jim Morrison-style curls, but the grizzled, balding veterans approaching my own age. Not that I, conscious of my budget, actually take a ride with any of them, but I'm happy to watch them from the *vaporetto* or from bridges, as they pass beneath my feet.

I'm leaning on the rail of a random bridge, over a random canal, watching a gondola loaded down with Japanese tourists, two middle aged couples. One pair have matching yellow sunhats, like sou'westers without the waterproofing. The wife wears hers with the peak down, while the husband has his folded upwards, Paddington Bear style. They look so ridiculous, and so unselfconscious, that I can't suppress a giggle. The gondolier, facing towards me and much closer to my height, catches my eye and gives me a wink. He's made my day.

Making plans
In the late afternoon I'm back in the hotel to charge up my phone before going out again. I'm determined to get some sunset pictures, and can buy a 24 hour ticket for the vaporetto, take the circular ride across the lagoon and back through the Grand Canal, and then have use of it for most of tomorrow.

Venice is that rare Eden, a McDonald's free zone. The hotel wifi is €4 for 1 hour, or €10 for 10 hours, but is that 1 hour continuous, or one hour total connection over a set period? I don't feel ready to make any decisions, and I don't want to spend my €4 and then have to pay more later.

Besides, I should really write, and having internet access is a terrible distraction from writing, because you feel as though you're doing something important and being busy when you're not necessarily achieving anything.

So I stick to writing, and when the phone has recharged, I head for the jetty and take my sunset cruise, the low light bouncing off the waves of the Lagoon, the sky streaked pink and gold above the Rialto, and when I return I find a restaurant for gnocchi in cream and a glass of chianti.

Back at the hotel, I pay for my €4 worth of internet. Leaving Italy means heading east to Istanbul, and this part of the journey is the least thought-through. I've managed to avoid thinking about it, just putting together each stage as I go along. In the original fantasy, Athens figured somewhere in the plan as well, but before I left England I found that international train services into and out of Greece were suspended from 13 February, because of the economic crisis.

I'm planning to ease myself into the Balkans gently, starting with Croatia and the eastern coast of the Adriatic. It looks on the map as though it ought to be straightforward just to get a train around the coast, heading for Trieste first, and then to Split. But I can't find any train service between Trieste and Split, only a ten and a half hour bus ride. Wonder if there's a ferry from Venice to Split? No such luck. There's a ferry from Ancona, but that will mean a train journey to Ancona first, and I don't want to go back down into Italy now I'm so close to leaving it. I'm getting stressed because I've only got an hour online and I also need to find a hotel. How about Zagreb? I know nothing about Zagreb, but I can get there direct from Venice in a day, so I find a hotel and book a room for two nights.

'Two Nights in Zagreb.' It sounds like a cold war thriller.

Murano – Friday 27 April
Right, today I'm going to tackle the Wardrobe Problem. I've bought a shipping box from the Post Office on St Mark's Square, and I'm going to pack it with assorted clothes and guide books and post it back to my daughter. I need tape as well, and I have no idea where to buy it. I ask the hotel receptionist and he directs me to the Ratti shop, a hardware chain. This is quite a revelation as I've never noticed it before, tucked in amongst the jewellers, tourist shops and cafés. It's strange how hard it can to be to find a general, run-of-the-mill shop selling normal stuff in the middle of a tourist area.

Next I head to the *vaporetto* jetty, to get my money's worth from my 24 hour ticket. This time I venture out into the lagoon and over to Murano, centre of the glass industry and location of the novel 'Through a Glass Darkly' by Donna Leon, which I'm currently reading. In a workshop store, I buy ear-rings for myself and my daughter, and pendants to take my son's girlfriend and her mother. Souvenirs? Yes, I've finally started to buy them. Well, they're very small. And I want to take presents to Dina and her Mum in Norway when I visit them in a couple of months.

Back at the main island, I leave the boat at the railway station and buy tickets for tomorrow. I can't get a train direct from Venice to Zagreb, but there's a regular service, by bus from Venice, change at Villach and train to Zagreb.

When I leave tomorrow, it will be just a day short of five weeks since I arrived in Italy – almost as long as the time I spent in Belgium, France and Spain, and longer than I'm planning to spend anywhere else. Ten weeks and three days since I left England. Almost half way through. And four weeks and six days in Italy is close to half of that.

That sort of thinking can get obsessive.

Arrivederci Venezia - Saturday 28 April

I wake early, I've got things to do before I leave. I go to the casement window, remove the socks and undies that I wedged in there yesterday to dry, and look out onto the narrow alley below. The casement isn't quite closed. I notice it will open quite wide, I could probably get through it easily. If I threw myself out of here, now, I wonder, what would Commissario Brunetti make of it? A mystery. What would he find out about the life of this strange woman who had come to his city, and would he ever get to the bottom of why I did it?

I take my parcel to the Post Office.

'What is inside it?' asks the lady.

'Clothes and books'.

'New clothes?'

'No, used clothes.'

'New clothes' she says, meaningfully.

'Oh… okay, new clothes then'.

It costs €30. I wonder if I'll ever see it again, but at least the Wardrobe is lighter now.

I check out of the hotel and drag the Wardrobe up and down the steps of the footbridge, across St Mark's Square, and to the *vaporetto*. There's a longer wait than I was anticipating - a traffic jam on the Grand Canal. Maybe it's always like this on Saturday morning, but the time's ticking away. I'm wearing my usual travel outfit of jeans, boots, tee shirt, waistcoat and leather jacket, and it's warm.

I get off the boat at Tronchetto, expecting a bus station with the usual international travel facilities. I walk as fast as I can towards the buildings, not much time before the bus leaves. I pass an information office but keep going, surely it'll be easy enough to find the bus? There are buses lined up ahead of me, but they're all tour buses, airport buses, not long distance.

I check at the information office, but it's only for a specific bus company, they know nothing about the long distance service.

'I think you need to go down this building to the end and the stop is on the right.'

I walk down the side of the office buildings along a dreary stretch of tarmac and bored-looking, flat mown grass. There's no sign of bus station buildings, or of buses. I double back on myself once or twice. I've missed the bus by now, and I don't know what to do.

At the end of the road there's a bus stop and a station for the monorail back to the main island. The timetable shows that the next bus to Villach will be leaving in two hours. But there's nowhere to buy a ticket and no one to ask.

I have no idea what to do. Once again, after paying €30 to post my parcel, I've run out of cash, and I can't see any cash machines. I'll have to go back to the railway station, and the simplest way to do that is to take the monorail. Luckily I've got a euro coin to buy a ticket.

At the railway station information desk, the man tells me my train ticket is okay, it's an open ticket, I can get from Villach to Zagreb on a later train, but I have to buy another bus ticket.

Time's getting on, I haven't found a cash machine, I have to get back to the bus stop again, and I haven't got anything to eat or drink. And I have a three and a half hour bus journey to look forward to.

Waiting for the monorail back seems to take longer than it did before. I've taken off my coat and bundled it up through the handle of the Wardrobe, but I'm inseparable as usual from my waistcoat with its essential pockets. An American student says to her friend, clearly not expecting me to understand English: 'Who would wear a tank top in this heat?'

'You should have seen me earlier when I was wearing a coat as well' I think, but I don't say.

I get back to the bus stop with my ticket and ten minutes to spare, but I still haven't got anything to eat or drink, not even a bottle of water.

V

The Balkans

Zagreb - Split - Mostar - Sarajevo - Belgrade
- Nïs - Sofia - Istanbul

Chapter 24 - Zagreb

Villach – Saturday 28 April

I didn't realise the change from bus to train would be in Austria – it wasn't on my planned itinerary. The last time I was here was Vienna for a workshop in 2005. At the breakfast buffet in the hotel restaurant, a complete stranger stood up, looked straight at me, and very loudly and pointedly hissed at me. I have no idea what I'd done to provoke him - and in case you think I was being paranoid (because the whole thing was so inexplicable that I sometimes wonder myself), the people I was with couldn't understand it either. It was very disturbing, as you can tell from the fact that it's stayed with me for seven years.

By the time we get to Villach, I'm pretty stressed out, with the hassles of the journey so far, this uncomfortable memory, and apprehension about entering a new country, Croatia, in a completely unfamiliar part of the world. I try to catch the announcement on the bus about the connection for Zagreb, it's not very clear but I pick up '25 minutes', which doesn't seem too bad a wait for my connection, hopefully there'll be a buffet at the station and I can grab a coffee and sandwich.

I can't see any sign of the connection to Zagreb on the electronic displays, so I go to the desk and ask the ticket clerk, who tells me gleefully:

'Next train at 19.25.' He pronounces the numbers slowly and precisely, with great relish.

'What?' I ask, hoping I've misheard. 'What time will it get to Zagreb?'

'Twenty three thirty four.' A four hour wait, a four hour journey, and I won't arrive in Zagreb till just before midnight. All right, it's not his fault, but does he have to enjoy telling me quite so much?

At least the kiosk's open. I buy a pastry, coffee and a bottle of water and eat it on a bench facing the escalator. I can't find a left luggage locker, so I drag the Wardrobe out of the station into a perfectly lovely afternoon. There's a river, sparkling and falling away from a vision of snow-capped mountains, people strolling along the banks, youngsters on skateboards. I've got an open ticket to Zagreb, and nothing booked after that. Maybe I could stay here for one night and leave in the morning?

Fortunately the details for the hotel in Zagreb are on my phone, so I check the penalty for cancellation. Then I read that I'm supposed to inform them in advance if I expect to arrive after 22.00. And there's no phone number for the hotel, only a UK number for the online booking agency.

I call and explain my predicament.

'I'll call the hotel and see what they say, then call you back.'

Here I am standing by a sunny Alpine river in Austria waiting for a call from England to tell me what's been arranged with a hotel in Croatia. There's a lot to be said for twenty-first century communications. The answer comes, and all is okay.

The café terrace by the river is crowded with families. I can't see any free tables, and I don't feel like dragging the Wardrobe between the chairs, so I trudge back to the station.

On the platform, I can hear a blackbird singing, waiting for the answering call somewhere down the line. Standing next to me is a young giant, at least six foot six tall, dressed in – well, not exactly *lederhosen*, but a green velvet costume with knee breeches, lots of embroidered edelweiss, socks with little tabs at the top, a green Robin Hood hat with a feather, and black-framed glasses. It's very difficult not to stare, and impossible to ignore his efforts to strike up a conversation. He tells me he's Slovenian, has been playing in a band and is heading home to Ljubljana.

'What instrument do you play?'

'The accordion' he lifts the large case behind him to show me. Now the costume makes sense. That sort of band.

'How do you like this weather?' he asks. 'You never see it at home, hey?'

'We do sometimes.' The afternoon is turning into what could have passed for a perfect English summer evening.

'Twenty five degrees?' he asks sceptically.

'Sometimes, in the summer.'

'I've read about the English weather' he says, in a you-can't-pull-the-wool-over-my-eyes tone. 'It rains every day and is very foggy. You never see the sunshine.'

'It's really not as bad as that' I protest, but it's pointless. He's clearly convinced that I'm lying, and strikes up a conversation, in his own language, with another waiting fellow passenger.

Villach to Zagreb – Saturday 28 April

A black dog, running through long bright grass, tinged with gold. A shimmering, glorious evening. Children running up a hill behind the houses.

We go through a tunnel – maybe 20 minutes, as long as the Channel Tunnel – and when we emerge the gold has drained from the light. The white blossom in the orchards is still like clouds, but the passing cars have their headlights on.

My smartphone buzzes.

The text says: *'Benvenuto in SLOVENIA'* and proceeds to tell me, in Italian, what the charges will be, and how I can recharge online. Then my other phone springs to life, the one with an English Sim, telling me a similar message. I should compare rates. Isn't 10p for a text cheaper than 13.3 cents? What about 42.4 cents for a minute vs 36p to send, 13.3c/minute to receive vs 11p, or 0.8c/kb vs £4/mb? It's been a long day and my brain isn't up to this.

In and out of tunnels. At some point I realise it has got dark, outside as well as in the train.

At Ljubljana station, the three Italian ladies on the seat opposite get out, and I have the compartment to myself. I pull the Wardrobe in from the corridor.

We are standing in the station for quite a long time. I think the young men in the next compartment have got out to buy wine. I hear them in the corridor talking. I have no idea what language they're speaking, but it's not Italian, it has a Slavic ring to it, and I think – I have left Western Europe behind.

The compartment is hot and clammy. The train whistles in the darkened station, and it sounds unexpectedly thrilling as we start to move. At last I'm starting to feel like a real traveller. Then a McDonald's poster glides past the window. Ah well!

I tweeted yesterday that 'Two Nights in Zagreb' sounds like a cold war thriller. This is the prequel: 'Night Train to Zagreb'.

Stations pass in the dark. Sometimes we seem to be passing a river, light reflected from the water.

At Dobrava we stop for a long wait, as officials walk through the train, and I am asked to show my passport, for the first time since I left Ebbsfleet. The couple in the compartment with me have dark blue passports, which surprises me, until I remember that Croatia won't join the EU till 2013.

Dobrodošli u Zagreb - **Sunday 29 April**

An unexpectedly sudden disjunction between west and east, after all the linguistic and cultural overlapping I've noticed up till now. Is it just knowledge of history that makes me think that? For the first half of my life so far – well, okay, more than half – 'Eastern Europe' was a distinctly Other sort of place.

The language has a Slavic sound to it, and the most I've picked up so far is *'da'* and *'nay'* (almost certainly not spelt like that, but that's how it sounds). I persuaded the receptionist at the hotel to teach me 'good morning' and 'thank you', the very least, in my opinion, that it's polite to know when you visit a new country, but they were so different from anything with which I'm familiar that I forgot them almost instantly.

The final part of that Cold War trilogy: 'Two Nights in Zagreb', 'Night Train to Zagreb' and 'Twenty Four Hours in Zagreb' (actually, more like forty hours). What strikes me is how quiet, if not downright sleepy, the place is. The surprisingly large number of groups of young British men makes me wonder if it's become a popular venue for stag parties, but if so, even they seem remarkably subdued and well behaved.

According to the free guide booklet I picked up in the hotel lobby, 1667 saw *'the last of the great mass brawls between the inhabitants of Gradec and Kaptol... Henceforth Zagreb becomes a much more united city'* which is reassuring to know. Incidentally, the translator/writer of 'Zagreb In Your Pocket' (or 'ZIYP' as it likes to be known) appears to have learnt English through studying American teen comedy films and associated websites, if this description of Nikola Šubić Zrinski Square is anything to go by:

'The combination of outdoor gazebo, expertly manicured lawn, flowers enormous trees, fountains and statues make this sucker a brilliant place to take

a load off. This is the park closest to Ban Josip Jelačić Square, and you'll be thrilled to see that its (sic) also a make-out point: local lovers show-off their most complex and passionate manoeuvres free of charge in this baby.'

Well I never.

What else to say about Zagreb? It's an attractive town, but it's hard to remember that it's a capital city, albeit of a country which didn't exist as a separate state twenty five years ago. Not only does it seem like an unlikely setting for Cold War intrigue, it's even more unlikely to think that within the last two decades this region has been involved in a hot war, and a very nasty one at that.

I set off with my guide booklet, including map, and, I think, a reasonably clear idea of where I'm going. Without exactly getting lost, I struggle to make what I see correspond to what I'm expecting. Stop; push sunglasses up on top of head; rummage in bag for reading glasses and map; study map; try to match map with street signs; replace map and reading glasses in bag; slide sun glasses back down over eyes. Now, what did I just read on the map? Yes, my short term memory really is that bad, particularly when trying to remember long, vowel-free strings of consonants which relate to nothing remotely familiar.

Eventually I find my way to Ban Josip Jelačić Square (or *Trg bana Josipa Jelačića*):

'this Austro-Hungarian styled square is the true centre of the city. There's a phenomenal variety of cafés, shopping, feeding and people watching everywhere. It was named after the impressive sculpture within its domain, that of Count Jelačić, his deadly steed, and a sword so pointy and sharp that it could poke your eye out' according to ZIYP.

I'm walking across the square past said statue, looking for some people to watch, when I hear the sound of drums. Four blokes on horseback ride into the square, followed by half a dozen others on foot playing drums, all dressed in lovely Ruritanian uniforms with flapping black cloaks and feathers in their hats.

Three of the horses pass me, but the fourth, a piebald one, seems to be coming straight towards me. He turns round to my left, and then another bloke, dressed very un-picturesquely with a high vis waistcoat shouts at me and waves me over to join the other bystanders. I thought I was standing out of the way, but actually I was right by the statue, which is where they're congregating, one either side and two in front.

There's a ceremony, with lots of standing to attention and a bit of shouting, then the drums start again and they all march or ride out of the square. I wonder if it's a special occasion, or does it happen every Sunday? Maybe it's the Croatian equivalent of the changing of the guard. There's not much of a crowd, just the dozen or so people who, like me, happened to be passing through the square anyway.

I walk around the Old Town in the sunshine, pretty but not very memorable buildings in white stone, cream and pink stucco and red roofs, churches with neat white bell towers, grey spires with spherical or curly embellishments and the odd dome. I find a café with an Italian menu for lunch, then walk to the Upper Town. The place is eerily empty, just me walking around a huge deserted square by the Church of St Mark, which has a tiled roof decorated with the coat of arms of Croatia. Everywhere is so quiet. Down below the street cafés are packed, but here in the Upper Town, the museum district, the streets are empty and the birdsong is deafening.

I keep seeing signs for the Museum of Broken Relationships. The Museum was founded by two Croatian artists, after their relationship ended, and they describe it as follows: *'an art concept which proceeds from the (scientific) assumption that objects... possess integrated fields - 'holograms' of memories and emotions - and intends with its layout to create a space of 'secure memory' or 'protected remembrance' in order to preserve the material and nonmaterial heritage of broken relationships.'*

I'm very intrigued by this – it feels like fate - so on the way in I chat happily to the woman on the desk, explaining about my trip, the reasons and funding behind it, the fact that I've just had an email from my solicitor saying the decree absolute came through on 16 April (when I was in Florence), and promising to send my story to be an exhibit, possibly with a copy of the Croatian stamp in my passport.

After walking round the exhibits, I'm more subdued. I've always said that this trip wasn't about the break-up of my marriage, that I'm okay with that, that it's the rest of life I'm trying to deal with. But there's something about seeing all that detritus of bitterness and sadness that touches me very deeply, and I can't really explain how or why.

Outside the Hotel Esplanade - Monday 30 April
Monday morning again. The train doesn't go till 14.00, but I get to the station about 10.00 and leave the Wardrobe in a locker. The botanic garden is close to the station and I head there for a walk. There's a woodland with bluebells, and spring is burgeoning into summer, full of hope after all that rain I've seen over the last month. I'm not sure I'll ever forgive Italy for that. The air is filled with a most peculiar noise, a mixture of quacking, rusty machinery and old hinges. I track it to its source, a pond full of hundreds of frogs.

Walking back to the station, I pass a neo-classical building with white marble columns, at the end of manicured lawns, where a huge fountain plays erratically. Maybe it's a former palace, or ministerial offices? No, it's the Hotel Esplanade, with tables and chairs on the terrace and waiters serving coffee.

Only an hour and twenty minutes till the train. I could go to McDonald's and get online, but I'd rather stop for a cappuccino at a shady table outside the Hotel Esplanade, watching the fountain and the people and the trams and the world going by. The horse chestnut blossom is pink and splendid, and the noise of the birds almost drowns out the traffic. On the way back to the station, I pass a street market, and buy a bag of apples.

Zagreb to Split
I'm heading for the seaside, and when I look out of the train window, the dark clouds are gathering again. Bother.

Oh, fantastic. Not only is the rain now coming down in torrents such as I haven't seen since I was in Turin, but I just reached for an apple out of my carrier bag full of supplies to find that the bag has split and at least one apple has gone rolling down the train. Ah well, there were more in the bag than I needed anyway. And as for the rain, we've got another five hours of the journey to go, plenty of time for the weather to change again.

More wonderful mountain scenery, empty moors, sparkling streams, isolated buildings. Stations with names like Gospić and Knin.

The train stops in the middle of nowhere. The stewardess comes through the carriage and says something. All the people at my end of the carriage get up and disappear, but leave their luggage.

What's going on? I start walking through the carriage - there are still other people up at the other end, including one woman who's asleep. In the next carriage I find the stewardess and ask her what's happening.

'We have to wait for the train coming from Split' she says with a smile. We had to wait for the line to be free, so they all got out and had a leg stretch and fag break.

Two more hours before we get to Split. Still in the mountains, but I just saw a road, the first for I can't remember how long, probably three hours or so. It's 18.40 now and we left Zagreb just after 14.00.

I've been wondering, as I used to when we drove across Texas, how people cope with being so isolated. At least here they have lovely mountains to look at.

A view of mountains from the Zagreb-Split train

Chapter 25 - Split

Dobrodošli u Split – **Monday 30 April**

When we arrive I let everybody get off before me so I can take the Wardrobe off the rack without getting in anyone's way. There's a cluster of people around the door apparently waiting for someone. I heft the Wardrobe down the three steps, but they don't get out of my way. Then they all start at once, an oldish man, a woman about my age, and somebody else on the left that I can't see clearly because I'm trying to get past them.

'Accommodation?' the man says 'You want accommodation? Tonight?' He waves a map in my face,

'No thank you.' I set the Wardrobe on its wheels and try to get clear of them.

He's still speaking. 'Is there anything else I can do for you?' I don't say 'get the hell out of my way' as I swing round him, though perhaps I should.

The woman manages to keep up and come alongside me.

'Accommodation?'

'No!' They're really starting to annoy me now. 'I wouldn't have come all this way if I didn't have somewhere arranged to stay the night. That's what the internet's for!'

I'm out of the station now and by the taxi rank. I've got some directions, but they're still following me so I go up to the first taxi, and show him the address.

I watch the meter like a hawk as it winds up to 42 *Kuna*. Divide by six, multiply by 4, my fuddled brain is trying to think it through. That would be €28.

'Where are you taking me?' I ask suspiciously.

'No traffic allowed in the centre' he says. 'We have to go round the back'.

A little later: 'This is the street, but it's one way, we have to go down to the end.'

We drive down the narrow street with cars parked along one side, and meet a car coming the other way.

'Someone doesn't know it's one way!' I say.

The car pulls in, but on the other side of it is another car with its reversing lights on. The taxi driver pulls up right behind it. The driver, a woman, climbs across the passenger seat, comes over and talks to the taxi driver, in such a calm and casual way that at first I assume she knows him. Then she gets back in.

'We'll have to stop here' my driver says. 'It's just down there' he points ahead. 'Forty please.'

He gets the Wardrobe out of the boot, while I offer him a 100 *kuna* note and make a point of checking the change.

The hand-written number on the house on my right looks like 13, and I need 11. The next one says 21, so I walk back and look again. It could be 23, I suppose. Further down I find 19, 17 and so on, past a metal gate and then 9. I double back, look again at the metal gate, and the array of bells next to it, ring one at random and say my name.

'Push the gate.'

I am walking up an alley that opens out into a yard. In front of me is a two storey building with four doors, two on the ground floor and two on the first, and an external staircase down which a man is coming. He shakes my hand and introduces himself.

His name is Frane (pronounced 'Franya'), tall and chubby with a round face and black-framed glasses, probably in his thirties. He unlocks the left hand door on the ground floor, and shows me into a flat, with two bedrooms, a kitchenette and a bathroom. In my room there are three beds but there are no other occupants, in fact I have the whole flat to myself.

'My family live upstairs' he tells me. 'If you want anything come up and ask, you can talk to my sister or me but my mother and father don't understand English.'

He asks to see my passport, and when I look for it in my backpack, I realise that the middle pocket is open. I may have left it open, can't swear I didn't, but I think about the people at the station and wonder if it was a scam to try and rob me. The only thing of value in that pocket is my Kindle, and it's still there (either they didn't have a chance to find it or they didn't know what it was or there is little resale value on them).

Frane tells me that tomorrow, 1 May, is a public holiday – 'for the labour day.'

When I settle in, I work out the taxi fare and realise I did the driver an injustice, the exchange rate is 7.4 *kuna* to the Euro so the rule of thumb is 30 kuna to €4, the fare was less than €6, and I feel bad for being so rude to him.

Split – Tuesday 1 May

May Day, and the swifts are calling outside fit to bust. I think back to when I heard them in Naples, then to watching swallows over the river in Rome, Florence, Turin… and where was it I saw the mud nests? I think that was Turin, down by the Murrazzi.

Well, there are swifts here.

I didn't see anything last night when I got here, so I head out to explore. When I find the harbour, I'm surprised to realise it's right by the railway station. I didn't notice it last night, possibly because I was just desperate to get into the taxi and away from the people who were harassing me.

I walk along the seafront and find a beach and a concrete harbour wall with steps going down into the water, as though it's a swimming pool. The water looks about the depth of a swimming pool too, maybe a metre or a little over.

I return to my room to get my swimming things. On the way back to the beach, the path goes along above the railway line, and I see a man, red tee shirt, jeans, rusty baseball cap, walking along the lines, stepping from sleeper to sleeper. I keep pace with him, step for step, wondering what on earth he's doing. As we approach the bridge over the railway I speed up to get there before him and watch him go under, then I cross the road to watch him come out the other side, like Pooh sticks. The railway line ends in buffers, and then there's a path leading to the bathing jetty.

It seems strange to use a railway track as a short cut, but that's not the only surreal aspect to the place. By the harbour is a giant fish hook with the caption: *'The thousand year anniversary of the first mentioning of fishing in Croatia'*. Then there's the ladder, randomly sticking up out of the water in the middle of the harbour.

Most surreal of all, though, is the origin of the Old Town as the palace of the Emperor Diocletian, with its narrow alleyways, originally corridors of the palace, and squares and buildings that must once have been rooms.

I swim for a while, from the jetty, the water is warm and comes up to my midriff. I'm nervous, as always, of leaving my things. The place is busy, it being a public holiday. I climb out and lie in the sun to dry, but there's no shade and it soon becomes uncomfortable.

I walk to the market and buy a bag of oranges. All the shops apart from Konsum (wonderful name for a supermarket chain) are closed for the May Day holiday. When I get back to the flat, the gate next to the entrance is locked with a grille over the window. It looks very mysterious and intriguing and I peer through. Hard to tell in the gloom, maybe it's an antique shop?

Morning thoughts – Wednesday 2 May

If I try to write what I'm thinking, the way I used to write my blog, I just can't do this. I didn't finish what I started yesterday, but now I feel like I should be writing about what I did yesterday, which means that all I have to post for the day before is the half-finished thing I wrote yesterday. But if I try to write just summaries, notes, bullet points, I'm worried that that will be it and my memory will get wiped and I'll never be able to write it up properly. I'm always behind with everything, running to catch up with myself.

There are loads of things I need to do while I've got wifi, like sort out where I'm going next, where I'm going to sleep and how I'm going to get there. I need to contact the people I'm planning to visit too, and fix dates with them, because I have to fit into their lives, and the overall time schedule is starting to slip quite badly.

I'm tired, but it's better if I get up than lie in bed awake. The swifts are making such a lot of noise, and I can hear music somewhere, just a radio, although yesterday evening there was someone playing a piano.

And the bells start ringing at 6.00. They seem to ring at random times, I think there might be a monastery somewhere in the town.

Single to Sirkeci

I walk to the baker's down the street to buy pastries. Back at the flat I make (instant) coffee (no equipment to make the real thing, sadly), and take my pastry and a couple of the oranges from the market out into the courtyard. There are some picnic benches, and I sit in the sun with the laptop as well as breakfast. I'm trying to find out how to get from here to Istanbul and then back to Budapest without retracing my steps.

'Good morning!' Frane comes down the stairs, so I smile back.

'What a beautiful morning.'

'You are lucky you weren't here last month. We had so much rain, it was terrible.'

'I was in Italy last month, and it poured with rain there too. I think it was the same everywhere.'

'I went on holiday to London in September last year for nine days. I had wonderful time, such an exciting city. Everybody warned me before I went that the weather would be bad, but it only rained a little on one day, the rest of the time it was sunny and warm, very good weather.'

'The weather isn't as bad as people think.'

We move on from the weather to the economy.

'Things are getting bad' he confides. 'Twenty years ago, we had industries, everybody had a job. Now the industries are going, all we have is tourism. We are dependent on the tourism and that is not good. What happens if the tourists stop coming, or decide to go somewhere else?'

'It's the same everywhere. Things are bad in England too. Lots of people have lost their jobs.'

I can see from his face that he doesn't believe our problems could measure up to Croatia's, comfortably ensconced as we are within the embrace of the EU. And considering how tourist London must appear by comparison with Zagreb, perhaps that's not so surprising.

Along the side of the courtyard, under a sheltering porch, there's a shelf of books left behind by past travellers. He pulls out a guidebook.

'What are you planning to do today?'

'I don't really know.' Walking, swimming, sitting in the sunshine.

He starts telling me about local attractions. The Marjan peninsula 'is a natural park, overlooking the sea, very beautiful views. You can walk there and back. There is a beach here' he points it out on the map '..and here. Very good to swim. And you should visit Trogir, a very beautiful place, like Split, on an island off the coast. You can get there on the 37 bus, it takes only half an hour, and they go all day from the bus station.'

I flick through the books when he's gone. There's a Lonely Planet 'Guide to Europe on a Shoestring'. Looking through its highlights, I'm gratified to realise I've done, or am planning to do, a fair few of the recommendations, including London (well, not on this trip) and Paris, not to mention: 'take the train' and 'walk around'.

These boots are made for walking

Walking out through Split I pass a shop in a backstreet that looks like it could be a cobblers. On closer inspection it's clear that the proprietor works in metal, even down to the Vespa that takes up most of the space in the shop – or maybe that's his transport and way of avoiding paying for parking. I mentioned before that I've been fretting over my boots. They're so comfortable, and they've carried me through Belgium, France, Spain and Italy, through mud, beaches, pebbles, over cobbles, up mountains. By the time they got soaked through in Sorrento they were showing signs of wear, first the heels, then the soles. In vain I searched for an Italian version of Timpson's. This place looks as cramped and chaotic as I'd expect of a cobbler's, but clearly key cutting is as close as it gets to Timpson's.

It's given me an idea though. Split seems like the sort of place that would have a cobbler's shop. I bet Frane would know. But I'd better do something about it now, while there's time to go back and collect them.

I turn back towards the flat to ask Frane, popping into Konsum en route. I buy eggs, bacon, butter, cheese and mushrooms, for the makings of an omelette, chocolate and a bottle of red with a picture of a donkey on the label, all for 36 Kune, just shy of €5. Then to the baker's for some fresh, seeded bread and a cake.

I'm just thinking about having to disturb Frane again, when I walk past the gate next door to the flats and see that it's open and, far from antiques, there are shoes on the counter.

I take my groceries into the flat, pick up my boots, then walk into the gloom of the cobbler's shop. It's dark after the bright sunshine, and seems deserted.

'Hello' I call, nervously.

'Two minutes' comes a deep, Slavic voice from the depths of the building. I wait, inhaling the smell of leather.

A body appears suddenly out of the darkness, a body to match the voice, dark eyes and beard, rough curls, the face of a mountain partisan. I catch my breath.

'Do you speak English?' I manage to whisper.

'A little.'

I show him my boots. 'Could you have them ready for tomorrow?'

'Tomorrow afternoon' says the voice. 'After 5 o'clock. One hundred *Kuna*.'

'Great! Thank you.'

Marjan

I head for the Marjan peninsula, with my swimming costume under my clothes and a towel in my tote bag. It's as beautiful as Frane promised, with stunning views over the harbour and the Old Town, but when I reach the top, I realise just how much of the city is laid out over the other side, round another bay.

The penisula is wooded, with a wonderful mixture of Mediterranean trees, succulents and flowering plants. I walk along winding paths, into shade and out into glorious clearings, rich with the sound of birdsong, small lizards slithering over rocks and mysterious rustling in the undergrowth. Precipitous views over sheer cliff edges down to the blue Adriatic, where a mis-step could take you fatally down over rough rocks.

Every so often I see signposts for the beach, but although I follow them I never seem to get there. I come upon a fitness trail, and follow that, passing equipment among the trees as incongruous as an agave plant in an urban gym. The path leads downwards, with the sun at my back, so I must be heading towards the north eastern shore of the peninsula. A gap in the trees opens out to smooth rocks rising from glorious blue water and a hazy view of buildings across the bay. It's not exactly a beach, nor is it completely deserted; there's a mother with two small boys, and a little further along a young couple. But it's perfectly beautiful, the water warm from the afternoon sun, and I slip in gratefully. I wonder if I'll be able to find my way back to town? Who cares?

The walk back is further than I'm expecting, but less difficult to navigate, in fact I'm rather disappointed at how quickly I get back to a tarmacked road. I stop for a cocktail at one of the bars on the seafront, then go back to the apartment and cook myself an omelette, which I eat sitting outside on the patio in the evening sun. I'm supposed to be getting on with the next bit of research and booking, or at least sorting out my blog – but instead I wander back down to the harbour again, where I have a stroll and listen to an all-woman choir. When the folk-dancing starts, I drift into the Old Town, where I sit on a cushion on the steps outside the cathedral, drinking a Bailey's coffee and listening to two men singing and playing Light My Fire on guitar. I can never resist live guitar music.

Planning – Thursday 3 May

Big dilemma. I was hoping to get to Istanbul via Bulgaria, and come out again via Romania. The plan was to go from Split to Belgrade and/or Sofia, possibly through Sarajevo, and thence to Istanbul.

However, I've found out two things: the only train connection from Split is with Zagreb, but it is possible to get to Sarajevo on the bus. And the overnight train from Sofia to Istanbul is not currently operating, because the line's being upgraded, which means getting off the train at the Turkish border (at 1.45 am) and going the rest of the way by bus.

I'm not a fan of buses, largely because I get travel sick if I read on them, whereas, for some reason, on trains I can quite happily read and even write on the laptop. The bus from Venice to Villach was three and a half hours, but the bus from Split to Sarajevo takes eight hours. And there's no direct connection from Sarajevo to Sofia, so I'd have to go to Belgrade to get back to Sofia to take the train that doesn't go all the way anyway.

The Man in Seat 61 website 'strongly recommends' getting to Istanbul via Bucharest, on the Bosfor Express, which has comfortable sleeper cars. Which means taking the same route into and out of Istanbul.

So it might make sense to retrace my steps to Zagreb, on the nice, comfortable high-speed train, and go back to the nice comfortable hotel in easy walking distance of the station, and start again from there. But to get from Zagreb to Bucharest, according to Raileurope, I have to go via Budapest. This is just silly. I want to go to Budapest on the way back, not the way there.

I've been up for two hours digging through websites, and I'm not getting any further forward. My brain is now saying: 'right, I've been awake for two hours, time to go back to sleep.' But if I go back to bed now (7.20), I'll sleep till some stupid time and waste the morning.

The Romania tourism site says I can get from Zagreb to Bucharest via Budapest or Belgrade. But if I go via Belgrade, how about going back to the plan of going from here to Sarajevo, and on to Belgrade from there? And what is Belgrade like? What is there to see? Might there be somewhere more interesting but less well known?

Deutsche Bahn says there is one train a day from Sarajevo to Belgrade, leaving at 7 in the morning and taking 11 hours. Raileurope (which I'm getting distinctly fed up with) says there aren't any.

I read on some site that it's possible to get a train from Sarajevo to Ploče, and bus from Split to Ploče, which reduces the amount of time on the bus to less than 3 hours. And the buses from Split to Ploče seem quite regular. But when I finally track down the train from Ploče to Sarajevo, it seems there are only two a day, at 6.30 in the morning and 17.00, arriving in Sarajevo at 21.00.

And after another look at the Man in Seat 61 I realise that the bus transfer on the last leg of the journey to Istanbul applies whether you're going from Belgrade/Sofia or Bucharest, so there's probably not much point in going via Bucharest. And either way, Sarajevo seems to be a sensible way to get there, so it's worth settling on Sarajevo for tomorrow.

So then I start looking for hotels in Sarajevo. And trying to work out how far they are from the bus station. And I find out that there's a train service between Sarajevo and Mostar. So I look up buses from Split to Mostar. And they take three and a half hours and go six times a day, including sensible times. And I look up hotels in Mostar and book myself a room for 2 nights.

And finally, finally, go and get a shower. I've only been awake 4 hours, and I have a plan for the next two days and nights.

Trogir - Thursday 3 May
As Frane's advice about the Marjan Peninsula was right on the money, I decide to take his other suggestion as well and spend my last day in Croatia by taking the 37 bus to Trogir.

The bus ride is interesting in itself, through the back streets of Split and along the coast. Trogir is attractive enough, but I can't help thinking I could have had just as nice a day in Split. There's a sign saying that it's a Unesco World Heritage Site, but I'm not sure why. I wonder, rather cynically, if places in the Balkans were given this status to protect them during the wars of the 1990s, or to boost the countries' esteem and place in the world after all their traumas? Perhaps I'm just getting jaded after all the beautiful places I've seen already. I walk around the marina, have a picnic lunch, buy postcards, wander through the Old Town in search of a post office, climb the clock tower and marvel at the views and the refreshingly relaxed attitude to health and safety that I also noticed yesterday on the cliff walks of the Marjan Peninsula.

Back in Split, I browse through the market, walk again through the Old Town and listen to the swifts, then pick up my boots, newly soled and heeled, from the cobbler. I end the evening with a walk along the waterfront, picking my way over unmade roads and past building sites under the full moon.

The 'beach', Marjan peninsula, Croatia

Chapter 26 - Mostar

Split to Mostar – Friday 4 May

From my balcony, I can hear the voice of the *Muezzin* over the sound of the birdsong. At least, I assume that's what's being broadcast, though it sounds less like a call to prayer than a lament. On the hill to my left I see a tall cross, and smaller ones, faintly along the ridge. Closer, on the wires, a swallow whistles and chatters, while dogs bark in the distance and the table umbrella flaps in the breeze. The view is stunning.

I don't know where to start, what to say. I don't want to be pretentious, or patronising, or melodramatic. I know it's my awareness of history that makes me feel this way. And I'm not sure I have the right to feel these feelings, to write about them, I who have no such experience in my life story.

So, back to my journey, from the coastal plain with its fruit orchards and views of the gloriously blue Adriatic, through an area where flat island farms seem to float on the water, and at last into the mountains.

From the bus station in Mostar, I start walking, but there's a construction lorry parked diagonally across the road, and behind it the surface is completely dug up. In some places there's a pavement on one side, in some places on the other, and the kerb stones stick up. I keep dragging the Wardrobe over the rough surface. The road leads into a square, and then a paved road, with a sign saying 'accommodation' outside the building. I press the intercom button, expecting someone to speak or open the door, but nothing happens. I press again.

A head appears out of a window on the first floor, just above me and to one side. Short spiky grey hair and blue eyes.

'I've got a reservation.'

'Linda?' he asks.

'Yes.'

'I'll come down.'

It takes a while before the door opens. A smiling man about my age lets me in.

'Shoes here please, with the others.' I take off my boots. There are about a dozen sets of footwear paired up along the wall.

He takes my case and leads me upstairs.

'You are Swedish?' he asks.

'No, English.'

'Ah. I lived in Sweden for a while. There are many Lindas in Sweden.'

On the first floor, there are two doors, side by side. He points to the one on the left.

'This is where I live, and this...' he opens the door to the right '...is where you will stay.' There's a kitchenette, sofa, table and chairs and a single bed along one wall. Patio doors lead out onto a large balcony with a wooden table big enough for six chairs, a parasol, a barbecue, a sink and some reclining chairs folded up.

There's a bathroom, with washing machine, and also a double bedroom, but it's clear that the first room alone is mine. That's fine, it's a palace as far as I'm concerned. We discuss the usual details, he gives me the keys. Then he says something that sounds like:

'You want drink?'

It's clearly a question, but I'm not sure what he's getting at. Is he asking me if I want a drink? Or is it...?

'You want to drink in here?' he repeats.

'Alcohol?' I say 'You're asking me not to drink in the room?'

He smiles and nods.

'Oh, okay, no problem' I say. I'm glad I finished off that bottle of Croatian red last night, rather than bringing it with me.

Dinner in Mostar

Paying the two nights rent in advance swallows up all the Bosnian Marks I took from the atm at the bus station, so I walk back there and get some more money. I'm looking for a supermarket - I've got a kitchenette so I might as well cook and eat there. It takes ages wandering around the supermarket – I would say there's something endlessly fascinating about supermarkets in strange countries, the brands you know, the ones you've never heard of, the things you can't identify no matter how you try – but actually, I'm just confused and indecisive. In the end I come away with far too much, two bags' worth: fresh tortellini; cream cheese, camembert and milk to make a sauce; tinned mushrooms and peas to add to the sauce; butter to fry the mushrooms; yogurt for breakfast; chocolate… No bread, because I think I will go out in the morning and find a baker's. Oh, crackers and pate. And sour cherry juice, as I can't have wine.

Now I'm laden with shopping and not at all sure where else to go. I was going to explore and try to find the 'old town', but I'm losing enthusiasm. On the main road, there's a shopping mall on the corner, with Zara, Pull and Bear, and – wait for it – McDonald's. I turn left, towards what looks on the map like a park or square, but it turns out to be a big concrete plaza with benches and fountains. There are people about, crowds of youngsters, a mother with children, old people sitting in the sunshine – it sounds lively enough, but somehow seems strangely subdued and dull. I turn left and walk back, over another bridge and to the square near my lodgings. There's a café and I stop for a cappuccino, watch the world go by.

Back at the flat with my groceries, there's almost no equipment you would expect in the kitchenette. Even to make an instant coffee requires boiling the water in a pan on the stove, which is fair enough, except that no matter what I do it takes hours. There are a couple of saucepans, an assortment of plates and cups which could be what has been left there by past guests who in despair have been out and bought what they needed. No utensils of any description - to make my sauce I have to stir it with a dessert spoon. When I open the tetrapak of milk it splashes over the floor, the front of the cooker and my skirt. The only thing to wipe it up with is one washing up scourer/sponge. There's a sparkly clean bin (the only time I've seen a bin that clean is the new ones in Wilkinson's), but no bag to go in it. No tin opener, so the mushrooms are out, although the peas are ok because they're in a ring pull. The bowls on the counter have been stacked still wet; I find out why, it's because there's no tea towel.

It's as though this flat, lovely though it is, has been kitted out by someone who has no idea of what might be useful to anyone who actually wants to use the kitchenette. I scrape together dinner somehow, leave the washing up in despair, and have a bath.

Morning in Mostar – Saturday 5 May

I'm looking for a baker's to buy pastries for breakfast, and somewhere that sells detergent, because there's a washing machine and I might as well use it, especially now I need to get milk out of my skirt. As my mother drummed in to me, you should always clean up milk straight away because it will turn sour and smell.

Walking back over the river, I watch the builders working on a structure going up on the bank. At the top and set back a little, three storeys of a hollowed out building, old arched windows, and in front and below, two storeys of unfinished concrete like rows of giant lego bricks. Five floors of hollow spaces, waiting to be filled, a hotel perhaps, or apartments.

Through the square where I stopped for coffee yesterday, I admire the posters for upcoming attractions: Igor Vokovic (moody with his guitar) at the Club Art, Dragana Mirkovic (dark and sultry in a glittery dress) at Disco Bar Strong.

Back at the flat, I put the water on to boil for coffee, then load the washing machine. I choose appropriate settings – 40 degrees, mixed fabrics. I press various buttons, lights flash, but the thing does not leap into action.

The landlord said he lived in the next door flat, and to knock on the door if I need anything. I feel a bit awkward – he's not as friendly as Frane, and there's something slightly creepy about his bright, staring blue eyes – but I pluck up my courage. I knock a couple of times, half hoping that he won't be there and I can sneak away again, but at last the door opens. I explain the problem, and he follows me into the flat. He opens and closes the round glass door, fiddles with the settings, turns the knobs and presses the button, and the washing machine springs into life.

Travel plans

I want to see the Old Town, of course, but first I want to get to the railway station and check the trains for Sarajevo, as they don't appear online. In fact, I've discovered something rather strange about Bosnia's online presence. As far as Google Maps is concerned, Bosnia is a non-place. It appears on the maps, of course, with names of towns and roads in between, and as usual if you zoom in, you get to see more and smaller towns. But zoom in further, and things disappear. Inside the towns, in

Mostar for example, even Sarajevo, there are no streets, although here and there are dotted the names of individual hotels, or landmarks like the 'Greece Bosnia and Herzegovina Friendship Bldg' and 'Presidency Bldg'. But no streets – and no distances, any request being answered with a terse message saying that that information is not available. It's disturbing to think I'm entering a part of the world where Google Maps fears to tread.

When the washing's finished and hung out on the patio, I walk to the bus station, and into a large, echoing, empty concourse at the far end of the same building. I walk around looking for timetables, ticket office, anything resembling what you'd expect to find in a railway station. There's a desk at the far left with a young woman sitting behind glass, but she's selling telephones or internet access, not train tickets.

At the far end of the bus station is a travel agency, so I go inside and ask about trains. The girl pulls a face as though I'd said I wanted to know about flying to the moon.

'I don't know from trains, only buses. Go to the train station.'

'Where's that?'

'Right past the bus station.'

That's the building I went into before. This time I ask the only human being I've seen in there, the girl behind the phone sales desk. She waves her hand in the air and closes her window in my face.

A young man appears behind the next window and opens it.

'You need to ask at the ticket office.'

'Where's that?'

'Over there' he gestures to the row of windows in darkness to his left, along the back of the building opposite the entrance.

'There's nobody there.'

'The lady maybe gone for coffee. Back 15 minutes, maybe.'

Well, now I know where the ticket office is. There's a couple there now, looking at a tiny notice. And they are talking English, the man dark and heavily Balkan in appearance and accent, the woman fair and bespectacled and sounding somewhat North American, but with something else in there. As I walk towards them, they drift into Bosnian (I presume), then back to English.

The woman smiles at me and says hello.

'Excuse me, do you know anything about the trains to Sarajevo?'

'That's what we're trying to find out' she says cheerfully, pointing to the A4 notice, which turns out to be a timetable.

There are two trains a day, at 8.05 and again in the afternoon.

'Do you know where you get the tickets from?'

'The ticket office will be open for an hour before the train goes' says the man.

We get talking.

'We're over here from Canada, staying with my husband's family' she explains. 'We want to go to Sarajevo on Monday.'

I tell them about my trip, and they're suitably impressed.

'I haven't been back to the UK for a while' she says. 'I've got family in London, but I'm from Belfast originally. And Marek's from here, it's his turn to visit family this year.'

They're both very nice, and it's good to talk to someone with some connections from home. Usually I run a mile from British tourists, but these two are different because they have a reason for being here.

I walk away from the station reassured now by Marek's confidence that the ticket office will be open in the morning, and determined to get there at 7.00 to make sure of getting my ticket. Now I can head for the Old Town of Mostar and make the most of the rest of my day.

And thinking about Marek and Christine, it occurs to me that, if she is from Belfast and he is from Mostar, they have a lot in common, a background of divided communities, bitterness and intolerance. I wonder how they met, and I imagine a twinning between the two cities, a conference, maybe, of reconciliators. Or perhaps that is just me romanticising a situation that deserves to be respected and faced up to.

Stari Most

I didn't know much about Mostar until I looked it up online in Split a couple of days ago. Before the war of the 1990s, Mostar was one of the most integrated cities in the region, but it was then involved in some really bitter fighting, and suffered a lot of damage, including the destruction of its old bridge ('Stari Most') from the Ottoman days, which had linked the Croat (Catholic) and Bosnian (Moslem) halves of the city. In 2004 the bridge was rebuilt jointly by the two communities (with a lot of support and prompting from the UN) as a symbol of reconciliation.

Well, that's how the story goes, no doubt with a bit of romantic embellishment. I do remember hearing something on Radio 4 about the bridge being reopened, with one of their reporters who was there in the war going back to cover the ceremony.

I walk towards the town, past the bombed out buildings and the reconstruction, the broken roads and the smell of freshly laid tarmac. Through the tourist-trap markets, past the mosque and the old Ottoman house, then I stop for coffee by the river with a view of the new Old Bridge where tourists cluster and watch for the posturing young men to dive into the green mountain river water.

People make symbols. A bridge is a good enough metaphor for reconciliation. I read something online by a Swiss man who came here in 1999, before the reconstruction of the bridge. He described it as 'Europe's apartheid city.'

People make wars, and people make peace, and people build and people destroy. And people are different, and the same, everywhere.

And I am in this place, which is beautiful and strange, but not as strange as if I'd just landed here straight from Luton. Air travel turns the whole world into a zoo, a theme park.

We make gods and symbols to protect us from the fear of the unknown, then we start to fear the symbols, forgetting that they came from us in the first place.

Through the touristic huddle of the Old Town I find that I am climbing the steps to the Old Bridge without realising it. I stand and look from the upstream, northern side. A man sits on a rock a little above the water, below the trees and the cafes and the souvenir shops. I can't see if he's fishing, but I think of the man on the boat near the Ponte Vecchio in Florence – *Ponte Vecchio, Stari Most,* they both mean Old Bridge.

A duck drifts, backwards and sideways, carried by the current. Or perhaps it's not drifting, perhaps it's paddling as fast as it can, but the outcome is still the same.

A young man is posing on the other side of the bridge, preparing to jump. The crowds gather round him, but with my typical perversity, I carry on watching the ducks. I hear a cheer.

In the tourist market, I buy myself a ring with a large green and black striped stone. It's the third one I try, and the first that fits, like Goldilocks, so of course I buy it.

'Five Euros' the girl says, in English.

'I don't have Euros'.

'Eight Marks.' I hand over a tenner. I think the mark price is better than the euro one.

When I left work, my friend Sue gave me three bracelets: tiger's eye, carnelian and malachite. I'm still wearing the carnelian and tiger's eye, but the malachite one got lost somewhere, left in a hotel room in the Languedoc.

'The tiger's eye is for protection' Sue said, 'the carnelian is for positivity and happiness, and the malachite is for creativity, but don't wear it when you're feeling down.' I've been looking to replace the malachite, starting in the crystal shops in Carcassonne and now I've bought this ring.

Sitting at the edge of the river, on a stone wall by a pebble beach, I take the ring from its bag and put it on. I don't know if it's malachite. But it fits. I have my symbols, too.

Believe, and protect yourself from the unknown. But believing isn't knowing, it's just telling yourself that you know. I don't believe, and maybe that's why I am so restless.

Clouds of white feathery seeds are blowing from somewhere, they cluster like dust-balls on roofs and in cavities in the walls and lie on the pavement and in fluffy bunches in the rich dark earth furrows of a raised flower bed.

A man in a Doors tee shirt walks by. Jim Morrison, eternally waif-like, pouts iconically over the belly of a stage of manhood he never lived to see.

Graffiti, in English, spray painted on a wall: 'Don't drink and drive, smoke a joint and fly'.

A man with hair in a half pony tail, like mine, scooped up on the crown of his head, eating strawberries straight from the punnet, holding them by the green stalks and biting off the fruits.

I visit the Turkish house, behind its walls, beautiful and calm with its octagonal tables, red furnishings and views over the green mountain river. In the courtyard, tortoises amble comfortably, camouflaged against the cobbles.

I enter the mosque, and climb up inside the minaret, taking endless photos of the town, the river, the bridge and the circling mountains with their crosses and monuments, where tourists are cautioned not to leave the roads because of the possibility of unexploded landmines.

I walk back to the railway station again, where the ticket office is manned at last in preparation for the early evening train, and confirm that I can get a ticket in the morning. At least I feel now that I've seen something of the town beyond the station.

Beer and *Ćevapčići*

When I get to my lodgings, the gate to the front courtyard is open to the street, and the landlord and another man are sitting outside in the sun.

'Linda!' he calls, 'come and join us!'

I smile and walk over. He indicates a picnic chair between them, and I sit down.

'Have a beer with us!'

Well, I was obviously wide of the mark about the 'no-alcohol' rule then. I take the proffered bottle and drink from it. It's a good day to be sitting in the sun.

'This is my friend Yakov' he gestures across the table to the other man 'and this is Linda.'

'How do you do Linda' says Yakov with exaggerated emphasis. He raises his bottle to mine. 'Cheers! And this' he gestures back to the landlord 'is Tibor'.

'How do you do Tibor!' I say, raising my bottle, 'cheers!'

'Ah, Linda, Linda, Linda,' says Tibor dreamily. 'In Sweden, it is always Linda. Linda and Erika.'

'And Ursula' says Yakov.

'Ursula Andress' says Tibor.

'Ah. Brigitte Bardot' replies Yakov, and they both laugh. I laugh too. They're harmless, and funny, the sun is shining and life feels good.

'Try this' says Yakov, passing me a plate of meatballs with pitta bread. 'Eat, please.'

I try to refuse, but he's insistent. He passes me a fork, and I eat.

'Very good!' I say with a nod. They are, too.

'Yakov is opening a café there' says Tibor, pointing to a ramshackle building across the road, with a couple of tables and chairs perched precariously outside on the edge of the pavement. 'Tomorrow.'

'Monday' corrects Yakov.

'Let's have more beer' says Tibor.

There's a crate on the floor by Yakov's side. He pulls out three bottles and passes them round, then launches into the story of his life.

Yakov is half German, and his wife is a quarter German, or three quarters German, I can't quite make it out. He's lived in Germany, but he also fought in the army during the war (presumably the civil war of the nineties, as he's not old enough for anything else). I have no idea which side that puts him on, but it seems best not to think about it. He has some kind of business which involves trading with Germany, I assume exporting Balkan foods, and now he's opening this café. Tibor, whose English is more patchy, has lived in Sweden, I know. They are probably both in their fifties, and I guess they've come home to settle after saving up enough from working in the West to set themselves up in business. Or maybe I'm just inventing stories again.

Anyway, the food is very good, not just the meatballs, but cheese, salad, olives. They try to teach me how to say *Ćevapčići*, without much success but with lots of giggles.

'When you have *Ćevapčići* in Sarajevo, very different from these in Mostar' says Yakov definitively, waving his beer bottle for emphasis – it's something to do with the size, but I can't work out which are larger and which smaller, and I don't honestly care.

It's a pleasant, if slightly surreal way to end my stay in Mostar, but I've got to leave early in the morning, and I still need to pack, so after the second beer I make my excuses and leave them to it.

Mostar, Herzegovina

Chapter 27 – Sarajevo

Mostar – Sarajevo – Sunday 6 May

I've enjoyed my brief stay in Mostar, if a little bitter-sweet; it's a bitter-sweet sort of place. The history – very recent – of this area is getting to me, I have that nasty sense of being a voyeur, a misery tourist. But I have to strive not to go the other way, to patronise, to think how wonderful it is that 'these people' have survived a particularly vicious civil war and are just getting on with things now. It's life. I think too much, I know.

The journey to Sarajevo is relatively short - three hours - through fabulous mountain scenery, so I get there by midday, find a taxi to my guesthouse, then go out to explore.

The phrase 'Single to Sarajevo' has lodged itself in my mind. Sounds like a good title, with the alliteration, the rhythm, the ambiguity of 'Single', and the resonances of 'Sarajevo'. I use it for a post on my blog. Of course, though, this is only a stage, not the end of the journey.

Café-sitting in Sarajevo

From my lodgings, it's an easy walk to the Latin Bridge, site of the assassination of Arch-Duke Franz Ferdinand, trigger of the First World War. It's not terribly impressive, particularly by comparison with the Stari Most in Mostar, and the river itself is shallow and confined between concrete, like the Tiber in Rome. I pass the 'Time of My Life' travel agency (slogan: *'Putovanja, Turizam i Avantura'*, or 'Travel, tourism and adventure') and head for the Old Town. I wander through the Ottoman bazaar, walk through a square full of pigeons and out into the modern town, past shops, a park where men are playing chess with giant pieces on boards laid into the floor, a modern metal statue of a human figure inside a globe, with the caption 'The Multicultural Man Builds the World'. It starts to drizzle, and I go back to the Old Town and find a café. In fact, I spend the rest of the day going from café to café and reading. Perhaps I'm getting jaded with the tourist thing, perhaps I'm intimidated by the recent history, perhaps I'm intimidated by sorting out my journey to Istanbul, perhaps I'm just tired and ready to spend a day quietly. No disrespect to Sarajevo, it is a very pretty city, and no doubt has a lot to offer, but I've seen so much, so many cities in such a (relatively) short time.

I return to my room and spend a couple of hours trying to sort out the onward journey to Istanbul, which, as I write on my blog, is 'challenging'. Still, every time I get a little further on the way, and actually get to a place, the journey turns out well and the places I stay (and people I meet) are lovely.

Rain in Sarajevo – Monday 7 May
Rain on the window. I was hoping to walk up into the hills a little. Sarajevo, like Mostar, is located in a river valley surrounded by mountains. I have that urge to get higher, to keep getting higher.

Hoping the weather will improve later, I go in search of a museum. Monday's not usually a good day to find museums open anywhere, but the museum by the Latin Bridge, dealing with Bosnia's occupation by the Austro-Hungarian Empire, from 1878 until the Empire's collapse in 1918, is the exception. It's a small museum, and naturally, focuses on the assassination, including photographs and film footage (presumably a reconstruction, but it certainly looks like an old piece of film). What startles me is how much it resembles the assassination of JFK, this grainy, black-and-white, silent film with the motorcade, the gunshot and the crowds gathered to watch the passing of the royal couple. With something of a shock, I realise that the time period between the two events is comparable to that since the second – 49 years between 1914 and 1963, and 1963 to 2012. It makes both the first seem much more modern, and the second (which is within my memory) much more historical.

I walk out of the museum into sunshine, and set off to climb up the hillside. I walk through a cemetery, gleaming bone white monuments in rows, I don't check the dates, or the names, I don't even know (or want to) what religion they belong to.

Spits of rain start to bounce off my glasses, and I'm looking for somewhere to shelter with a cup of coffee. I can see the river below, and instead of retracing my steps, I take what seems to be the most direct way downwards. The rain gets heavier, soaking my hair and trickling irritatingly down the back of my neck; the path grows slipperier and I have to watch my steps on the muddy slope. Across the river I can see a building on stilts out over the water, which looks like a restaurant. I cross a bridge and head for this sanctuary. Inside it's dark and empty, but a waiter appears out of the gloom.

'Cappuccino?' I say hopefully, and he nods and shows me to a table in the middle of the huge, echoing space.

Once I've sat down and ordered, I peer out of the misty windows onto the river, and convince myself the rain has stopped, but by the time I've drunk my coffee it's pouring again and hammering against the wooden roof.

'Maybe if I'd kept going I would have got into town before it started again' I think gloomily. Instead I bow to the inevitable and order lunch. The service takes an inordinately long time, giving me plenty of time to read the posters, which suggest that the place doubles as a ballroom on balmy summer nights, explaining the presence of a grand piano in the corner. The restaurant fills up somewhat, in that people come in and sit at two other tables, and in the end there are maybe as many as ten or fifteen customers, as opposed to the 200 or so which I'd guess was its capacity. The food is pretty grim too, something fried with bread and cheese and soured cream, which sounds intriguing on the menu but is hard to finish.

I go back to my room, convinced the rain is setting in for the day. I'm still fretting about how I'm going to get to Istanbul – however many websites I look at, I can't seem to work out what will be the best plan. So I give up and have a bath.

Sarajevo to Belgrade - Tuesday 8 May
I get on the train at Sarajevo, find an empty compartment and settle myself in with the Wardrobe and my backpack. I'm assuming this is the right train, there's always that uneasy feeling, when you can't understand a word of the station announcements, that maybe you've just made a terrible mistake.

An older lady with a walking stick and an overnight bag on wheels comes into the compartment, frowns at the Wardrobe, and says something to me.

I shrug. 'Don't understand. English' I say. She continues talking in Bosnian. I smile and shake my head.

She gestures at me to move the Wardrobe out of the way so she can sit in the opposite window seat. She is determined to get me into conversation.

I think she might be asking about the train.

'*Beograd*' I say.

She says something else.

I pull out my ticket and show it to her.

'*Ah, Beograd, Beograd!*' she agrees. We could be completely at cross purposes, maybe she's asking me for confirmation that this is the train for Beograd, and thinks I've just given it, whereas as far as I'm concerned, it's the other way round. I'm still confused. I decide she's just a nice lady looking for someone to chat to.

Somehow she manages to get over to me that she won't be going all the way to Belgrade, but to somewhere en route that begins with D. She borrows my watch and points somewhere between the 2 and the 3. I take it back and point to the 8, pulling a face.

Next she investigates my luggage labels. They are TGV ones, picked up months ago, and she is completely nonplussed by the printed messages in French. So am I, to be honest: '*Decouvrez une gamme complete de services adaptes aux besoins de chacun*'. I've never read it before, but I think it means: 'Discover a complete gamut(?) of services adapted to the needs of each'.

She turns it over and finds my name. She struggles over my surname but picks up on Linda. I confirm and smile.

Then she pulls on the ring finger of her left hand, and says something interrogative. I shake my head. I notice she isn't wearing one either.

'Was' I say.

'*Kaput*' she says. Ah, so she knows some German. I wonder whose marriage she's saying is broken, hers or mine.

She's been staying with her sister in Sarajevo and is on her way home to Doboj. She's very nice, but I'm completely at a loss. I take out my book and start to read. I hope she doesn't think I'm too rude.

Some hours later…

A woman passes through the train in jeans and a smock, and with rubber gloves pulls my rubbish out of the bin.

A little while later, we stop in the middle of nowhere, and I see the woman who emptied the bin walking across the tracks to the platform. She's carrying a small backpack. What the heck was she doing with my rubbish? She talks to a man in a red tee shirt with cropped hair. He gets on the train and walks past the compartment, then I see him pass back, get off the train again.

Now someone with a uniform cap and shirt-sleeves opens the compartment door.

'Passport?' I ask. I pull it out, he studies it and stamps it.

After a while we move off, but soon stop again.

Someone else opens the door.

'Passport.'

I hand it over. He stamps it. When I check the stamp, I realise that the first was for Bosnia and the second was Croatia (I can see that because it's the same as the one I got on the way to Zagreb). But not for Serbia.

Before we start again, another man sticks his head into the compartment. He also wants to see my passport. But he doesn't stamp it.

A fourth man comes in. He wants to check my ticket.

Finally we start moving again.

And we are back in Croatia. We still have at least one more border to cross.

Sure enough, the same procedure again. We stop, somewhere, who knows where?

A man comes into the compartment. I hand him my passport. He looks at the Croatian stamp that was added to the page a couple of hours ago and passes it back to me with a nod.

There is a pause while he passes through the train, repeating the procedure for all the other passengers. Then he gets off and the train starts again. We move for maybe ten minutes, stop again.

Someone checks the passport and stamps it.

Someone checks my ticket.

The last one is a woman. She takes my passport, and checks the stamp that the previous person but one added about half an hour ago. The stamp for Serbia is surprisingly feeble by comparison with the one for

Croatia.

Now we are moving again. After a while I look out the window to see, after what feels like months of mountains, a landscape that could be Bedfordshire. Flat fields, crops, tractors, hedgerows with elder trees in blossom, telegraph poles, electricity cables, pylons. On the horizon low grey hills – that'll be the Greensand Ridge then, or the Chilterns. On the outskirts of towns, people digging in allotments.

I travelled all that way… for this???

Evening falls. At last we are passing through suburbs, and I realise that this is the first time since Turin that I am coming into a city, a big city with suburbs and factories and distribution centres and low-cost housing.

We come into a station and I try to read the name in Cyrillic. This has to be Belgrade.

I get up with my luggage and go out into the corridor. I move out into the space between the carriages and hesitate by the door. I see someone and say:

'Is this the main station?'

'No' he says, then, pausing, struggling to find the words: 'Next one.'

'Thank you!' I smile.

I don't think it's worth trying to get back to a seat. Someone is coming up the corridor, I try to get out of his way, but as I turn, my backpack swings around, still blocking his way. At last he gets past me and goes into the toilet.

I am right next to the door, leaning against the outside end of the compartment. There is no door into the space between carriages, or rather, if there is, it is open. I sway and listen to the carriages sliding and screeching against each other, and… what's that smell? Urine, of course. I try not to block the corridor, I look through the window and we are crossing a suspension bridge. In the darkening evening, lights reflect from the water of the Danube.

It feels as though I am standing there for half an hour before we finally pull into the station, a big city station, and I walk down the platform, find the cash machine. I know that there are 112 dinar to the euro, I checked online, but still it seems crazy to be withdrawing 2000 of anything. The notes come out, ten 200 dinar notes. I look at them and think – each one of those is worth less than €2.

I show my notebook with the name of the hotel to the taxi driver, and he says, apologetically: 'Read it please, my eyes not good'.

'Hotel Slavija?' I hope I'm pronouncing it correctly, that's why I always write things down, but it's okay, he knows it.

'600' he says before I get in, the first time this has happened to me. 'Always agree the fare before you get in the cab' I read somewhere online a couple of days ago. I have been ripped off by taxi drivers right across Europe, I know, but I am just so pleased to have some way of getting to where I need to go, it seems like a bargain.

Pigeons in Sarajevo, Bosnia

Chapter 28 - Belgrade

Nightlife at the Hotel Slavija – Tuesday 08 May

How to describe the Hotel Slavija? A concrete finger pointing to the sky, a block of cement rabbit hutches glued together, lifts, doors, staff, smartly dressed young receptionists in a wide lobby that looks deceptively like that of a large international hotel. No help as I drag the Wardrobe to the lift and rise creakily to the nth floor.

My particular rabbit hutch is tolerable, though the orange patterned tiles in the bathroom, and the general architectural ambience, take me irresistibly back to the 1970s. Still, it's a room and a bed for the night.

I head back down, following signs to the Aperitif Bar, but it's closed even though it's prime aperitif time. Here's the restaurant - a huge, empty space, with a bar at one end - hard to tell whether it's open, given the absence of people. At the opposite end of the room, about as long as a railway station platform, are a few tables with people sitting at them. I walk that way, sit down at a table near the window and pick up a menu. It only lists drinks. I wait. And wait some more. After a while, I walk back to the serving area, and hover. A man comes out from the back and starts setting tables for breakfast, even though it's only 21.00.

'Can I order a coffee please?'

He turns with a start and stares at me, then waves towards the tables at the far end.

'Sit, please, someone come.'

I return to my table and start waiting again. It's dark outside, and the hotel is on an intersection of at least six roads, car headlights bearing down from all directions, bouncing back from the falling rain and wet tarmac. Is that the gleam of a McDonald's sign in the distance? Should

I venture out and try to find it? Hmmm. Maybe not such a good idea. I give up and go to bed.

The Danube and Kalamegdan – Wednesday 9 May

Belgrade reminds me of my first experience of Eastern Europe, Hungary in 2000 - same lack of finesse in the accommodation, same unhelpfulness of staff in hotels, restaurants and shops.

I feel literally disoriented, too, not sure where I am relative to 'the sights', or even what 'the sights' consist of. The hotel advertises that it's in walking distance of the Cathedral of St Sava, but which of the several roads leads towards it? Anyway, I'm not a great fan of cathedrals – I'd rather see the river and the Citadel of Kalemegdan, overlooking it. After I've had breakfast and sorted out my next steps.

I can take the train from Belgrade all the way to Istanbul (with the obligatory bus journey at the end), the Balkan Express, a 24 hour trek, leaving and arriving at 8.00 in the morning. Or I can stop over at Sofia, making two 12 hour journeys. Or I can try to find somewhere to stop before Sofia. I've more or less decided to stop at Niš, between Belgrade and Sofia. I don't have much idea what I'll find in Niš, but there are hotels there that I can book online, including the Prenociste Linda. The best translation Google can offer for *'prenociste'* is 'quarters for night', but this sounds good enough, and given the name, it seems fated.

I set off in search of the Danube, which I crossed last night. I can't get that Paul Simon song out of my head: 'the nearer your destination, the more you're slip-sliding away'. Sometimes I wonder if I'll ever get to Istanbul. It's Zeno's paradox – with each step approaching my goal, I'm bisecting the distance left, and if I continue to do that, I'll never actually get there.

I walk through rather grim city streets, past more bombed-out buildings, reconstruction sites, railway lines, bus stations, dreary dual carriageways. Then, as the dual carriageway goes over a broad concrete bridge, there underneath is the river, wide and beautiful, reflecting back the sunshine. I walk into one of the few cafés, and sit with a glass of lemonade, looking out across the water.

From here I can see Kalemegdan, white fortifications on a broad green hill overlooking the river, but there's a high fence, wide dual carriage-way and grass slope in between. I have to retrace my steps quite a way along the riverbank before I find the end of the fence and a place where I can cross the road.

The large, grassy park of Kalemegdan, on a peninsula overlooking the confluence of the River Sava with the Danube, has been the centre of settlement since the third century BC (according to Wikipedia), and was extensively rebuilt during the Austrian rule of the 18th century, so presumably that's when most of the present impressive buildings date from.

Ivy crawls over the walls of the fortress; white towers and crenellations silhouetted against deep blue sky, and in the old moat, higgledy-piggledy displays of armaments from cannons to tanks. Not really my thing, so I skip the museum in favour of a red-roofed church on the slope overlooking the river; steps down into a sunny courtyard beside the chapel, pots of white daisies and a mosaic of the Virgin Mary, with bright blue robe, gold-leaf halo and in the background, an image of the church with its red-tiled dome. It's undoubtedly a beautiful place to wander around or just sit on a bench high above the river, gazing at the view and losing myself in my thoughts.

I need to eat. There doesn't seem to be a café in the park itself, and walking back into the main part of the city I can find lots of international eateries, pizza palaces, noodle shops, burger bars, fried chicken establishments, but nothing more authentic. I head back towards the Slavija and en route I stop to eat pizza and drink Aperol spritzer at a pavement table, trying to ignore the buzz of traffic and, on the far side of the road, the bomb-damaged masonry

Morning in Belgrade – Thursday 10 May

My train's not till this afternoon, so I leave my suitcase and backpack at the hotel and go for a last stroll through Belgrade, up to the cathedral, a blocky white Orthodox church laid out in an equal-armed cross with shining gilded domes on each arm and every tower, the largest, of course, being in the centre. The sunlight is so bright that when I try to take a picture all I can see on the camera screen is the reflection of the ice cream van behind me, so I point in the right place and hope for the best.

It stands in the middle of a wide park. There's a honey market - a dozen stalls selling nothing but honey and honey products, and one selling lollipops. The air is filled with the scent of honey and wet grass, with the noise of sprinklers and fountains and crows cawing. Magpies, looking very like the magpies from home but with grey feathers instead of white, are dodging among the sprinklers with wet feathers. I wonder if they're trying to get wet, or just confused?

I wander back down past the hotel to Republic Square, past a bookshop, and of course, I can't resist window shopping, even if everything's in Cyrillic. There's a display of notebooks on sale – hey, I left mine in the backpack and my thoughts are particularly buzzing, which seems a perfect excuse to buy a lovely one with a sepia drawing of Belgrade on the cover.

I walk past the pavement café outside the Hotel Moskva. The man at the end table, looking out over his cigarette, watches me as I walk past him. I watch back, through my sunglasses. Then I turn and look again, over my shoulder. He's sitting at a table for four, but he's alone.

I hesitate at the entrance, step in under the umbrellas, between the fake rattan chairs and low glass tables, sit down at an empty table and check the time on my phone. Half past twelve, an hour and a half till I need to collect my bags from the hotel. Plenty of time for a lemonade, even given the speed of the average Serbian waiter.

I take my new notebook from my bag, and that's when I notice that the building in the cover picture is the front of the Hotel Moskva itself.

People watching in the café of the Hotel Moskva
The man with the pale blue shirt, sunglasses and thick mane of grey hair is still lounging in his chair, still watching the street. Maybe he's looking out for someone specific: wife, business contact, girlfriend, colleague, friend. Maybe me? Hardly. A group of young women walk past him, and I tell myself his head isn't following them the way it followed me, but there's no way I can tell.

Wherever I go, I watch people, in cafés, in parks, on buses, at railway stations, on the street. I watch men (of course, why not?) though I'm seldom (never) aware of them watching me back. I like to look at men, I admit it, to see who's out there, watch their faces, the way they move, to wonder if they're watching me.

I like to look at pretty girls too, and elegant women - their clothes, their posture, the way they wear their hair. At one station, I noticed a girl on the platform who held herself like a dancer – feet in first. She had a dancer's body too, slim and straight, and was wearing leggings and a flimsy top with a diagonal neck that left her right shoulder bare. Her hair was thick and long, in a pony tail, but her face was round and she was wearing thick glasses, and this somehow made her seem unattractive – to me, at least, but then, I'm not a man.

On the train from Turin to Venice, a woman about my age got on at Milan and sat opposite me, reading a style magazine. She had long, untinted grey hair, down to her waist, braided into a single plait over her left shoulder. She was wearing the minimum of makeup and jewellery, tight fit jeans, boots, a simple tee-shirt, and she looked stunning – comfortable in herself and with who she was.

I like watching old people and children, families and couples. I like to watch how they interact, how they speak to one another, how they ignore each other. Yesterday in the park at Kalemegdan I saw an old man with a small boy on a tricycle, his grandson presumably, the child was misbehaving in some way, the grandfather was standing no nonsense. Parents, myself included, stood around remembering, smiling in sympathy, grateful they weren't the ones having to deal with it on this occasion.

In the bazaar in Sarajevo, another small boy, desperate, separated from his mother. I had seen her with him earlier, distracted, fussing over an even tinier child in a buggy, while he chased some toy. A friend of the mother, or perhaps an aunt, appeared and took charge of him.

In a pastry shop in San Sebastián, very early on, I sat over my coffee one afternoon and watched through the window as two people, a man and a woman, met casually on the corner and got into conversation. It was clear that they were acquainted, but not yet that well, and I watched their body language, wondering where their story was going.

Sometimes I hear music, not just from the ubiquitous street musicians but through windows, out of buildings. In my hotel room in Zagreb I swear I heard the piano being played. I turned down a leafy street in Belgrade and heard what at first I took to be a ring tone turn into an exercise played on the flute. Further along an operatic female voice practising scales. I thought perhaps I was passing a music school, and suddenly I was back in Brussels, a season ago when winter was peering through the drizzle towards spring, but then I turned a corner and realised that I'd been walking past the back of the National Theatre.

Belgrade to Niš

The big international railway stations – St Pancras, Brussels Midi, Paris Gare du Nord, Rome Termini – are shopping malls. The main station at Belgrade is more like a pavement café.

It's fortunate that Niš is one station name I can recognise the Cyrillic characters for (НИШ), so I can pick it out on the departure board, though I'm slightly worried that I don't know which is departures and which arrivals. And I have no idea what platform it leaves from. Lucky I've got plenty of time to spare.

Suddenly I spot the boy who played Buttons in panto with my am-dram group in Bedford last winter, though god knows what he's doing in Serbia. Things like that happen to me all the time. I guess I must have seen thousands of people over the last three months, so some of them are bound to look like people I actually know.

Did I mention that the station announcer at Zagreb sounded as though she was reciting Russian elegiac poetry, or reading out the names of the glorious and heroic dead? The announcer here in Belgrade is marginally more cheerful, though I still can't understand a word. But as she speaks, there's a sudden movement of people towards a platform on the far side of the station.

'Niš?' I ask a passing lady. She smiles and nods, so I follow the crowd.

I pull the Wardrobe into a compartment where a middle aged couple are sitting in the window seats. Turned parallel to the sides of the train, it takes up the space between the sets of seats on either side. The woman looks at it, glares at me, and speaks in Serbian.

'Don't understand' I say. 'English.' I drop the backpack onto one of the four free seats.

She says something else. I shrug.

'Well I don't understand what you're saying' I say, not rudely, because she clearly can't understand me either, and I keep my tone pleasant and even. 'I don't know whether you're saying it's okay or not okay for me to come in here.'

The man, very carefully and deliberately, with a nasty expression on his face, shakes his head and wags his finger from side to side.

I drag the Wardrobe back out into the corridor, where a queue is building up behind me. What gives them the right to refuse to share 'their' compartment with me? After all, I've bought my ticket just like they did, in fact if anyone asked me to, I would happily pay another 784 dinar (about €7) for a ticket for the Wardrobe.

I find another compartment with one middle aged man sitting by the window and his bags on the opposite window seat. He doesn't seem too bothered by me or the Wardrobe. Next an elderly woman gets in, and takes great exception to the Wardrobe, but starts berating him rather than me. She bullies him into sliding the Wardrobe down between the two window seats and at right angles to the window, reducing his leg room by about half. I feel rather guilty about it, but he doesn't complain or make any sort of fuss. Later in the journey we end up with five people sitting in the compartment, so nobody has much leg room.

Gradually the train empties and darkness falls. I start to feel as though I'm the last person left alive on the train, if not in the whole country, when at a station in the middle of nowhere an entire extended family appears, with tots on trikes, buggies being wheeled up and down the corridor, at least four different generations, loud music blaring, possibly even a couple of accordions being carried in cases. They never settle, just keep moving up and down the corridors for the rest of the journey.

I start to wonder – will I know the station, is it really the terminus, can we have passed it already and me not know? – when we crawl into a town of some size, over a river bridge, and limp into a gloomy station, where everybody gets off and piles down a flight of stairs into a dark tunnel under the lines and back up the other side to the station entrance.

I drag the Wardrobe up the last few steps and out through the bleakest station buildings I've ever seen to a forecourt that seems even bleaker. It's only nine o'clock, but if it was the stroke of midnight on Halloween I don't think I would have felt more apprehensive and crushed.

I have the address and phone number of the hostel written in my note book. I can't see anything that resembles a taxi rank, but along a road and past a piece of scrubby waste ground is what could be a bus shelter. If I walk that way, maybe I'll find my way to the road, and if there aren't any taxis around, at least I can ring the hostel and see what they suggest.

But lo and behold, behind the bus shelter is a bright yellow taxi, with a sign and a driver. I show him the street address, he nods and opens the boot for the Wardrobe. I climb in the back seat with a mixture of relief and renewed apprehension, as we drive over a river bridge and down a road leading out into the suburbs.

'What's the number?' he asks.

'Fifteen.'

We're both looking at the buildings, when I spot it on the other side of the road, a neon sign with 'Linda' on it – unmissable.

At the entrance, I'm met by a vision, a minor Greek deity, who, evidently bored with Olympus, has decided to move north for a while and slum it in provincial Serbia.

In the small office/reception, he takes my passport, checks my particulars (oh I wish!), lifts the Wardrobe with one finger and floats me up the stairs to the second floor and my room. He shows me the bathroom, the light switches, the air conditioning, the TV remote, the spare blankets, explains to me about the breakfast… at least, I assume that's what he's telling me – it's not that his English isn't perfectly good, you understand, it's just that my concentration is away somewhere in the mountains.

'Any more questions, just ask me. I'll be downstairs where you found me.'

'Oh – oh yes…'

'Yes?'

'About the… the wifi? The password?'

He smiles, a deep, deific smile.

'No password is necessary. The wifi is just there'.

Before I can coherently utter my thanks, he is gone.

Health and safety, Serbian style, Belgrade

Chapter 29 – Niš

A Day in Nis – Friday 11 May

My room includes breakfast so where do I go for it? I'm hoping for another encounter with the Greek god, but on the desk there's just a young Serbian man, who directs me to the café next door. I take a seat outside overlooking a wide but very dull road. The waiter offers omelette: 'with cheese, ham, bacon?'

'Bacon please.'

He comes back with two rashers of bacon and two fried eggs sunny side up.

'Milk or yogurt for drink?'

'No coffee?'

'Coffee extra madam.'

It's a sunny morning. I drink my milk and wonder where I am and what there is to do. According to the Internet, the top three attractions are the Fortress, the Tower of Skulls and the concentration camp, none of which sound terribly appealing. There's a bus stop, but which is the way to the city centre? I know from Google Maps (thankfully, Serbia, unlike Bosnia, is recognised by Google), that this road (the E-80) runs roughly parallel with the river then turns towards it and runs along the north bank for a while, and I suspect this is the way to go, since river cities tend to centre around the river and have a bridge or bridges at their heart.

I take a chance and join a crowd of people waiting at the bus stop on this side of the road. Before long we're riding along the river embankment, and everyone gets off by a large bridge, so I follow them. Good plan. The Fortress is to my right, and I head across the bridge in hope of finding coffee.

I come into a square with an equestrian statue in the centre, an ice cream shop-cum-café and McDonalds on the right and a hotel, tourist information office and Costa Coffee on the left. I head for the tourist office and pick up a map. I'm determined to avoid the Costa and McDonalds, so I take a seat outside the ice cream shop and try to catch the waiter's attention.

'Cappuccino? I say hopefully.

'No madam, only the other kind of coffee.'

'Okay' I say, meaning I'll have that, and settle back to wait while he takes the order from two ladies at the next table. After a few minutes, he brings lemonade for them, but where's my coffee?

One of the ladies smiles at me and says kindly in English:

'Very good place for coffee, over there'. She's pointing at the Costa.

'Thank you.' I get up and walk across the square. The hotel near the Tourist Information office also has a terrace with chairs outside. I sit down, and ask the waiter for a cappuccino. This time, it works.

Seems the Fortress is the most touristic place, so I cross the bridge. Very similar to Kalemegdan in Belgrade, it's a green open space with occasional buildings. A tourist road train drives around, carrying one passenger. I climb up and along the walls for a little way, looking down over a clutch of market stalls. I walk down to investigate, and find a standard market: fruit and veg, cheeses, meat, random household goods, cheap jeans, fake labels, traders shouting.

Back over the bridge, I go past McDonald's into the back streets and take a seat outside a restaurant. Two men on the next table seem to be having a business lunch, and what's that they're eating? I ask the waiter by pointing at it. When it comes, it's a rolled and stuffed piece of meat served with vegetables and a creamy sauce. I ate something similar for lunch on my first day in Sarajevo, but there it was disappointing and here it's delicious.

By the time I finish lunch it's mid-afternoon. Should I go looking for the Tower of Skulls (built by the Turks out of the skulls of Serbs killed in the uprising of 1809) or the concentration camp? Nah, I'll just take a walk by the river Nišava. Here's another place where the river banks have been reinforced with ugly white concrete, but the fishermen are happy enough watching the floats bobbing, though I don't see any of them catch anything.

I cross a bridge to the north side of the river and walk up a quiet residential road that brings me out not far from my lodgings. Back in my room I check the train for tomorrow, leaving at 12.37, getting in about half past five, so I'll get to Sofia in daylight and not have another uncomfortable arrival at a strange city in the dark.

Getting out of Niš – Saturday 12 May

In the morning I have a go at unpacking and repacking the Wardrobe. Even though I got rid of a whole parcel of stuff in Venice, it doesn't seem any better. Things slide around more than they used to. Everything settles at the bottom if it stands on its end for a long time, and because the sides are soft it drags on the floor. But anyway, it's got this far, despite what my brother-in-law said.

The railway station looks even more gruesome in daylight. There's a man stretched out snoring across a bench, and as far as I can see, the staff behind the glass are asleep too. The sign over the left hand desk says 'International connections', but the man sitting behind it really does have his head on one side, eyes closed and mouth open.

I hear the sound of a grille being pulled back, and the woman in the middle window is glowering at me.

'Sofia?' I ask, nervously.

She sneers at me, picks up a pen, and I assume she's going to write out a ticket, but instead she gets a scrap of brown paper from somewhere, scribbles, '2.55' on it and pushes it through the opening.

What is she trying to communicate? I stare at it for a moment, then she points at the numbers, points over my shoulder and says:

'Clock.'

And then, with emphasis:

'Morning.'

What? Is she really saying what I think she's saying?

'You mean, in the night?'

She nods, slowly and triumphantly.

'But the website says…'

She doesn't exactly say 'Ha, website, I spit on your website!', but her eyes say it.

'Bus' she says.

'From here?'

Single to Sirkeci

'Bus station.'

'Where's that? How do I get there?'

'Two kilometres' she says, pronouncing each syllable separately and with great emphasis. And then she closes the window in my face and goes back to whatever evil spell she'd been working on before I interrupted her.

I walk out of the station again, as forlornly as when I first got here. There's a bus - just pulling away. I guess any bus must go to the bus station, so I just have to wait for another. Yes, here's another one, and someone's getting off.

'Bus station?' I ask.

The man who's just got off the bus looks at me sympathetically.

'Best to take a cab.'

'What about a bus?'

'There is a bus, green and white, it go round and round and it will come to the bus station. Ask the driver. But better get a cab. The cab stops are over there' and he points to the road. 'Look, there are some waiting.'

Sure enough there are. We drive back through streets I don't recognise, and then into a street market. Stalls and people spill onto the road as we creep along.

'Bus station is here' the driver gestures to the left and stops the car.

'One hundred sixty five.'

I rummage around trying to sort out the notes, so many notes of so many different denominations, all worth less than a euro. I find a hundred, a fifty, a ten, a second ten but no five.

'It's okay' he says, taking the 160. I try to give him the other ten as well but he waves it away and drives off. How often does a taxi driver do that?

I trudge into the bus station, and up to the ticket desks, where there's a hum of activity, and the employees look quite human. Some are even smiling.

There's a bus to Sofia at 16.00, arriving at 21.00. A five hour wait followed by a five hour bus journey. So much for my idea of getting there at half past five in daylight, as promised by the timetable on the Serbian Railways website. Ah well. I've got a ticket, and a metal token to get through the turnstile to the platforms.

Where am I? And can I leave the Wardrobe somewhere and get out for a while? I need to check my tourist guide, but it's buried somewhere in my backpack. There's an octagonal building with glass doors to the right of the ticket office, and I push the door and go in. It's cool, so I sit down and start rummaging through my bag.

On a bench opposite me are two teenage girls, laughing at something in that embarrassing way that's impossible to suppress once you get started, however unfunny the initial cause. Maybe they're laughing at me? I will be dignified and rise above it.

Then I notice a number of screens hanging from the ceiling at the centre of the room, showing electronic displays which change every few seconds, like a powerpoint presentation. It's a series of sepia-tinted still photos of people in old-fashioned clothes, with subtitles in Cyrillic, and when it comes to an end it starts over again.

Gradually I'm drawn in. It tells the heroic tale of the construction of the new Niš bus station, over the years from 1977 to its glorious opening ceremony in 2011. Now I can see why the girls were giggling, I can't help it, I join in. It's unintentionally hilarious, even though I can't understand the captions.

I guess you had to be there.

I still haven't found the map, I think it must be packed inside the Wardrobe, so because I can't think what else to do I walk out of the bus station, dragging the Wardrobe behind me. I turn left through the market stalls, and recognise that stall with the jeans, and the watermelons across the aisle – this is where I was yesterday - and there's the wall of the fortress up there. So, if I keep going along this way I'll come to the bridge, and over that the square with Costa Coffee and McDonalds.

But I'm not going to drag the Wardrobe all that way, so I return to the information desk and ask if there's a left luggage office.

'Yes, but it's on the other side of the turnstile, turn right and it's at the far end.'

'If I use my token will I be able to get back through again?'

'When you leave your bag you'll be given a ticket. Show it to the man at the turnstile when you come back, and he'll let you through.'

Hmmm. I'm not sure I want to give up my token, but with a deep breath, I put it in the slot, push the turnstile, and go through.

I spend about half an hour wandering up and down trying to find the left luggage office. There are plenty of cafés on this side of the barrier, and even a 'Stop and Shop', which is empty and closed-down - presumably its customers Stopped Shopping. But what I can't find, apart from the left luggage office, is a cash machine. I quickly count up my money, and I've only got about 300 dinar left, which won't buy much in the way of food and drink for the journey.

So I really need to get out again. But to do that I need a ticket from the left luggage office, so that I can get back in again to catch my bus. You know, sometimes I think these Eastern European countries still have quite a way to go.

The information desk lady said the luggage office was right at the end, but all I saw there was the toilet. Better ask the toilet man.

I get to his booth and try to explain what I want, pointing to the Wardrobe. He starts to speak excitedly in Serbian, and circles with his arm to show that he wants me to go round the other side of the toilet block, where there's a door with no sign and no indication that it's ever been opened. I wait by this door for him to open it and present himself in his other incarnation as the left luggage attendant. But then when I want to speak in English, he has to go and find an interpreter.

I don't know what this other guy's official role is, but he's very affable and happy to talk to me about what's required in terms of showing my passport so that my details can be written down – by hand – in the ledger.

'How's the weather in England now?' he asks cheerfully.

'I have no idea' I say. 'I haven't been there for three months.'

When all paperwork is completed, signed and duplicated, he helps the toilet/left luggage attendant to stow the Wardrobe at the back of his office, tells me there will be a 100 dinar charge to be paid when I collect it, and gives me a ticket.

'Show this to the man on the gate and he will let you back in' he explains. 'Don't lose it. Your ticket for the bus won't get you back in, but this will!'

At last I leave the bus station a free woman, without the burden of the Wardrobe, and happy in the knowledge that I'll be readmitted. All this activity has comfortably killed two of the five hours between the purchase of the ticket and the scheduled departure of the bus. I walk to McDonald's, taking 1000 dinar from the cash machine en route to buy myself a burger, fries and drink, and settle myself with my laptop to write.

Chapter 30 - Sofia

Добре дошли в София (Dobre doshli v Sofiya) – **Sunday 13 May**

Outside my window, a woman with a blonde pony tail, dressed in orange high-vis trousers and smock, is sweeping the gutter with a flat triangular broom - the kind that looks more like a Halloween decoration than a household utensil - and a long-handled dustpan. I'm so used to unfamiliar sights that I stare at her for a few minutes before it dawns on me that this really isn't a terribly efficient way of cleaning the gutters. Perhaps it's a community service punishment.

I haven't been watching long before a man in a high-vis waistcoat over normal dark blue trousers and shirt, and a white baseball cap, walks over and speaks to her. He has a plastic cup of drink in his hand. He sits on the kerb under a tree and offers her a cigarette. She walks out into the road - is she coming to get a coffee from the machine in the hotel lobby? No - she walks back to him with a handful of twigs picked up from the road, then takes them with her dustpan round the corner, presumably to empty them.

I'm suddenly reminded of the mornings when I watched the passing show from the window of my second-floor flat in Bedford. I'm at about the same height, and it's a similar street, apart from the trams, and the Cyrillic names on the shops.

The journey yesterday wasn't that bad. I noticed when I got on the bus that the clock at the front was an hour ahead of what my phone was showing me. Sure enough, we crossed into a different time zone, and in a way it's quite staggering to think about how far I've travelled, from San Sebastián, west of the Greenwich Meridian and most of England, to the border of Bulgaria, without changing time zones. At the border, the bus stopped and as we waited to be checked through, a dog strolled towards the gates, tail held jauntily erect.

Otherwise, the journey was uneventful. I listened to the audio version of 'Around the World in Eighty Days' on my mp3 player and stared out at the mountains. I'd already been travelling for nine days longer than Phileas Fogg.

I can't get onto the hotel wifi in my room, so I take the laptop down to the lobby, and crouch in the corner sipping a filthy 'cappuccino' from the machine. The young male receptionist is pottering behind his desk, doing whatever receptionists do when there's no one to receive. On top of the desk there's an ad for the free Sofia walking tour, leaving at 11.00 every morning, no need to book, so I ask him about it.

'Go right out of the hotel, cross two little roads and that is Boulevard Vitosha. The walk goes from the left hand corner of Boulevard Vitosha.'

Sounds like a plan. I return the laptop to my room and head out, down the road past the Café Athene – got to be my spot for breakfast, the café of the goddess of Wisdom in the city of Wisdom – but I'll check out the meeting place first. On the corner there's a white neo-classical building guarded by a black stone lion. This is it, and I've got over an hour to find breakfast before the tour leaves.

Back at the Athene, I can't see anything that looks like breakfast, just small biscuits and large gateaux, a bit rich for this time of day. Three young waitresses are standing around talking, but no one shows any interest in me or the possibility that I might want to order, so I walk out.

Boulevard Vitosha is quiet, pavement tables and chairs still neatly stacked. I go into a cafe and ask if they serve breakfast. They smile and offer me coffee. A waitress comes out and wipes a chair for me to sit on the empty street with my cappuccino, a little chilly in my sleeveless top, as the umbrella flaps above me in the breeze. Astronomically I am out an hour earlier than I'm used to for this time of day.

I've booked the hotel for two nights, expecting to take the night train to Istanbul tomorrow, but how about extending my stay for one more night? I'm getting weary of moving on, searching for hotels and packing up and checking out and getting taxis and making connections. It might be nice to settle, just for a few days. This last fortnight, since I left Venice with Istanbul as my goal but no clear plan for getting there, has been exhausting. Four capital cities in a fortnight – actually, three in a week

- Zagreb, Sarajevo, (I believe even Mostar is capital of Herzegovina), Belgrade, Sofia. And now, on the verge of reaching Istanbul, I'm hesitating.

What's the date? Check my phone – it's 13 May. Tomorrow will be exactly three months to the day since I took the Eurostar from Ebbsfleet to Brussels, the first, small step. It's too late now to get to Istanbul on the 14th, but at least if I leave tomorrow I'll arrive exactly 13 weeks after I started.

Tomorrow it will be.

Free Sofia Walking Tour

When I get back to the stone lion, a lively group of walkers is assembling, a mix of nationalities and ages. A petite, dark-haired, young woman sticks out her hand to shake.

'Hi, I'm Elena' she says in an American-tinged accent, 'I'll be your guide, and this is the first time I've done it, so please don't be too hard on me!' She was born in Sofia, but went to the States as a student, and returned recently after twenty years away, to look after her elderly father. She's a university lecturer, but she's volunteered as a guide '...because it's my home town, and I want to share the best of it with people.' Her homecoming was a culture shock, and this is part of her way of dealing with it. 'It's not the easiest place to live, but it's home, we're putting the hard times behind us and building a better future.'

I get chatting to Tim, a young Australian, who's just come from Istanbul, heading west as I'm heading east.

'Did you come on the train?'

'No, by bus' he replies. 'Much simpler.'

It's good seeing all the sights with a local person, this strange mixture of Byzantine, Hapsburg, Ottoman and Stalinist architecture, overlaid with a thin veneer of twenty-first century gloss, just as the dome of the Alexander Nevsky Cathedral is plated with gold. Elena describes the huge and ugly statue of a woman on a high column as Saint Sofia, but the owl on her arm makes her connection with Athena the goddess of wisdom obvious. The statue was erected in 2000 to replace a statue of Lenin which was removed from the same site in 1991.

It's a friendly group, and afterwards Elena takes us to a restaurant for an extended lunch of fish soup and salad. I'm sitting next a young

Romanian woman, Monika, who persuades me that I need to spend some time in Romania. I've been wondering what I should do after Istanbul, my next fixed point is visiting my friend Gabriella in Budapest, but I've got a hankering to see some of the Black Sea coast, maybe even the Danube Delta. Tim gives me the web address for the hostel where he stayed in Istanbul, while Monika writes some place names in the back of my notebook. 'And Timisoara, you must go there. And see the rose garden. You will love it.'

After lunch, and many farewells and good-lucks, we go our separate ways. I've got to make my bookings for tomorrow. Back at the hotel I still can't get online from my room, so I take the laptop to McDonalds on Vitosha Boulevard. Tim's recommended hostel is full, but I've got a single room in another one, only a couple of tram stops from Sirkeci station.

I can't buy my train ticket online, so I walk to the station. The road from the hotel takes me past the main buildings I saw this morning, but the cityscape grows progressively less glossy as I walk. When I get to the station, they can't sell me a ticket in advance, but at least now I know where to go.

I walk back past the parliament building, and smile at a young sentry yawning in his box, who glowers back. I head for Tsum, the communist-era department store now converted into a shopping mall. I have to walk around three sides of the building before I even find a way in, and when I get there it seems weirdly empty and quiet.

In the 'wifi area' I check my phone and find there's a signal- hooray!

Not the Orient Express – Monday 14 May

Next morning I return to Tsum with my laptop, and order a cappuccino in the coffee shop. The atmosphere is strangely threatening, the coffee foul, and I can't pick up the wifi. I'd be better off in McDonald's.

The weather is colder than yesterday, and drizzly. There's a weird feeling everywhere – is it the city, or is it me? Yesterday, with the group from the walking tour, I had a lovely time, but now I feel restless and disturbed.

I go back to the hotel, pick up my bags and get a taxi to the station. It's hours till the train leaves, but I might as well be there as anywhere.

The Wardrobe is in the left luggage, and there's no cafe on the station concourse, just a kiosk. It's only mid-afternoon, but the sky is so dark and the rain pounding so hard against the glass doors that I can't really see the buildings clustered outside the station. Surely one of them must be a café? I push my way into the deluge, hanging on to my umbrella, cursing and wishing I still had my leather jacket. Most of these places look like bars and gambling arcades, and judging from the way those young women are dressed, that's not the only business going on. Okay, this place serves food. Grubby plastic tables and chairs, pictures of hot dogs and burgers behind the counter, a group of men smoking in the corner, who look up when I walk in. I try not to inhale and order a hot dog and coffee. By the time I've finished, the weather's still not improved, so I order the same again, to pass the time and fill my stomach because I don't know how long it will be before I eat again.

Back in the main station building, by the international ticket desk, there's a timetable for direct trains to St Petersburg. St Petersburg? How far, I wonder? How long would it take? At the far end from the ticket desks there's a supermarket, so I stock up with sandwiches, bananas, yogurt, biscuits, chocolate. Supplies for tonight and tomorrow.

The wet, dark afternoon drags on towards evening. I gather my belongings and walk out onto the platform. A pack of stray dogs is running through the station, along the empty platforms. One drops down onto the lines and all I can see above the platform are the tips of its ears and tail.

The Balkan Express, both graffiti-splattered carriages of it, stands waiting for passengers. I show my ticket to the man.

'You know about the Turkish visa?' he asks.

'Yes.' I've read about it online. I can buy it at the border.

'You know you have to pay cash?'

No, I didn't. I've been doing my usual trick of trying to get rid of as much local currency as possible before leaving a country where I don't expect to return. 'How much is it?'

'Fifteen euros.'

That's about 30 Bulgarian lev. I don't have that much left. I thank him and make my way back into the concourse, to the cash machine and withdraw the notes. The smallest denomination available is 20, so I take 40 lev.

Back at the train, the steward shows me to my couchette, brings my sheets, pillow and blanket, and asks if I'd like a cup of coffee. At last, after a long, wet, dark day, I start to relax. I am on the train to Istanbul. It may be small, and graffitied, and not the most luxurious train I've been on, but I have a ticket, a room booked for tomorrow, and soon I'll be moving again.

Curving shapes of mountains – or clouds or reflections of mountains - through the train window. A flat plain stretching away towards them. Bands of cloud, then the mountains above and more clouds above them, merging and disappearing like the Alps behind Turin on gloomy days.

Small cattle or large goats in a field, hard to judge the size, except that there is a man standing in their midst.

A stork stands in the middle of a field then slowly takes off and flaps away from the train.

Silhouettes of trees against a white sky. Fingers of pines pointing to heaven, and the trembling tips of the poplars. Above and behind them, specks of swallows.

Red tail lights of passing cars reflected on the wet roads. Then, further into the mountains, there are no cars because there are no roads, and mist lies in the valleys, almost tangible beyond the window.

River tumbling over rocks, dam, hydro-electric plant.

We stop somewhere to let more passengers on. I can't see the name of the station, and I hope I'm not getting room-mates. I'm thinking of getting my bed ready – even though it's only 21.30, it's dark, and I'm tired.

As we leave the station, a row of low buildings, single storey, with a narrow platform in front, look almost as if they're on wheels too, as if they could drive off somewhere, all in a row with their little tiled roofs.

I set up my bunk. Snuggling down, feeling the motion of the train, I feel safe and secure. Waking and dreaming merge, like the clouds and the mountains, so I don't know or care where one ends and the other begins.

...And not (quite) Midnight Express

I'm awake and the train is still. It's 1 o'clock. Someone's knocking on my compartment door.

'Okay' I say, and the steward opens the door.

'We come soon to Kapikule.'

'Thank you'.

I lie on the bunk for a while longer, then get up. I need the toilet, but I know not to use it while the train is stationary. I fold up my bedding, pack my stuff together, get ready to leave the train.

Assembling on the platform, there are more passengers than I thought, maybe twenty or so, mostly youngsters. We form a queue for passport control. What happens about the visa? Well, I guess we're all in the same boat, presumably the passport officer will take the money.

I get to the front of the queue, and he looks at my passport.

'You need visa' he says. 'Go to police station. Round corner.'

Everybody else has gone through without question. They are standing by the bus. I start to panic.

'Where?'

'Out this building, to your right, other building' he says, none too patiently.

I am staring at two huts, the one I've just left and another a few metres away. It is open, light spilling through a window looking out onto the platform, and people behind it. I walk towards the window clutching my passport and my two 20 *lev* notes.

'Fifteen euros for visa' the man says.

I try to give him the Bulgarian *lev*, but he shakes his head and waves them away.

'Where you from?'

'England' My heart is pounding now.

He gets out a ledger, looks something up.

'Ten pounds.'

'I don't have pounds. Or euros. I've just come from Bulgaria, this is all I have!' I pull out my cards, debit cards, credit cards. He shakes his head again.

'Fifteen euros, ten English pounds, or twenty American dollars.'

In the middle of the night, in the middle of the mountains, I am screaming at a Turkish policeman while his colleagues watch with interest, armed soldiers and border guards are moving towards the fracas, and the rest of the passengers are boarding the bus to Istanbul.

'You've got to let me through! This is all I have and I need to catch the bus. This is all the money I have, what am I supposed to do about it?' I don't even have any Turkish lira.

A man appears by my right shoulder and removes the money from my trembling fingers.

'Give me your passport.'

I stand frozen. I don't want to let go of my passport.

'Your passport' he repeats. 'Please.'

I give it to him, and he starts to walk away.

'Where's he going?' I yell. 'Where's he taking my passport?'

'To the shop' says one of the border guards.

Somewhere, buried deep in the Wardrobe, there is an emergency €50 note, and buried even deeper, some pounds. The Wardrobe is still in the passport control office. Of course, none of this passes through my mind. All I can think is: 'I want my passport. What the fuck happens next?'

The man has returned, he's talking to the policeman, who scribbles something into my passport and hands it to me, with a handful of euros. And a piece of paper.

'Sign this madam, please.'

'What?'

'It's okay madam, you must sign this, it is the receipt for the money I changed in the shop' explains the smiling guard. 'That's why I needed your passport. Now it is all legal.'

He escorts me back to passport control. I am apologising to everyone for the scene. The bus hasn't left without me. The ink is still wet on my Turkish visa as the man behind the desk checks it and adds his stamp. The bus driver helps me to stow the Wardrobe. I climb onto the bus and find a seat.

It's three in the morning, Tuesday 15 May 2012, and I am on the last stretch of my journey to Istanbul.

Chapter 31 – End of the Line

İstanbul'a hoş geldiniz – **Tuesday 15 May**

The bus from Kapikule shakes and rattles but I fall into a deep sleep and wake suddenly as people start moving past me down the aisle. We've stopped. Through the window, it's still dark. I follow the group across the car park and into the bright lights of a supermarket, with the tantalising smells of hot coffee and pastries. I prowl the aisles looking for a cash machine - I don't have any Turkish money. The cashier, surly at having to deal with all these foreigners at this unsociable hour, takes one look at my credit card and shakes his head. Back on the bus, I doze fretfully the rest of the way, watching the suburbs grow under the rising sun until we reach the heart of the city and morning.

It's 6 o'clock when we pull up outside Sirkeci station, terminus of the old Orient Express and now undergoing extensive building work. There's a bank across the road, so I dodge over between the tram lines and join two young Aussie backpackers by the cash machine. With money in my pocket and the prospect of breakfast I'm starting to feel more cheerful. The Aussies are heading for a coffee shop on the other side of the intersection, so I tag along. It's buzzing with breakfast preparations and little clusters of travellers from the bus.

There's fabulous coffee, and a dazzling array of pastry, but I'm too bamboozled to choose so I play it safe with *pain au chocolat*. I emailed the hostel yesterday and warned them I'd be coming on the night train, but I didn't get a reply. I sip my coffee and hope there'll be someone to let me in and somewhere to leave my luggage.

Two stops on the tram up the hill to Sultanahmet. It's still empty and quiet, but the sun is shining and the city's starting to wake up. The door to the hostel is between a souvenir shop and a café, and opens on a flight of stairs up to the reception desk on the first floor. As I'm dragging the Wardrobe over the top step, a friendly young man appears.

'I'll check if your room's ready, but if not you can leave your case with me, no problem. And please, help yourself to some breakfast.'

More stairs, past the second and third floors, where the bedrooms are, but then I'm out onto the roof terrace, coffee, bread, eggs, jam, sunshine, the city waking up below me.

Thirteen hours ago, I left Sofia on a rainy Monday evening, riding a train that rattled so much I can barely read the notes I jotted down, and now I'm sitting in the sunshine with a cup of coffee, listening to the seagulls and gazing down on the minarets and dome of the Blue Mosque. Thirteen weeks ago I said goodbye to my brother on Ebbsfleet station, at the start of a journey that has brought me 10,000 kilometres across a continent (and under a scrap of sea).

My room is a box, a single bed with barely enough room beside it to lay the Wardrobe open on the floor, and shared bathrooms across the corridor. But who cares? I'm in the heart of Istanbul, and I've got five full days to enjoy this place which has haunted my imagination.

I walk out of the hotel, through the trees, lawns and cobbled terraces of Sultanahmet park, past red and white bunting flying between lamp-posts outside the Blue Mosque; blue and white mosaic-tiled fountains where the seagulls stop to drink; carpets hanging on the walls behind stalls piled with Iznik pottery, copper plates, and trinkets outside the russet walls and minarets of Hagia Sophia; a white stone lion and a bed of blue and yellow pansies in Gülhane Park, down to the waterfront. Then onto Galata Bridge across the Golden Horn, past the waiters trying to entice me into their cafés, the fishermen intent on any hint of movement among the forest of fishing rods stretching out across the water, to stare at the far bank and the low pyramid shaped hill of Galata, a mass of higgledy piggledy cream, yellow and white buildings clustering around the yellow central tower with its conical top; ferries and fishing boats and ships of all sizes; the smell of fish and the crying of the gulls. Everywhere is exciting and magical and wonderful and beautiful, and I am here at last.

Extract from 'The Long Way Back'
Sequel to 'Single to Sirkeci'

Farewell to Istanbul - Saturday 19 May

In a quiet back street near Gülhane Park, I find carpet stalls and dozing cats. This is the first time I've really spent much time in the park itself, wandering among the trees and open lawns. Bill Bryson ends his book 'Neither Here Nor There – Travels in Europe' here, dreaming of the Asian shore, but acknowledging, reluctantly, that it's time to go back. At least I'm taking the long way home, I've still got that to look forward to. I find a table at the café, overlooking the Sea of Marmara, and drink my tea, Turkish style, from a double tea pot, with hot water in the bottom half. I walk through the spice bazaar and surrounding shops looking for snacks to take on the train, with surprisingly little success, then have a late lunch/early dinner at one of the fish restaurants on Galata bridge.

Back at the hostel, the receptionist helps me carry the Wardrobe down the stairs and to the tram stop.

'You will come back?' he asks.

'I hope so.'

'You like Stamboul?'

'Yes, very much.'

At the station, I buy my ticket and stow the Wardrobe in a left luggage locker. Then to Hafiz Mustafa's overlooking the station, where I went that first morning, for baklava dripping with honey and walnuts, ice cream and coffee. Walk down to the waterfront one last time to smell the fish and watch the lights starting to twinkle on the far shore and the passing boats. Back at the station I settle myself with my Kindle for the last hour or so before the bus leaves. There's a relaxing massage chair in the station concourse, but it's occupied by a ginger and white cat, probably waiting for someone to put some money in and get the thing going.

The bus arrives and I collect the Wardrobe and join the other passengers congregating around the stop. I find a seat among the overhead lights and hear the doors closing and the grumbling of the diesel engine as the bus starts up. This is it. Time to go.

On the way to Kapikule, the bus stops again at the supermarket, but this time I have money to buy nuts, dried fruit and chocolate for the journey. The bus arrives at the station about two o'clock, and it dawns on me that there's just the one bus (and the one train), exchanging passengers in the middle of the night. I get chatting to a middle aged English couple, who've already been to Bucharest and exchange worrying glances when I tell them that's where I'm heading.

'Be careful' they tell me. 'Watch out for the taxi drivers, and don't walk around the area near the station on your own.' I've already picked up this advice from the travel sites, but it's depressing to hear it confirmed. I think of the places I've been already, especially Naples, and think, well, I'm not as naïve as I look, at least I've got this far.

'Are there any particular sights I ought to see while I'm there?' I ask. They look at each other and the wife grimaces.

'Well, there's the Great Hall of the People' says her husband.

'I suppose that's worth seeing, just for curiosity value' she concurs, half-heartedly.

When the train arrives, I have a compartment to myself again, so I set up my couchette, snuggle down under the blankets, and sleep till morning light comes through the window.

On the move again, in the Carpathian Mountains